An Epidemic of Rumors

An Epidemic of Rumors

How Stories Shape Our Perceptions of Disease

Jon D. Lee

UTAH STATE UNIVERSITY PRESS
Logan

© 2014 by the University Press of Colorado

Published by Utah State University Press
An imprint of University Press of Colorado
5589 Arapahoe Avenue, Suite 206C
Boulder, Colorado 80303

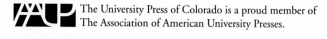 The University Press of Colorado is a proud member of
The Association of American University Presses.

The University Press of Colorado is a cooperative publishing enterprise supported, in part, by Adams State University, Colorado State University, Fort Lewis College, Metropolitan State University of Denver, Regis University, University of Colorado, University of Northern Colorado, Utah State University, and Western State Colorado University.

Cover design by Dan Miller

ISBN: 978-0-87421-928-9 (paper)
ISBN: 978-0-87421-929-6 (e-book)

Library of Congress Cataloging-in-Publication Data
Lee, Jon D., author.
  An epidemic of rumors : how stories shape our perceptions of disease / Jon D. Lee.
    pages cm
    ISBN 978-0-87421-928-9 (pbk.) — ISBN 978-0-87421-929-6 (ebook)
1. Epidemics. 2. Epidemics—Social aspects. 3. Communicable diseases—Public opinion—Psychological aspects. I. Title.
  RA649.L44 2013
  614.4—dc23
                        2013033548

Cover illustration: Photograph of Earth © MarcelClemens/Shutterstock; photograph of mask © Jinga/Shutterstock. Photo composite by Dan Miller.

For Lynnette and Joshua

Contents

Acknowledgments

Writing any list such as this is stressful, to say the least. I began researching this project while working towards my doctoral degree in Folklore at Memorial University of Newfoundland (MUN), and completed my first draft roughly five years later. In that time I no doubt discussed my various and ever-changing ideas with hundreds of people. Dozens more helped me in subtler ways. It takes a village to raise a child, as the saying goes, and it took the support and encouragement of everyone around me to help create this work. The impulse to therefore include in this section anyone and everyone I've talked to since March of 2003 is strong.

More stressful still, after narrowing down this list of contributors, is the task of placing them into some sort of order. Whose name should be first? Will I offend anyone by placing their name last? Or by leaving them out altogether, even if by accident? To this last question I can only say, I tried my best to include everyone, and if a name is not on this list it is only due to my oversight, and not because I did not appreciate what that person did for me.

As for ranking names by importance, any such feat would be self-defeating. I cannot say, for the most part, that one person helped me more than another. Like the butterfly in Ray Bradbury's "A Sound of Thunder," the removal of any one person from the history of this project could result in catastrophe. The lists of people that make up the rest of this section will therefore be random, written down as they occurred to me, with no differentiations made as to importance or usefulness.

Save one. I met my wife, Lynnette, only a few months before beginning this project. She has, in faith and love beyond my comprehension, remained beside me throughout my struggle to bring this work to light, offering condolences where necessary and, as was more often the case, Drill-Sergeant-like encouragement during my periods of sloth and torpor. For putting up with me (and putting me up, given my graduate student's salary), I will never adequately be able to express my gratitude. Thank you, my love.

In random order, I also wish to thank the following people.

None of this could have been possible—quite literally—without the time and space volunteered by my interviewees: Jennifer, Angel, Rosita,

Luis, Mike, Jonathan, Annie, Mayee, Justin, Ann, Seny, Benjamin, and Heather. For answering my questions, for providing me with data, and for making me realize new areas of research that I wasn't aware of, I am forever indebted. In addition, several friends gleefully and torturously filled my inboxes with more jokes, conspiracy theories, cures, and other narrative forms than I could possibly analyze. Kristian, Cara Nina, Christine, Lynne, Philip, and Gillian are most notable in this light.

My former roommate Robert "Robbie D" Dennis was instrumental in not only helping me procure a place to stay while I conducted my research in Toronto, Canada, but for introducing me to one of my informants, and for providing me with bibliographic resources. Robert's sister, Hollie, and her husband, Michael Peter Carter, were kind enough to offer me a bed and an Internet connection in Toronto, and more importantly, free use of their coffee maker.

My friends and fellow graduate students in the Folklore Department at MUN also deserve to be mentioned, and none more so than that fond fable of folklorists, Lynne S. McNeill and Andrea Kitta. Together, the three of us suffered the long road East, and logged hundreds of hours of encouragement, diversion, ideational dissection, and support. Without Lynne, I could not have written sections of chapter six; without Andrea, I would not have survived theory class.

Many of the professors in MUN's Folklore Department buttressed me at one time or another, and none so much as Dr. Diane Goldstein, dissertation advisor extraordinaire, who challenged me at every turn and forced me to greatly hone my mental skewers. Committee members Dr. Paul Smith and Dr. Cory Thorne provided additional assistance, slipping relevant mailings and printouts into my mailbox and otherwise providing new ideas and sources of material. Dr. Martin Lovelace, who served as Department Head for most of the years I was at MUN, offered constant encouragement, and more importantly, believed in me enough as an educator to consistently offer me courses to teach. In addition, Dr. Lovelace was generous enough to step in last-minute, and at considerable cost to his free time, as a committee member when circumstances left a different member unable to continue. Dr. Hiscock performed brilliantly in his role as teaching mentor, and offered better bibliographic advice than even my *Chicago Manual of Style*. Dr. Peter Narváez's CD *Some Good Blues* played constantly in the background, as did his theory lectures from Folk 6030. Dr. Diane Tye's clarifications of proper dissertation format and length kept me buoyant during mental storms. And the patience and grace of departmental secretaries Sharon Cochrane and Cindy Turpin cannot be underestimated for keeping me out of trouble, for helping me organize my academic life, and for providing me with the resources I needed to make it from one class to the next.

MUN was not the only university to provide me with useful folkloristic mentors. Drs. Jeannie Thomas, Steve Siporin, and Barre Toelken of Utah State University are singularly responsible for getting me interested in folklore in the first place. Dr. Mikel Koven has provided excellent information on the publishing world, and both he and Dr. Elliott Oring have given helpful feedback on conference papers, sometimes providing jaw-dropping alternate views of key elements that have forced me to reconsider my theories. And I can only send out a broad thanks to the dozens of folklorists—both professional and student—who have come up to me at conferences and offered positive, unsolicited reviews of my papers.

Outside of the academic world, no two people have been more influential and supportive than my parents, David and Jan. Together with my grandmothers—Ruth and Willa—they have provided shoulders strong enough on which to support the world. For assistance both financial and emotional, I offer the following prayer: May your beer be forever cold and never flat. *Gracias.*

I also wish to extend my appreciation to everyone who has ever encouraged me to write, regardless of genre. Special mention must be given here to Sam Green, Michael Donovan, Bill Holm, Robert Hodgson Van Wagoner, Primus St. John, J.V. Brummels and Eddie Elfers at Logan House Press, Charles Cuthbertson, Robin Parent, Micah Schicker, Chris Okelberry, Ian Brodie, and Jodi McDavid.

Finally, a note for the fallen. Ellen Meloy, Leslie Norris, Bill Holm, Ken Brewer, and Bill Kloefkorn—all wonderful people, all brilliant writers, all fast friends—did not make it to see the completion of this work. I know they would have been proud to see me succeed. From whatever vantage point they're watching, I hope they're smiling.

An Epidemic of Rumors

Introduction

The Yellow Brick Road

What has been will be again,
what has been done will be done again;
there is nothing new under the sun.

—Ecclesiastes 1:9

IN 2003, FOR A FRANTIC FEW MONTHS, A virus assaulted humanity with a fury that seemed apocalyptic. This novel disease came from China but quickly slipped that country's boundaries to bound halfway around the world in a matter of hours. Its speed left doctors and researchers gasping in the wake, struggling to erect walls both physical and intellectual against the onslaught. But their reactions were nothing compared to the fear that gripped the nations of the world as they suddenly confronted a strange, invisible, and unexplained foe that killed one out of every five people it touched.

Panic ensued. Thousands of people were involuntarily quarantined. Thousands more simply chose to stay home rather than risk catching the new virus from a coworker or stranger. The tourism industry ground to a near halt. Airlines, theaters, restaurants, hotels, and other businesses showed record losses. Chinatowns all over North America virtually emptied. And people were dying: not only laypersons, but doctors and nurses, too, cut down by the very disease they were struggling to understand.

For a frantic few months, the virus was everywhere. Even when not physically present, its name was everyday writ large on television screens and the covers of newspapers: Severe Acute Respiratory Syndrome, known far better by the acronym SARS. Headlines screamed the death tolls. The nine-o'clock news mapped out the new geographical areas where the virus had spread overnight. Radio announcers warned people to wear protective masks and avoid public places at all costs. The messages were impossible to

DOI: 10.7330/9780874219296.c000

1

avoid. SARS equaled fear. SARS equaled the unknown. SARS equaled the uncontrollable. SARS equaled death.

And then, almost as suddenly as it had arrived, the virus disappeared. No cure or vaccine prompted its departure; no great medical breakthrough hastened the world toward a SARS-free future. Instead, in the end, simple measures proved most effective: isolating the contaminated, regular temperature checks, public announcements on proper hygiene measures, vigilance.

Thousands of questions could be asked of an epidemic such as this. Where did it come from? Why did it appear? Why didn't it prove more lethal? Is there a cure? Medicine is able to provide answers for many of these questions. But there are many more questions that lie beyond the normal interests of virologists, and many perspectives that do not appear in the pages of such prestigious publications as the *British Medical Journal* (*BMJ*) and the *Journal of the American Medical Association*. For instance, what is the story-making process that underlies the disease narratives that circulated among laypersons? Why was SARS so prone to these kinds of narrative constructions? What do these stories reveal about popular conceptions of disease?

Questions such as these deserve answers as deeply investigated as the conclusions that appear in medical journals, precisely because the kinds of questions that the layperson asks about a novel disease are, in part, the same questions that a doctor asks. That is, am I vulnerable, who is infected, and how can I assure my safety? The answers to such questions may ultimately be different, and even highly contradictory. This, however, does not lessen their importance. Regardless of how the answers are ultimately phrased, the act of creating those answers—the act of understanding anything that is new—is accomplished initially by creating for that novel item a story, and that story is created by taking what is known about a similar item and laying that knowledge over the rough form of the unfamiliar. The differences that exist between the answers given by a doctor and a layperson thus emerge not because of the question, but because of the different worldviews held by those groups as a result of their training and experience. Understanding how and why these worldviews shape those reactions, and especially understanding why the layperson's answers often feature entirely different areas of concern, interest, and conclusion, should therefore be considered a task of paramount importance; without such an understanding, a divide will always exist between medicine and the public, between doctor and patient, between what is considered important and what is not.

At this point a folklorist may begin to offer answers that a doctor cannot, for while the latter offers a skill set that focuses on treating and preventing disease, the former brings an interviewee-centered approach primarily concerned with attempting to understand how the world looks through the eyes of the people who experience that world. The historical, largely quantitative methods used by many researchers to study items of folk belief stand in sharp contrast to the heavily qualitative methods used by the folklorist, and the folkloric approach often results in a greater understanding of these belief systems, since it seeks to comprehend the data from the perspective of the interviewee, not the researcher. The work of David J. Hufford, especially in *The Terror That Comes in the Night: An Experience-Centered Study of Supernatural Assault Traditions*, provides an illustration of the differences between the quantitative and qualitative approaches. Hufford's deconstructions of historical studies of folk belief systems revealed a disturbing set of assumptions held by the researchers, three of which he found most pernicious:

> (1) That statements which do not appear to allow for materialistic interpretation may be rejected out of hand; (2) that "the folk" are always poor observers and consistently confuse subjective with objective reality—a confusion which the scholar can unravel rather easily at second hand; and (3) that informants therefore cannot maintain memorates separate from legends.[1] (Hufford 1976, 73)

Because of assumptions such as these, which at best marginalize the opinions of storytellers on the meanings of their own stories, Hufford created a new hypothesis, the "experience-centered approach," which he explains as essentially following the rule that, when collecting data, "we should suspend our disbelief and not start wondering immediately what *really* happened—that is, what would be an explanation we could accept" (Hufford 1976, 73–74). Instead, Hufford claimed that interviewee-oriented fieldwork should begin with the stance that the material the interviewer is to receive is coming from "accurate observations interpreted rationally" (Hufford 1982, xviii), and as such, "When an informant relates a bizarre but believed experience, we should try to ask some of the questions that his friends and neighbors might, as well as those that occur to a university professor" (Hufford 1976, 74). This valuing of informant belief systems and narratives is of critical importance when it comes to understanding disease narratives.

Any examination of the types of narratives that circulate during disease epidemics must therefore take into account both the opinions and conclusions of medicine and the public. The juxtaposition of these is initially problematic and confusing. Medicine is, after all, the rationalized, highly scientific study of the body and those objects that attack it. Medicine is often seen as austere, detached, objective. Its practitioners are regularly accused of dehumanizing their subjects, of treating living, breathing human beings as little more than broken vessels whose wants and needs, opinions, and cultural mores are irrelevant and unwelcome. Medicine is good at treating diseases and shoddy at treating people.[2] What could this discipline possibly have to offer in the way of understanding how humans think and act, behave and react? Folklore, on the other hand, is the study of culture—a discipline dedicated to understanding the reasons behind many aspects of human thought and action, behavior and reaction. Folklore is grounded in the human condition, and its practitioners highly value the wants and needs, opinions, and cultural mores of the people they study. And any folklorist who attempts to make a medical diagnosis is obviously overstepping the bounds of her training.

Rather than serving as opposing constructs, these theoretical stances can in fact function well together, dovetailing into a mechanism that can—at least in certain areas—provide answers that either discipline by itself could not. Medicine can tell us how to transplant an organ; folklore can tell us why ethnic groups such as the Hmong often refuse such lifesaving procedures—since they view the organs as the seat of the soul—and what may be done to deal with such situations. In contrast, folklore can tell us that people have used the foxglove plant since the Middle Ages to treat various maladies; medicine can tell us the name of the plant's relevant medicinal compounds and provide standardized, safe preparations to treat individuals with atrial fibrillation. In the areas where these disciplines meet, it is safe for both practitioners to wander and point out questions and answers the other side may not have considered.

From these questions, these recognitions, emerged this book, which studies the interactions between diseases and disease narratives. The work that follows is based largely on the 2003 SARS epidemic, but the lessons learned from this epidemic stretch across time and space. Ultimately, this work begins with the approach that the names, dates, and places associated with any particular disease are of secondary consideration to the narratives in circulation that pertain to that disease. And an examination of these narratives quickly reveals that the similarities between disease narratives are astonishing: when a SARS narrative is compared to an AIDS, H1N1, or influenza narrative, the stories often bear parallel forms and meanings. Take the opening paragraphs of this introduction, for example: change the date to 2009, the word China to Mexico, and the name of the disease from SARS to H1N1, and with little further effort we have a new etiological narrative that still proves surprisingly accurate in describing the H1N1 pandemic. With a just a few more changes, we could have a series of paragraphs describing the origins of avian flu, Ebola, or AIDS. Such an exercise is far from the overly simplistic and easily dismissed example that it may seem, for these same processes—akin to using a word processor's find and replace tool on a series of oral narratives—are the very ones that appear over and over again in actual disease epidemics. The SARS epidemic may provide the skeleton of the research in this study, but narratives from dozens of other diseases will help flesh out those bones.[3]

This book is organized as a series of studies, fronted by an extended timeline of the SARS epidemic. Chapter 1 provides this timeline in the form of a chronicle of public information. The focus of this chapter is twofold, simultaneously presenting the epidemic as various media sources revealed it to the public as well as showing the medical version of the epidemic disclosed through academic journals. The ultimate goal of this chapter is to demonstrate the key differences in what the public was receiving versus what the medical world was discovering and announcing. Especially in the areas of published rumor and legend, the story of SARS that the public received from the media in 2003 was not the story that the medical establishment was telling. This chapter sets the stage for the examinations occupying the central studies of this book.

Chapter 2 begins this series of studies by focusing on etiological legends. Dozens of narratives dealt with the origin of SARS, including why it arrived and where it came from. Providing glimpses at legends as widely varied as government conspiracy theories and animal origin stories, this chapter will demonstrate that the narratives that arose during the SARS epidemic closely resembled the narratives that emerged during the initial years of the AIDS epidemic. In doing so, this chapter attempts to establish the first in a series of arguments that ultimately demonstrate that disease narratives are recycled from previous epidemics.

Chapter 3 moves the examining lens from the field of etiological legends to narratives that deal with gathering places. Beginning with a historical overview of narratives concerning the negative consequences of eating in Chinese restaurants, the chapter moves to the world of SARS, where modern and historical narratives are once again found to be similar in tone and plot. These modern narratives are examined as they appeared in media sources and oral forms. Beginning a theme that will thread throughout the remainder of the book, this chapter addresses the racial and ethnic fears caused by such narratives and their consequences.

Chapter 4 continues the investigations into the xenophobic nature of SARS narratives by examining those legends and rumors that involved individuals conducting private actions in public spaces. Many of the narratives that circulated during the epidemic had at their roots incomprehension as to the different meanings that cultures place on actions. These misunderstandings and miscommunications led to scenarios in which Asians were wrongly blamed for misconduct, when in fact the conduct was often completely appropriate according to Asian standards. Such blame was not just the province of the public; media sources assisted in the spread of negative rumors by both publishing those rumors and continually printing stories that fomented anti-globalist sentiments.

Chapter 5 uses the lens of stigma theory to further examine the racism and xenophobia that came packaged with the coronavirus. But stigma theory is found to be lacking in key areas when held up to the types of stigma experienced by interviewees during the SARS epidemic. As well, the mediatory reactions developed by the public in many ways belied the seriousness of the epidemic. This chapter therefore highlights these underdeveloped areas, pointing out avenues for further classification rubrics and suggesting new criteria for the types of stigma that could be studied.

Chapter 6 examines the state of folk medicine during the epidemic. Several SARS cures are noted and discussed, and the types of these cures are compared to the preventative and curative measures employed by laypersons during other epidemics such as AIDS. What will result from these studies is proof that SARS is unique in the types of cures that laypersons created in response to the threat of disease. In addition, this chapter looks at the longstanding battle between folk and "official," "Western," or "hospital" medicine and the interconnections and fragmented pathways that lie between these realms. More specifically, this section addresses the reasons why folk medicine has remained a vibrant, growing presence in the modern world, suggesting that the medical establishment may be doing itself and its patients a great disservice by attempting to quash the public's interest in it.

Chapter 7 presents the book's largest focal shift. In the spring of 2009, swine influenza A/H1N1—later referred to only as the H1N1 virus or flu—swept the globe. Even within the first few weeks of this new outbreak, it seemed clear that the narratives surrounding the H1N1 flu followed the same basic structures and formats as those found in SARS as well as many of the other diseases discussed in this book. There were some differences, but overall the stories that came across televisions, radios, and computer screens were remarkably familiar. This chapter provides an in-depth analysis of the parallel structures that existed between H1N1 and SARS narratives and highlights the dangers associated with automatic acceptance of rumors, many of which are not only racist and xenophobic but factually inaccurate and manipulative.

Chapter 8 presents the last study, involving an in-depth scrutiny of the nature and problem of rumor and legend in disease epidemics. These forms of narratives are often deleterious and damaging, and this demands the question of what can be done to prevent or stymie their spread. Unfortunately, the answer to this question is difficult, for rumors and legends have proven to be notoriously difficult to eradicate. Yet some recent studies may shed new light on possible solutions to these problems.

For a frantic few months in 2003, the world buckled under the onslaught of SARS. Then, just as suddenly as it arose, it vanished. SARS remains, for all intents and purposes, a dead disease. Like the Latin language, this epidemic provides scholars with a perfect specimen to examine: an ideal, non-evolving thing-in-a-bottle that can be placed under a metaphorical microscope and seen from end to end, all of its connections fixed and unchanging, even if undiscovered. The following series of examinations are by no means exhaustive in scope but will hopefully provide at least a ray of light in a previously dark chamber and give voice to people whose stories would have otherwise been forgotten.

NOTES

1. A memorate is a firsthand account of an experience.
2. This concept will be discussed at greater length in chapter 6.
3. The narratives in this book have been gathered from multiple sources, and include contributions from professional and amateur writers, formal and informal sources, and oral and written interviews. Except for corrections made for clarity, the original spelling and grammar of these sources has been retained.

1

Chronicle of a Health Panic

THE ORIGINS OF THE SARS CORONAVIRUS CAN BE traced to China's Guangdong province, though it was some months after the disease's initial outbreak in the Western world that a full timeline could be constructed. Secrecy on the part of the Chinese government is the main reason for this, followed closely by the difficulties of tracing public disease pathways in reverse. But even after locating the earliest-known examples of human-related SARS, investigators were still left questioning where the virus had come from before entering the human population; viruses aren't created *ex nihilo*, so the disease had to have its origins elsewhere. But where? An animal? Which animal? And how did the virus manage to cross thousands of miles of land and open water to simultaneously spring up in Hong Kong, Hanoi, and Toronto but miss the places in between?

This chapter will discuss these issues. A full-scale timeline is not necessary for the purposes of this study; more to the point, it would add potentially several hundred pages of largely irrelevant information. It is, however, necessary to cover the basics: to point out how the brief ripples caused by skipping a rock over the pond intertwine. The materials used to create this chapter largely consist of newspaper articles; the methods used for gathering them can be seen in some ways as evidence of public concern about the disease at various points in time.

From April 2003 to summer 2004, the daily news regularly featured reports on SARS. The bulk of these articles, however, were printed between April 2, 2003, and July 2, 2003. The decrease in available articles after this point in time can be seen as evidence of waning public interest in the disease in concordance with the virus's declining worldwide presence. July 2, 2003, for example, is the day the World Health Organization (WHO) removed Toronto from its list of infected cities. Not coincidentally, North American news sources soon began to focus their attentions elsewhere. By

8

DOI: 10.7330/9780874219296.c001

2004 media sources only printed two or three articles a week on SARS, and the last of the series of regularly published stories sputtered out in July of that year. Subsequent journalistic contributions do exist but dwindle to sporadic thrashings, barely managing one or two contributions a month, and by mid-2005, even those were gone.

These news reports can be seen as a chronicle of public, media-based information concerning the epidemic. That is, they constitute a selective progression of events based on journalistic customs and biases, which are largely based on considerations of assumed public interest. The narratives that construct the media's version of events are therefore suspect, for though this version does contain much that is true and factual, it also bends at times toward the sensational at the cost of objectivity. Why then use media sources to construct a timeline, as rife as the result will be with biases? Because the media was in many cases the primary disseminator of data for the public, and large sectors of the population were directly influenced by what they heard on the evening news or read in the morning papers. Many of the informants interviewed for this book said that they kept their televisions turned on constantly throughout the SARS epidemic and always tuned to a local news channel. And if the news reported rumors, it is only logical that those rumors became part of public consciousness.

Such reliance on media sources is problematic for several reasons. Steven Epstein has noted that the media's continual use of a specific set of reporters and "experts" to discuss a situation not only mirrors "the internal stratification of a social movement or a scientific community, but can even *construct* such hierarchies" (Epstein 1996, 335, emphasis in original). In this sense, media reports cannot be seen as simply a record of the events in an epidemic but must be considered a functional part of those events, both shaping them and being shaped by them. If a media source designates Doctor X as an expert on the topic and continually uses his sound bites (perhaps because he is simply more photogenic or better at paring down complex jargon than his peers), then Doctor X literally *becomes* the expert on the subject in the eyes of the public—despite the fact that he might not know as much as Doctor Y, who is simply not as effective at communicating with media sources.

Seen in this light, the media plays a complex role in epidemics, particularly because media outlets largely attempt to deal with a large quantity of information by filtering it into small, journalistic sound bites that take up only a few columns in the daily newspaper or a few minutes on the nightly news. Actions such as these, especially when they involve something as technical and rapidly changing as a disease epidemic, are troubling, since many of the problems with and confusions about SARS that resulted in panic and xenophobia came from the interactions and communications (or lack thereof) that took place between official medicine, the media, and the public. For example, it took the scientific community some time to isolate the SARS coronavirus and locate its source in the Chinese civet cat. During that time the scientific community advanced many hypotheses concerning such details, and, as is the nature of scientific work, many of those hypotheses were ultimately proven incorrect and were retracted. Regardless, media sources reported every piece of news relating to the origin of SARS they could glean from the scientific community, resulting in a flood of information that was sometimes only "accurate" for a matter of hours. But an information-hungry public made the media's actions possible by purchasing in mass quantities any newspaper with the word "SARS" in its headline. And this information-hungry public absorbed that information, leading to laypeople discussing the epidemic in both public and private conversations—the accuracy of their conversations only as good as the last newspaper article they had read.

Two critical problems arise from this scenario. First, distinct levels of vocabulary exist in all three layers of this picture—from the highly technical medical jargon of the scientific community to the simplistic vocabulary employed by most newspapers, to the widely varied communication styles employed by laypeople. The problem is that the media, which has arguably the simplest language of the three, is the main source of communication between the scientific and lay communities. Any information that comes from the scientific community must therefore be pared down to its bare bones and rephrased in such a fashion as to make it understandable to the general public. Considerable loss of nuance and meaning results from such paring, a consequence that can result in miscommunication and misunderstanding.

A second area of concern in this relationship is the accuracy and completeness of information flowing between sources. The media is a problematic source of information because it is a business and therefore has as a primary interest the creation of profit. News stories that sell newspapers will get published as a result while news stories that are of lesser interest or impact will be put aside, pushed to later pages of the paper, or left uncovered altogether. As such, access to information curtails the coverage of the thousands of newsworthy events that take place around the world on a daily basis but so do economic judgments concerning which of those events will be seen as the more interesting by the public, and will thus sell more product. S. Elizabeth Bird (1996) has commented on the nature of this relationship at length, stating specifically,

> News reflects and reinforces particular cultural anxieties and concerns. It goes in waves; many scholars have demonstrated, for example, that waves of reporting about teenage suicide or child abuse do not necessarily reflect actual changes in the rates of these problems. Rather, they reflect waves of interest, and in turn feed the anxieties that have produced the interest in the first place. (Bird 1996, 47)

What appears in the pages of newspapers and the special reports on the evening news cannot thus be assumed to be an unbiased and accurate reflection of daily events. Instead, it must be thought of as a subjective representation of them, sifted through numerous political, economic, social, and cultural filters.

The effect that the media ultimately has on the public is contentious. There are some who argue that the narratives dispersed by media sources are ultimately helpful. After all, the media does disseminate useful, correct information on a regular basis, including articles that debunk popular misconceptions or warn of the negative consequences of certain actions. The title of Marshall Goldberg's (1987) article epitomizes this stance: "TV Has Done More to Contain AIDS than Any Other Single Factor." Goldberg's piece defends television-based AIDS reporting, arguing that, despite the problems to the contrary (inaccuracy, sensationalism, etc.), television has ultimately improved the public's mediatory responses to the epidemic, having taught the basics of transmission, susceptibility, and prevention. This article is admittedly not scholarly, appearing as it did in the pages of *TV Guide*, but as it was written by a physician and appeared in the pages of a magazine with a purported circulation of 16.3 million in 1989 (Jones 1989), many of its readers no doubt considered it authoritative.

On the other side of the argument lie those who claim that the narratives circulated by the media have done varying degrees of harm, largely due to their inaccuracy, misunderstanding of key concepts, or misrepresentation. Benjamin Radford (2005) provides an example of the sometimes-inaccurate nature of news reports in his article "Ringing False Alarms: Skepticism and Media Scares." Radford only briefly mentions SARS in his work, mainly as an example of a disease that is regularly given "alarmist headlines." But he does present four major stories that appeared in newspapers between 1990 and 2001, including missing/exploited children, racism-fueled church fires, the dangerous nature of bounty hunters, and the 2001 case of a Nigerian "slave ship." In all four cases, the nature of the threats and the numbers associated with the stories were grossly overexaggerated by the media—as in the case of the slave ship, which turned out to be an innocuous ferry transporting job-hunting (and free-living) teenagers to Cotonou, Benin. Radford claims that the most exaggerated series of stories involved the presence of missing or lost children, a number estimated by the US Department of Justice to reach 400,000 each year. But a study by the Crimes Against Children Research Center found that 73 percent of those children were home within twenty-four hours, and parents, usually as a result of divorce, absconded with most of the remaining children. In fact, between 1990 and 1995, the National Center for Missing & Exploited Children handled only 515 cases of children abducted by strangers (Radford 2005). Thus, the media cannot be assumed to consistently provide accurate reports.

In reference to SARS, the media has often been criticized for making matters seem worse than they actually were. Peter Washer, in "Representations of SARS in the British Newspapers," which appeared in 2004, closely examined news articles that appeared in all major Sunday national newspapers in the United Kingdom for a four-week period after March 16, 2003. Any article that mentioned SARS was noted, coded for any of twenty-four key themes, and entered into a qualitative software database. Washer made his first observation upon examining his results:

> In the very first reports of SARS on 16 March, all the articles referred to the new illness as a "killer bug" or to a "mysterious" "lethal" "deadly pneumonia virus." This new "threat" was described as "moving at the speed of a jet" and people affected were not responding to traditional treatments. Combined with adjectives like "untreatable" were some graphic descriptions of how the "victims' lungs swell and they suffocate." (Washer 2004, 2565)

For the first two weeks of the period Washer studied, newspaper articles revolved around several themes, including the origin of the disease, the attempts by Western doctors to combat it, the search for a "patient zero," and the idea that SARS could be the next plague. By the third week, however, only three types of stories dominated the papers: (1) Chinese corruption and inefficiency; (2) the death of a major researcher, Dr. Carlo Urbani, who contracted SARS while in Thailand; and (3) the negative effects of SARS on the economy. By the fourth week the only remaining major thread concerned the effect of the epidemic on global economies. Constantly mixed in with these threads over the four-week period, however, were comparisons of SARS to other diseases such as AIDS, Ebola, and Spanish flu. Washer notes that these comparisons are significant because the referenced diseases all came from somewhere other than the United Kingdom—in other words, the newspapers constantly pointed out how recent epidemics all came from elsewhere. This reporting contributed to the United Kingdom's xenophobic reaction: "the social representation of SARS resonates with representations of infectious diseases throughout history: we lay the blame for the new threat on those outside one's own community, the 'other'" (Washer 2004, 2570).

Stephen L. Muzzatti's (2005) "Bits of Falling Sky and Global Pandemics: Moral Panic and Severe Acute Respiratory Syndrome" gives an even harsher criticism of the media's handling of the epidemic, especially in regard to foreign peoples:

> The media's construction of Asian communities as breeding grounds of contagion was not focused exclusively on Canada. Rather, news coverage in the United States saturated viewers with images of East and Southeast Asians wearing masks and creatively-framed camera angles provided footage of deserted Chinatowns in American urban centers, further fueling the stigma. (Muzzatti 2005, 123)

Muzzatti unequivocally blames the media for coverage that was "little more than sensationalism and xenophobic fear-mongering," and that contributed to the "victimization of already disenfranchised groups" (124–25).

The media, while valuable, are often guilty of inflammatory exaggerations, inaccurate statements, and in regard to disease epidemics, scaremongering. Of course, the version of SARS represented through media coverage is not the only way to organize the data. In fact, there may be dozens of potential versions—personal, cultural, etc.—all filled with biases and exclusions based on what was and what was not seen as important. For the purposes of this chapter, two of these versions—the media's and medicine's—stand out. Media sources may have been the primary source of information for the public, but journalists were not, for the most part, the people on the epidemic's front lines, fighting to understand the disease, treat its victims, and prevent its further spread. This honor goes to the doctors, scientists, and health care workers who spent those few months risking their own lives—and sometimes dying—to save the rest of us. So throughout this chapter, the media's version of SARS will be periodically interrupted by a side discussion of the medical version, as represented through articles published in the *British Medical Journal* (*BMJ*) and *The Lancet*. This construction will allow for a glimpse at the differences in focus between these two sources of information, showing that what one source considered relevant and necessary was not always seen as such by the other.

Epidemics fade. This is the natural progression of such things. Equally true is that epidemics rise, and when this happens, rumors begin regarding where the disease came from; who is responsible for it; how long it will take to find a cure; how virulent it is. But in order to see the connections between rumor and fact, it is first necessary to set down said facts so that we may have a corkboard on which we can later pin our analyses. Let the following timeline be that board.

WEEKS 1–4 (FEBRUARY 1–28)[1]

In mid-February 2003, China's government reported 305 cases of atypical pneumonia in the Guangdong province. Five of these cases had resulted in death, but the government refused to divulge more information. Despite this secrecy, the WHO learned on February 10 that such cases had been occurring with some regularity in China since at least November 2002. China's government reassured them that these were not significant and on February 14 issued a statement claiming that the disease was under control ("Timeline for SARS" 2003).

Then, on February 21, 2003, an elderly professor from Guangdong checked into the Metropole Hotel in Hong Kong, having traveled there to attend a wedding. He took a room on the ninth floor. He had a cough and fever and soon infected twelve other guests at the hotel, possibly by sharing elevators with them. These guests left the hotel, traveling to Vietnam, Canada, the United States, and Singapore. They carried the virus with them, infecting people in these new countries, spreading the disease more rapidly and efficiently than virtually any other illness in human history (Goudsmit 2004, 140–41).

Within days these travelers and those they infected began arriving in hospitals, complaining of symptoms such as fever, coughing, and shortness of breath. Puzzled medical staffs attempted to interpret these symptoms, as they seemed in some ways to indicate flu, but also pneumonia. It took only five days for doctors in Hong Kong to diagnose this as a separate disease altogether and to give this set of symptoms its own name. On February 26 they introduced the world to Severe Acute Respiratory Syndrome or SARS. Other cases soon followed, and only two days later the first reports of this new disease emerged from Vietnam.

WEEKS 5–6 (MARCH 1–15)

Less than two weeks later—on March 12—the WHO issued a global health alert to health care workers, stating that a new flu-like disease was spreading and seemed to be highly contagious. Two days after that the disease was reported in Toronto, and within twenty-four hours the WHO issued an emergency travel advisory, warning that the new disease was spreading worldwide. At this point such guidelines did not restrict travel to any specific part of the world but merely advised travelers to be wary of SARS symptoms and report to airport personnel if any fellow passengers showed signs of such symptoms ("Timeline for SARS" 2003).

WEEKS 7–8 (MARCH 16–29)

On March 18, German doctors made the first step in identifying the physical structure of this new virus, claiming to have found evidence of a paramyxovirus in blood samples taken from a patient who had SARS. Scientists in Hong Kong, who found evidence of the virus in two other patients, confirmed this. The paramyxovirus belonged to a family of viruses that can cause, among other diseases, measles. The findings reported in Germany and Hong Kong immediately concerned medical staff worldwide, as pneumonia can be a complication of measles ("Timeline for SARS" 2003).

On March 20, Hong Kong officials hypothesized that the global spread of SARS may have had its origins in a guest at a local hotel. With this information, epidemiologists traced the illness back to the professor from Guangdong, and thence to China, shifting the focus in the search for the origins of the new disease. The Chinese government made the investigation official on March 21 by formally asking for help from the WHO in investigating the outbreak in Guangdong ("Timeline for SARS" 2003).

The last ten days of March marked the onset of panic and quarantines on a global level. Scarborough Grace Hospital in Toronto closed temporarily on March 23 due to an outbreak of SARS, and the chief of Hong Kong's Hospital Authority was admitted to a hospital on the same day, complaining of pneumonia-like symptoms. On March 24, researchers claimed to have found strong evidence that a coronavirus—also responsible for the common cold—caused this new disease. They also noted that coronaviruses were known to infect animals, raising the possibility of an animal-human crossover in the search for the origins of SARS ("Timeline for SARS" 2003).

On March 26, the government of Ontario declared a public health emergency in light of the recent spread of SARS. Thousands of people were ordered into self-quarantine and told not to leave their homes. New quarantine issues arose the following day when a small number of passengers on international flights contracted SARS from fellow passengers, the extended contact and sharing of air on the flights having provided ideal conditions for the disease to spread. The WHO, in response, requested that Canada, Hong Kong, and Singapore begin screening passengers for SARS symptoms. The airlines complied by passing out self-diagnostic leaflets to passengers containing a series of questions concerning health status and possible prior exposure. The relative laxity of measures such as these was not echoed elsewhere, as on the last day of the month, Hong Kong's health department issued an isolation order that required all residents of an entire apartment block into self-quarantine until April 9 ("Timeline for SARS" 2003).

At this point in the epidemic, the stories told by the media closely approximated those in official medical journals. For instance, in his article detailing how the British media represented SARS, Peter Washer noted:

> In the *British Medical Journal* of the 22 March, there was already speculation as to the origins of the virus which was thought to be an influenza virus or the Hong Kong Avian Flu. In *The Lancet* of the same day, while focusing on the Western Authorities which were investigating the illness, they also said that 'a WHO team is working closely with the Chinese authorities.' Both journals mentioned that chlamydia was also found by the Chinese authorities in the lung tissue of many of the early cases. *The Lancet* also mentioned that bioterrorism had not been ruled out as a possible cause. (Washer 2004, 2565)

In the March 29 edition of the *BMJ*, an editorial set a grim tone in its discussion of this new epidemic by opening with "Plagues are as certain as death and taxes" (Zambon and Nicholson 2003, 677). At least one academic voice subsequently claimed that this pessimistic tone set the stage for the subsequent week's worth of newspaper reports (Washer 2004). The *BMJ* article was largely fact-based in its estimations of the dangerous nature of the disease while simultaneously recognizing what was not yet known about the new virus. Researchers had determined incubation periods, symptoms, the virus's mode of dispersal through airborne droplets, and the progression of the disease in the lungs, where X-rays of the infected revealed "small focal unilateral diffuse interstitial infiltrates" (Zambon and Nicholson 2003, 677); they simultaneously noted that these nodes were often overlooked and might not appear at all in certain individuals. The clinical presentation of the virus was noted to "suggest an illness of variable severity ranging from mild illness to death. The speculation is that the most severe illnesses occur among first level contacts of an index case" (Zambon and Nicholson 2003, 677). But the article stopped short of attempting to locate an origin for the breakout, noting only that it appeared to be linked to the aforementioned cases in Guangdong province. Rather than providing a hopeful ending, or even a guess, the article ended with a sobering description of the state of affairs:

> The techniques of tracking a new disease parallel those of tracking a war and involve documenting death and detritus, progressing up blind alleys, reporting spectacular highlights, and asking unanswerable questions, emphasizing that emerging infectious diseases and mortal combat may still have much in common. Our mastery of the microbial world is less complete than we might imagine and more subject to chance interactions in the environment than we might care to admit. (Zambon and Nicholson 2003, 678)

WEEK 9 (MARCH 30–APRIL 5)

On April 1, American Airlines Flight 128 from Tokyo was quarantined briefly on the tarmac at San Jose International Airport in California after five passengers reported SARS-like symptoms (Sloan 2003). On the same day, the first suspected SARS case was reported in Australia; the first three cases were reported in Indonesia; a Malaysian hospital admitted that several patients had been quarantined for a number of days under suspicion of infection; and Singapore reported three new cases after screening processes at airports led nurses to send seven people to hospitals. At this point some 1,770 people in five countries had been diagnosed with SARS and 64 had died ("US Holds Plane in Virus Scare" 2003).

The WHO declared a travel advisory on April 2, asking potential passengers to "consider postponing all but essential travel" to Hong Kong and Guangdong province. The US Centers for Disease Control and Prevention (CDC) echoed these concerns, adding Singapore and Hanoi to its list. Canada managed to avoid the list, having convinced the CDC that the spread of the disease in Toronto had been checked (J. Cohen 2003). A day later, the residents of the quarantined apartment block in Hong Kong were relocated to isolation camps after the initial quarantine proved ineffective. US President George Bush echoed concern over infectious spreaders, issuing an executive order on April 4 that permitted the quarantining of healthy people suspected of having SARS but not yet displaying symptoms ("Timeline for SARS" 2003).

Both the *BMJ* and *The Lancet* were curiously devoid of SARS-related articles on April 5. It was, admittedly, too early in the epidemic for scientists to have begun publishing peer-reviewed papers describing their work with the disease, but in the *BMJ*'s first April edition, the only mention of the disease came via a report in the journal's news section. For the most part, this article reviewed the death tolls and gave a brief history of the WHO's actions in responding to the crisis. But there were two critical pieces of information revealed. First, microbiologists at the University of Hong Kong believed that they had isolated the virus involved in the epidemic as a coronavirus—a finding that confirmed the suspicions that were reported on March 24, which agreed with similar studies at the CDC. Second, the same Hong Kong team had provided hospitals in the Hong Kong area with a simple test for the virus, based on polymerase chain reactions—though the test was noted by the team's spokesperson as in its initial stages and therefore still in need of fine-tuning. The article was clinical in its presentation of this information, and all of its sources were medical; there was no mention of rumor or gossip, only data and arguments pertaining to that data (Parry 2003a).

WEEK 10 (APRIL 6–12)

On April 7, a team of WHO investigators traveled to Guangdong to ascertain the origin of SARS but was hampered significantly by the secretive nature of the Chinese government. Eventually researchers followed the chain back to a single man: a Shenzhen-based cook who had checked into the Futian Hospital of Chinese Medicine on August 20, 2002, having already infected his wife and two of his sisters. This patient would proceed to infect a number of doctors and health care workers. The elderly professor was one of those infected, though probably through an indirect route; it is unclear whether he and the man in the Futian Hospital ever met. What was known was that the cook regularly prepared, as part of his job, meals containing animals caught in the wild (Goudsmit 2004, 141).

On April 8, Chinese doctors declared that there were more SARS cases in China than the government was reporting. As if proving the veracity of this statement, Hong Kong reported 40 new SARS cases a day for three days in a row. The WHO investigators' initial report on April 9 declared that China might be withholding information about SARS ("Timeline for SARS" 2003). Initial forays into discovering the disease vectors responsible for the mass contamination occurring in Hong Kong led health officials to state that cockroaches might be responsible for carrying the disease from one residence to another (Lyn 2003a). Worldwide, the effects of public concern over travel were already apparent: Australia's Qantas airlines, for example, cut one thousand jobs—or 3 percent of its workforce—on April 9, and carriers such as Finland's Finnair, Germany's Deutsche Lufthansa, Japan Airlines System, Japan's All Nippon Airways, Hong Kong's Cathay Pacific Airways, Korean Air, and Garuda Indonesia reported financial losses and cuts in flights ("SARS Hits Airlines, Qantas Cuts Jobs" 2003).

The April 12 editions of the *BMJ* and *The Lancet* lacked SARS-related information compared to the editions published the previous week. *The Lancet* ran only a single news article. The *BMJ*'s coverage consisted mostly of a news article, penned by the same author as the April 5 *BMJ* article, which was once again clinical in its reporting, using official sources as its references and avoiding discussion of rumor and hearsay. The article gave the death toll and remarked that the argument over the cause of the disease had come down to isolating whether the coronavirus identified the previous week was the sole cause or whether it was operating in conjunction with another factor to create the symptoms associated with SARS. The author also noted the WHO's declaration that the disease did come from one of China's southern provinces, but that it could not yet confirm a link between animals and humans in the disease's transmission (Parry 2003b). The only other mention of SARS in the April 12 edition of the *BMJ* came in the obituary of Carlo Urbani, the WHO official who brought the disease to the world's attention and who had died from SARS-related complications on March 29 ("Carlo Urbani" 2003).

WEEK 11 (APRIL 13–19)

April 14 marked a banner day in the scientific and medical study of this new disease, with Canadian scientists successfully sequencing the DNA of the coronavirus believed to be responsible for the epidemic. Scientists in the Netherlands confirmed a day later that a coronavirus was indeed responsible for SARS. According to an MSNBC.com report, April 17 was another day of discovery, as Hong Kong officials reported the infection vectors of the apartment complex where residents had earlier been relocated to isolation camps, an accomplishment that traced roughly a quarter of the territory's 1,300 cases. SARS had, according to their investigations, spread through a leaky sewage system ("Timeline for SARS" 2003).

In Canada, churchgoers in Toronto attending mass on Good Friday were either asked to change or voluntarily changed their religious rituals, avoiding dipping their fingers in holy water, receiving bread in their hands instead of on their tongues, bowing to the cross instead of kissing it, and avoiding altogether the sharing of wine. Choir members with sore throats or coughs were asked not to sing, as the act could spread expectorant— and thus disease—over the congregation. On Easter Sunday—considered by many the most important celebration of the Catholic Church—Bishop John Boissonneau of the Archdiocese of Toronto excused from attending mass those who were sick or in quarantine because of SARS (D. Brown 2003).

The April 19 edition of the *BMJ* contained another news story, this one remarking on the difficulty in controlling the virus's spread (Parry 2003c). But this edition also marked the first time that month that the virus was mentioned in an article outside of the news section. In fact, the journal's first section, "This week in the *BMJ*," had as its opener a blurb titled "Severe Acute Respiratory Syndrome Demands Strict Control." The blurb itself was only a short summary of the contents of the two pieces in the journal that did discuss SARS, but it is indicative of the larger state of affairs that it opened the edition. Also indicative was that the first of these two pieces, a lengthy editorial, fronted the editorial section. The editorial itself was written by the deputy director of the Enteric, Respiratory and Neurological Virus Laboratory at London's Health Protection Agency and summarized the scientific advancements that had been made in the investigations of SARS since it was brought to the attention of the Western world. SARS was noted to almost certainly be caused by a coronavirus, but the disease's symptoms also seemed to be associated with a human metapneumovirus isolated in 2001. The editorial ended with a note that laboratories around the world were racing to check these correlations (Zambon 2003).

The second major piece in the April 19 edition of the *BMJ* was a professional paper by two researchers—a professor and a physician—at the University of Hong Kong. The short paper reviewed Hong Kong's rising number of deaths from SARS, summarized laboratory and pathological findings, recommended courses of treatment, and provided a list of precautions for doctors to take when treating those infected by SARS. The paper was largely a review of previously available information, but the recommendations for treatment and prevention did cover new ground, including advocating quarantine as the best method of inhibiting the disease's spread and noting that public education of proper hygiene measures would be critical in dealing with the epidemic (Chan-Yeung and Yu 2003).

The April 19 edition of *The Lancet* similarly focused on SARS but contained even more works relevant to the epidemic. In total, the edition devoted seven of fifty-six articles to the disease: one editorial, two commentaries, one article, one news piece, and two letters in the correspondence section. All of these pieces were clinical in nature and tone, discussing infection control measures and the identification of the coronavirus as the possible source of infection.

WEEKS 12–13 (APRIL 20-MAY 3)

The continuing aggression of SARS led to China facing increasing pressure and criticism over its lack of openness in discussing the disease and revealing pertinent and timely information. In response, the Chinese government promised to be more open and on April 20, reported the number of SARS cases in China as rising from 1,512 to 1,807 and that it had fired the Beijing health minister and mayor ("Timeline for SARS" 2003). A report filed by journalist Dexter Roberts on April 21 does not show evidence of this new openness, however; he quoted a Beijing doctor as saying, "I am not allowed to talk about my country's public health . . . I'm sorry—but the ministry has just informed me of this order" (D. Roberts 2003). Roberts went on to discuss the serious shortcomings in China's health care program, where 90 percent of the rural population had no health insurance, and 45 percent of the urban self-employed suffered similarly. Those who did have health care were either rich or struggling to stay insured, China's health care costs having jumped 500–600 percent since 1993.

Several hundred miles south, Hong Kong was experiencing its own set of problems, its economy sputtering miserably in the wake of SARS. Tourism had dropped to an all-time low, leaving hotels and airplanes virtually empty. Experts such as James Hughes of the National Center for Infectious Diseases in Atlanta, Georgia, did not help the situation; he said in a newspaper article, "It would be hard for me to see how [SARS] could be eliminated from places like . . . Hong Kong at this point . . . I think it would be prudent to say it's here to stay" (Stein 2003). Similar comments were made worldwide, with experts beginning to think that SARS had become so widespread that its eradication would prove impossible. They predicted SARS would crop up seasonally, much like the common cold.

April also continued to bring bad news to residents of the Toronto area. On April 22, the CDC sent specialists to the city to help contain the spread of SARS, Toronto having been deemed key in successful North American containment. At this point some 66 Ontario-based hospital workers had been listed as probable or suspected SARS cases, their numbers comprising roughly 25 percent of the 259 SARS cases in the province. In the Toronto area alone, some 7,000 people had been quarantined. However, there were only 57 cases of SARS reported elsewhere in the country, and all 14 SARS-related deaths had occurred in Toronto ("CDC Team Arrives in Toronto" 2003). Because of these numbers, on April 23, the WHO extended its travel advisory to cover, among other places, Toronto, giving this Canadian city the dubious honor of being the only location outside of Asia to have warranted such a warning ("New SARS Travel Warning Issued" 2003). Reaction to this new advisory was swift and, in some cases, scornful. Toronto Mayor Mel Lastman went on record as saying, "Let me be clear; it's safe to live in Toronto, and it's safe to visit Toronto" ("City of Toronto Disputes World Health Organization Travel Advisory" 2003). Despite such reassurances, major league baseball teams were advised against visiting hospitals, using public transportation, mingling with crowds, and signing autographs ("MLB Issues Guidelines for Toronto" 2003); and high-profile players like Alex Rodriguez of the Texas Rangers made public statements to the effect that they would confine themselves to their rooms between games to avoid possible exposure ("Rodriguez, Rangers Taking SARS Precautions" 2003).

The effects of the WHO warning on Canada were immediate, the travel advisory functioning for many as the straw that broke the camel's back. Store owners reported business falling by half overnight, and traffic in shopping malls ground to a near halt. Customers canceled reservations at already-strained hotels; the occupancy rate in some hotels dropped to 20 percent or lower. Conventions were cancelled en masse. Air Canada was hit especially hard, the travel advisory coming only three weeks after it had been forced to file for bankruptcy as a result of losses sustained due to the war in Iraq. Planes arriving in Toronto after April 23 were almost empty. Most telling, however, were the words of J. J. Johnston, chief economist at the Royal Bank of Canada, who said, "Our feeling is that probably now [SARS] is going to take about a half percent off of the national growth rate for the second quarter" ("Toronto's Economy Takes SARS Hit" 2003).

Other areas of the world were suffering similarly. On April 23, Beijing ordered 1.7 million primary and secondary students to stay home until May 7. On April 24, a major hospital in Beijing was sealed off under government orders, the 2,300 people inside forced into quarantine until further notice ("Timeline for SARS" 2003). The International Air Transport Association (IATA), the governing body over international flights, predicted that SARS would cost the industry some $10 billion and would affect airlines on every major continent ("SARS Hits Asian, European Airlines" 2003). Not even the Olympics were safe. Officials overseeing preparations for the 2004 Games in Athens, Greece, some sixteen months away, began questioning the process of admitting several hundred thousand athletes and visitors—any one of who could be infected—into the country and did not immediately rule out postponing the event (Bondy 2003).

Even the United States—largely untouched by SARS, with only 39 probable cases and no deaths—felt the effects. Chinatowns in every major US city reported sluggish business, with restaurants and other Chinese-run businesses saying traffic might be down as much as 60 percent. One walking tour in San Francisco's Chinatown reported that no one showed up for its Saturday excursion for the first time in twenty years. Travel agencies in Los Angeles said that 90 percent of their booked flights to Asia were cancelled and school groups in New York cancelled field trips to the Museum of Chinese in the Americas (Hopkins 2003). So potentially serious were the economic effects that on April 24, the US National Institutes of Health formally asked for assistance from US-based drug manufacturers in developing a vaccine, drug, or immunotherapy system to help combat SARS (Pearson 2003).

By late April, few places in the world had not been touched by SARS, either directly in the form of the disease itself or indirectly in the resulting economic problems. More troubling were reports that the virus had apparently grown stronger in recent weeks, and the worst was yet to come. As of April 24, 263 people worldwide had perished because of SARS—a relatively small number, but recent studies pointed to a troubling rise in the worldwide death rate: from 3 percent in the initial weeks to 6 percent in late April. The studies did recognize that these numbers could have been skewed by China's recent admission of hundreds of previously undocumented SARS cases. But news reports were still issuing constant reminders that hospitals around the world were encountering difficulties containing and treating the disease, and that a large number of the initial cases had involved infected hospital workers, who tended to be younger and better capable of fighting the infection. And as SARS spread through the general population, some experts hypothesized that it could prove far more harmful to children and the elderly. Hypotheses such as this were at least partially substantiated by reports from Hong Kong, which showed that the death rate among those younger than fifty-five was 3.6 percent, while 18.9 percent of those aged sixty-five to seventy-five and 28.6 percent of those older than seventy-five succumbed (Vedantam and Stein 2003). A CNN.com survey conducted on April 28 showed that public perception of the disease was also one of pessimism; in answer to the question "Have we seen the worst of SARS?" 30,858 of 39,544 voters, or 78 percent, answered "no."

Yet at the same time, a small but growing number of reports detailed successes. On Tuesday, April 22, Hong Kong allowed 200,000 secondary students to return to school after a three-week state-enforced absence, under condition that they wear masks and take their temperatures daily (primary students, however, were told to remain at home). This decision may have been made in light of reports from Hong Kong's health officials of a decline in the numbers of new SARS cases for three days in a row ("CDC Team Arrives in Toronto" 2003). Hong Kong had also created a novel warning system for its people in the form of text messages sent to cell phones: "Those opting for the service will have their phones tracked and will be told via short message service (SMS) which buildings within a kilometer of their location have had SARS . . . cases occur, as declared by the Hong Kong Department of Health" (Lui 2003).

Also in late April, the WHO officially recognized Vietnam as the first country to effectively control the disease, with no new cases appearing in two weeks ("How Vietnam Beat the Bug" 2003). And in the most promising statement yet, on April 28, a WHO official stated that he believed the worst of SARS was over in Vietnam, Canada, Singapore, and Hong Kong—though China still remained a large problem. Canada seemed to have recovered especially rapidly, as no new cases had been reported outside of a hospital in twelve days ("WHO: Worst of SARS Over in Some Countries" 2003). As a direct result of this, the WHO lifted the travel advisory for Toronto on the last day of the month. As a final positive note, banks around the world reported that SARS had done something they had struggled to achieve for years: encourage people to do their banking online. This allowed banks to save costs by "trimming branch networks and cutting payrolls," as conducting business online was more cost effective (Zhu 2003).

While April's last issue of *The Lancet* had only two pieces on SARS—a news article and Carlo Urbani's obituary, the last April issue of the *BMJ* had no fewer than seven pieces concerning the epidemic. None were peer-reviewed papers—two were news articles, three appeared in the "Personal Views" section, one was a letter, and the last was a review of the websites that various official sources, such as the WHO and the CDC, had set up to discuss SARS—but every section containing a piece on SARS opened with it. The news reports detailed that the coronavirus had been definitively identified as the source of the epidemic (Parry 2003d) and summarized the disease's progression in Canada (Spurgeon 2003a)—neither of which offered any great insights into the medical community. But it was notable that the three pieces in the "Personal Views" section constituted the *entirety* of that section, a clear signal that SARS was uniquely aligning the medical community. One of these deserves special consideration, for it marked the first time in the *BMJ* that the connection between racism and SARS as promulgated by media sources was openly discussed (Schram 2003). In addition, the letter that appeared in the same edition noted the problems that Chinese foreign exchange students were having when attempting to return to school after vacations (I. Wong 2003). Thus, for the first time since SARS was given a name, the *BMJ* had begun to pay attention to the role of rumors in the progression and effects of the disease.

WEEK 14 (MAY 4–10)

Still, the disease had not yet been eradicated and the worldwide economy was suffering as a result of global panic. A poll in early May revealed that roughly half of Americans believed an outbreak was likely in their country, though only 8 percent of respondents were seriously concerned about it ("Poll: SARS Epidemic Likely in U.S." 2003). Reports from Hong Kong were mixed, some claiming that the epidemic had peaked while others discussed concerns scientists had over mutations of the virus and relapses among patients, not to mention the fivefold increase in deaths over the previous month ("SARS Relapses Stump Doctors" 2003). In Beijing, the government ordered elementary and middle schools to remain closed for a further two weeks, issuing an additional threat of punishment to those home-quarantined in Taipei who had violated their sentences. Taiwanese hospitals groaned under the strain of SARS cases, which had tripled to 116 in the past ten days. On May 4 alone, 13 new deaths were reported in Asia: 7 in China, 5 in Hong Kong, and 1 in Singapore (Foreman 2003a).

On May 4, WHO officials in Hong Kong reported a significant breakthrough in the tracing of disease vectors, as data from recent studies showed that the SARS virus could live for up to four days in human waste—four days for diarrhea and two days for urine or fecal matter. Hong Kong scientists had long suspected that the virus could live in sewage and was at least partly responsible for the contamination of an entire apartment complex after sewage pipes leaked, but they had no proof. The WHO's findings confirmed these suspicions and necessitated entirely new worldwide containment strategies. Japanese researchers made a similarly significant report the same day, recording the presence of live viruses on a chilled plastic surface four days after their placement. This finding necessitated further global changes, as health officials now understood that the virus could survive for dozens of hours on something as unsuspecting as a refrigerated bottle of soda. On a positive note, CNN.com reported that experiments with basic household cleaners demonstrated that the virus died within five minutes of exposure to chlorine bleach, offering a simple household strategy to prevent infection ("WHO Sheds New Light on SARS" 2003).

The brightness of this message apparently failed to find purchase in China, as villagers protesting the local government's SARS policy in Zhejiang province stormed local offices, breaking windows and office furniture and assaulting officials. Beijing officials, apparently fearing mass retribution, sent policemen to guard eighty reservoirs around the capital city to protect the drinking water supply from SARS contamination (Foreman 2003b). Hospitals in the capital also suffered after scores of support staff quit their jobs. Their timing couldn't have been worse, as on May 5, China reported 160 new cases of SARS and 9 new deaths, with no indication that the infection rate was leveling off. In fact, Chinese officials expressed public concern over rural health care resources, especially as migrant workers fled the capital for their hometowns, increasing the possibility of new disease vectors ("Hospitals in China Battle SARS Burden" 2003). On May 6, Chinese Premier Wen Jiabao called the situation "grave" and warned that for China to contain the epidemic "arduous work" was ahead. The same day, the Chinese media reported 138 new cases and 8 more deaths ("China: SARS Battle Remains 'Grave'" 2003). The following afternoon, MSNBC. com reported that Beijing citizens, fearing that domestic animals such as dogs and cats may have been responsible for spreading the virus, had killed or abandoned hundreds of pets in recent weeks; some communities had apparently begun demanding such action even though local governments did not authorize these rules ("SARS Drives Chinese to Kill Pets" 2003).

Hopeful Asian exchange students felt the repercussions of China's situation, learning on May 6 that the University of California, Berkeley would not be accepting around five hundred students from China—as well as Hong Kong, Taiwan, and Singapore—for the summer session ("Berkeley Turns Away Students from SARS-Hit Regions" 2003). Other US educational facilities soon followed suit. John Holden, president of the National Committee on United States-China Relations, said on May 7 that he was "not aware of any [exchange] programs that are going forward at the moment, or plan to go forward over the summer," and some Asian exchange students in the United States forfeited trips home over fears of not being allowed to return for school in the fall ("SARS Impacting Higher Education" 2003).

In the nonacademic world, customs and immigration agents, trained to watch for airplane passengers who exhibited SARS-like symptoms, were given the authority to detain anyone suspected of contagion. Hong Kong led the way in this detection, having installed infrared sensors around its airports to read the body temperature of all incoming passengers, a high body temperature signaling possible infection. The system seemed to work, as 37 passengers were identified in only a few days. The United States, however, relied mostly on the abilities of agents to recognize telltale symptoms in passengers—high fever, dry cough, and breathing trouble ("Federal Agents Trained to Spot SARS" 2003). On May 9, Italy became the first country in Europe to introduce obligatory checks on all incoming passengers from China, reserving the right to also check those arriving from European countries "where they may have made connections from Asia" ("Italy to Check for SARS on Travellers" 2003).

Perhaps because of such efforts, this week saw a number of success stories. Although the rest of China was still struggling, Beijing declared on May 9 that its efforts to contain the epidemic appeared to be successful: the number of new reported daily cases had declined from 70 to 80 per day—a plateau prior to May 2—to 30 to 40 per day. Medical staff also reported contracting the disease less frequently, dropping from a daily average of 15.8 percent to 6.3 percent in the same period ("Beijing Hopeful of SARS Decline" 2003). For the exchange students who had previously been told they would not be accepted into US programs, slight relief came when the University of California, Berkeley rescinded part of their earlier ban and announced it would allow roughly eighty students from China, Hong

Kong, and Taiwan to attend school over the summer—though the school still planned on barring over five hundred others ("Berkeley Eases SARS Restrictions" 2003).

In the pages of medical journals, the first two editions of *The Lancet* published in May had eleven SARS-related articles between them, including three fast-tracked and peer-reviewed "Research Letters" that revealed the results of studies designed to investigate optimal diagnosing methods as well as treatment and preventative measures. News articles and editorials concerning China's failure to deal adequately with the disease in late 2002 and early 2003 made up the bulk of the remaining pieces. Unlike the *BMJ*, the pages of *The Lancet* had so far remained free of discussions of rumor and narrative in the progression of the epidemic.

WEEK 15 (MAY 11–17)

Global efforts to stymie the spread of SARS had been relatively few in early May but by mid-month had increased drastically. On May 12, the WHO added India to its list of countries with suspected cases of SARS after a man arrived at a hospital in Calcutta with a fever and cough ("One 'Probable' SARS Case in India: WHO" 2003). In China, the number of diagnosed cases passed 5,000 on the same day, with 75 new cases and 12 deaths added to the list ("China SARS Numbers Pass 5,000" 2003). And at roughly the same time the UK announced its first confirmed SARS case ("UK Has First Confirmed SARS Case" 2003), China reported that the disease had entered its countryside, where millions of people lived in towns that were entirely unprepared and unequipped to fight an epidemic. The worst of it seemed to have been located "in Qingxu, 270 miles southwest of Beijing, where dozens have caught the disease and several have died" (Pomfret 2003). Only twenty miles away, in Taiyuan, there were an estimated 300 cases and 15 deaths, though the provincial government only acknowledged 162 of the cases and 7 of the deaths. More telling was a report from a governmental spokesperson who said that Shanxi hospitals needed 453 more respirators—on top of the 80 already employed (Pomfret 2003).

These reports came the day after the Chinese cabinet passed a $2.56 billion fund to help the impoverished pay for treatment, assist in modernizing impoverished hospitals, and support research. But many people in Qingxu—and, it can be assumed, in other parts of China—doubted they would ever have access to that money; one local interviewee told a reporter from the *Washington Post*, "A peasant's life in China has never been worth anything" and referred to a general belief that local officials had stolen funds intended to alleviate poverty. Those same officials, anticipating reactions to these beliefs and concerned about the spread of SARS, began to ban migrant workers from returning home. But with a population of 1.3 billion, enforcing such a ban was impossible; there had been reports of patients known to have SARS fleeing to their homes, preferring to die there than in the hospitals, which many believed were useless (Pomfret 2003).

Also alarming were reports from journalists that rural regions didn't seem to understand the dangers of SARS and were not following governmental notices to disinfect public buildings. Even in hospitals, those with SARS-like symptoms were kept in waiting rooms with SARS-free patients until doctors were free to see them. But government officers also seemed to misunderstand the importance of quarantine, breaking it regularly in the process of following a tradition wherein local officials were expected to visit party secretaries in hospitals. This tradition may have actually led to the initial outbreak in Qingxu: Communist Party Secretary Yue Shoubin contracted SARS in Beijing, was hospitalized in Qingxu, and was visited in the hospital by several members of a delegation, at least two of whom subsequently tested positive for SARS and one of whom died (Pomfret 2003).

Despite their earlier agreement to be more open, China censored a CNN International report on May 15, refusing to air it because it "positions a negative coverage of China," according to one official. The seven-minute segment criticized the government's handling of the SARS crisis, pointed to inadequate health care systems, and accused the government of ordering doctors to underreport the number of SARS cases (FlorCruz 2003). Two days later, Beijing reported 4 new deaths and 19 new cases, raising the nationwide total to 282 deaths and 5,219 cases. The WHO, however, issued what was by this point almost a standard warning that these numbers could be higher ("Key Developments with the SARS Virus" 2003). The government in Beijing also found it necessary at this time to crack down on rumors spread by mobile phone messages. A new tracking system helped officials locate those who sent over one hundred such rumors an hour— rumors which included that Beijing officials were ready to impose martial law, that crop dusters were spraying the city with disinfectants at night, and that smoking and drinking helped ward off SARS. This new tracking system quickly resulted in city police detaining a dozen people ("China Checks SARS Rumor Messages" 2003). At the same time, Yahoo! News covered the government of China's increasing fight with the populace over widespread use of the occult to ward off the disease. The officially atheist communist government, which had attempted to rely heavily on science, found itself confronted with people who hired sorcerers, lit firecrackers, burned fake money, and practiced other such magical rituals to protect themselves. There were even rumors of a child born with the ability to speak who prophesied that "green bean soup" would prevent infection—a rumor that drove the sale of mung beans up sharply in large parts of the country (Ang 2003).

In the midst of this panic, China's Supreme People's Court, faced with the increasing problem of enforcing quarantines, threatened imprisonment for up to seven years for quarantine violators and a possible death penalty for those who caused death or injury by deliberately spreading the virus. The first arrest under these new laws came the day of the announcement, when a doctor in the northern city of Linha was charged with having previously violated quarantine, resulting in the infection of more than one hundred people. The doctor received the maximum sentence of three years (Bodeen 2003a). These drastic measures drew immediate criticism from the United States and international human rights groups ("US Criticised China over Death Penalty for SARS Quarantine Violations" 2003), and China's world-wide standing wasn't helped by yet another WHO declaration that its doctors were still under-reporting SARS infections—a criticism that had by this point been leveled regularly against the country since early April (Ansfield and Peng 2003). Perhaps because of this, China's President Hu Jintao said in an interview the following day, "We are ready to further strengthen our cooperation with Russia and the whole international community in prevention and treatment of SARS," acknowledging that more financing, better research, and coordinated efforts would help to stop the epidemic (Chuang 2003).

May in Hong Kong, although nowhere near as worrisome as in China, still proved hectic. Five people died of SARS on May 17, raising Hong Kong's total number of deaths to 243 ("Key Developments with the SARS Virus" 2003). And just across the Taiwan Strait, Taiwan had recorded its highest number of new cases on May 12, confirming 8 deaths and 23 infections, "the highest one-day rise for the area since the outbreak two months ago" ("China SARS Numbers Pass 5,000" 2003). Ranked the second-highest country in the world in terms of the number of new cases reported on a daily basis, Taiwan faced increasing criticism over the way authorities were handling the crisis. These complaints concerned "disorganization, lack of effective crisis management planning and political bickering" and eventually led Health Minister Twu Shiing-jer to resign his position ("Taiwan Health Chief Resigns in SARS Crisis" 2003). Still, by mid-month, 274 people had tested positive for SARS in Taiwan, and dozens of new cases were reported daily. Hundreds of doctors and patients in two hospitals in and near Taipei were quarantined and a hospital in the southern city of Kaohsiung might, by itself, have had dozens of cases, though officers said they couldn't be sure until the end of a ten-day incubation period. Sources close to the Taiwanese government told reporters that the battle was at a crossroads: "unless officials move quickly to contain the outbreak in hospitals and do a more effective job of tracing contacts of suspected patients, the epidemic risks taking a further turn for the worse, with potentially serious consequences for the country's health-care system" ("Taiwan Health Chief Resigns in SARS Crisis" 2003).

Taiwan's information came on the heels of a Taiwanese Interior Ministry report detailing the difficulties in fighting the disease due to locals who refused to cooperate: 42 percent of people who were supposed to register with local health officials after arriving at airports had neglected such duties. Officials were also having trouble keeping track of the 23,000 people in quarantine—most of who were disease-free—and had so far spent $350,000 on two thousand video cameras that had been installed inside the homes of quarantined residents. In Taipei alone, some 200 residents disappeared, breaking quarantine, after their housing project was closed following the discovery of a body and 2 people suspected of having SARS. As Loh I-cheng, a former deputy ambassador to the United States said in regard to this, "Everyone in Taiwan thinks he's special and smart—why should he observe the rules? He knows the police won't strike him or arrest him" (McNeil 2003).

Similar reports detailed a lack of concern in other areas of the world, or at least a perception that the SARS epidemic had been overblown. While US universities denied entrance to large numbers of Asian exchange students, some American exchange students in China chose to stay and study, ignoring the calls of parents and educators who urged them to return home. And some US educators were frustrated that their universities had cancelled planned research trips to China ("SARS Impacting Higher Education" 2003). In mid-May, two US doctors pointed out to a journalist that SARS, at this point, had only claimed the lives of 23 people in Canada and none in the United States, making the West Nile virus far more deadly, as it had killed 284 people in the United States and Canada in 2002. One of these doctors—Paul Epstein of the Harvard Medical School Center for Health and the Global Environment—said, "The attention focused in recent weeks on SARS is extraordinary and, it can be argued, excessive" (Fox 2003a).

Reactions such as these may be, at least in the United States, somewhat understandable. America had managed to avoid contamination for the most part and had not seen a single SARS-related fatality. Members of the CDC continued to express concern over the capacities of US hospitals to deal with a large-scale epidemic, should one occur, as hospitals lacked the necessary quantities of negative pressure/infection control rooms to deal with widespread contamination. But almost in the same breath they admitted that the current measures seemed to be working ("U.S. Hospitals Ready for SARS Outbreak?" 2003). Media reports in large part influenced public reactions to the disease, indicated by headlines in many mid-May news articles such as "So Far, U.S. Succeeds in Containing SARS" (Yee 2003a) and "CDC Doctor Suspected of SARS Recovering" (Yee 2003b). Judging by these articles, the United States had the outbreak under control; there was no need to worry.

Singapore appeared to be another bright spot, thanks largely to some of the strictest anti-SARS measures in the world. At the end of April, Singapore had the world's fourth-highest death rate, with 28 confirmed mortalities. But by the middle of May, the country had gone over two weeks without reporting a new case, and government officials were hopeful the city would be declared SARS-free by the WHO. Such a turnaround came thanks to the quarantining of over 3,000 people, temporary school closures, visitors being barred from entering hospitals, and agents checking people's temperatures at borders. Complications did arise briefly when 27 people, including three nurses, at the country's largest mental hospital were isolated with SARS-like symptoms on May 14 ("Fresh SARS Outbreaks Feared in Asia" 2003). But three days later none of these cases had been confirmed as SARS-related; the scare seemed to have been a false positive ("Key Developments with the SARS Virus" 2003).

Other signs of hope—and levity—occurred worldwide. On May 12, China announced that SARS would not delay the launch of its first manned space flight later in the year ("China: SARS Won't Delay First Human Space Trip" 2003), and in a public statement covered by Yahoo! News, Vitaly Zverev, head of Moscow's Virus Research Institute, asserted that the SARS scare was overplayed, that Russia would not have an outbreak, and that "100 grammes of vodka" was the best cure ("Russian Experts Downplay SARS Scare, Say Alarm 'Unjustified'" 2003).

Good news also came from the medical front, as a laboratory study in Germany suggested that a modified version of an experimental drug designed originally to treat the common cold showed potential usefulness in blocking the SARS virus from reproducing. A similarity in protease enzymes between SARS and the rhinovirus the drug was intended to treat provided the link, though no studies had yet been conducted on the viability of such a hypothesis (Recer 2003).

For Torontonians, probably the best news of all arrived on May 14, when the WHO officially removed Ontario's capital from its list of areas with "recent local transmission," as twenty days had passed since Canada had isolated the last reported case of SARS. According to the WHO, this meant that "the chain of transmission [was] considered broken," after 321 probable or suspected cases and 24 deaths ("WHO: SARS No Longer Spreading in Canada" 2003). Only a score of people in the country remained active caseloads, and 5 of those were released from hospitals the day before this announcement, leaving only 16 active cases in Canada ("Canada's Active SARS Caseload Falls by Five to 16" 2003; Public Health Agency of Canada 2003).

The origin of SARS, however, still puzzled researchers worldwide. As covered by MSNBC.com, a growing number of experts believed that it could have come from an animal but had few leads on which animal was to blame. Some said it could be a bird, drawing such conclusions from a 1997 outbreak of flu in Hong Kong spread by poultry that resulted in the slaughtering of 1.4 million chickens in containment efforts. Other researchers eschewed the animal theory altogether and said that SARS might simply be a mutation of a previously harmless human virus. Researchers had earlier hoped that decoding SARS's genetic makeup would help eliminate such concerns and point to a specific human or nonhuman origin, but the results had proved inconclusive ("Origin of SARS Virus Still a Puzzle" 2003).

The lingering confusion over the origin of the coronavirus was not the only remaining problem. On a global scale, businesses all over the world were still reporting losses, and none worse than the airline industry. Thomas Andrew Drysdale, regional director for the International Air Transport Association, called the situation a "crisis of major proportions," and stated that 9/11, the Iraq war, and Britain's foot-and-mouth disease combined hadn't created as much financial damage to the airline industry. Estimated worldwide losses topped $10 billion, despite SARS having only been on the global scene for nine weeks ("Airlines: SARS Worse than 9/11 on Industry" 2003).

Moving to the medical literature, the last three editions of *The Lancet* published in May had sixteen SARS-related articles between them, including several research letters, editorials, and commentaries. Once again, all of these articles were clinical in nature. The only piece that looked at the nonmedical world's impressions of the disease came in the form of an article titled "SARS, Lay Epidemiology, and Fear," published in the May 17 edition. The article began promisingly, summarizing the increase in stress and fear in a German hospital's outpatient department, which was said to be due to a graph published in a local newspaper, wherein a journalist had attempted to lay down an exponential curve on the epidemic, predicting an increasing surge in case numbers over the next few months. But the remainder of the article was an academic discussion of the journalist's failure to understand disease prediction methods, including examples of the difference between exponential and linear graphs and the failure of graphs to take into account basic prevention and intervention measures (Razum et al. 2003). In other words, with the exception of a small opening story, *The Lancet* was once again free of discussions of rumors.

WEEK 16 (MAY 18–24)

Canada, noted only days earlier as improving, continued that trend by marking a thirty-day dearth of new cases by midweek. But this lull, which had provided Ontario's capital city relative freedom from WHO and CDC scrutiny, proved an unreliable measure of success. On May 23, Toronto health officials revealed that they were looking into 25 possible new cases. This new outbreak covered two hospitals—St. John's Rehab and North York General Hospital—and prompted the CDC to reissue their Toronto travel alert three days after lifting it. Of those infected, two of the North York patients had died and three of the St. John's patients were in critical condition. Microbiologists studying the new outbreak were not immediately clear how it had spread and assumed all vectors as potentially infectious: health care workers, family members, and even other patients. Toronto officials issued a statement declaring that anyone who had passed through North York General between April 22 and May 13 and St. John's Hospital since May 1 should commence self-monitoring and immediately call a Toronto Public Health hotline to identify themselves; officials expected that over 1,000 people met these criteria ("Toronto Reports 25 Possible New SARS Cases" 2003).

Canada was not, however, alone in its growing number of problems. Taiwan, continuing the escalating problems that had arisen the previous week, had swiftly become the country with the fastest-growing caseload of SARS patients in the world. On May 20 alone, 39 new cases and 12 new deaths were reported, the latter bringing the island's toll to 52. This marked the third day in a row where the number of reported cases had set a record. Taiwan, still third on the list of worst-hit countries (following China and Hong Kong), was the only country where the number of daily cases was still rising ("SARS Tally Soaring in Taiwan" 2003). Over the next two days, 8 deaths and 120 new cases were reported and 991 suspected cases had yet to be conclusively diagnosed. Members of US teams assessing Taiwanese SARS control procedures weren't even safe; one man, despite following all recommended precautions, was transferred to the United States via air ambulance after developing SARS-like symptoms ("Taiwan SARS Crisis Worsens" 2003).

In contrast, Singapore appeared to be improving remarkably and by midweek was fast approaching three full weeks without a problem. But one day shy of the "twenty days free of new cases" mark set by the WHO to qualify a country as free of SARS, a single Malaysian man was positively diagnosed. Officials, though disappointed, still remained positive; one case in twenty days was considerably better than the large number of deaths reported in April. "Singapore should take this in its stride," said Health Minister Lim Hng Kiang (Chuang 2003).

Bright spots such as these stood in sharp contrast to the losses that businesses continued to suffer. Worldwide, tourism was down and business travel was stymied as workers avoided meetings. A survey of 2,015 Japanese companies that conducted business in Asia revealed that roughly 70 percent reported financial damage. The largest numbers came from China, where 86 percent of Japanese businesses had been affected, including the temporary closing of two plants after five workers were diagnosed with SARS. In other areas of Asia, 8 percent of Japanese businesses in Hong Kong reported damages, with 84 percent in Singapore, 39 percent in Indonesia, and 38 percent in Thailand making similar claims ("Japan Businesses Report SARS Impact" 2003).

Internet business, however, was booming, as consumers relied more on methods of shopping that avoided crowded marketplaces. As covered by CNN.com, in China, "Internet sales had risen as much as 60 percent at firms pitching joke books, antiseptic cleaners or DVDs to keep the housebound clean and entertained during the virus-induced panic" ("SARS Driving Shoppers Online" 2003). One store, which in 2002 sold roughly 100 million yuan worth of goods (about $12 million US), reported daily sales of 500,000 yuan in April and May, a 182.5 percent increase in sales. Another business reported April sales doubling from 2002 and expected May sales to triple ("SARS Driving Shoppers Online" 2003).

For the medical community, the last half of May brought breakthroughs in discoveries of viral transmission vectors and origins. Although some stories reported that SARS might prove to be a reoccurring disease with seasonal patterns, cropping up during flu seasons over the next few years (Miles 2003; Ross 2003), researchers remained hopeful that the virus could be understood and eradicated. In moving toward such an understanding, most of the virology community saw some theories as ridiculous, such as the CNN.com report of a British scientist claiming the SARS virus might have had outer space origins (Compton 2003). An ever-growing number of researchers, however, were focusing on the animal markets in Guangdong province, theorizing that the virus likely had animal origins. Some of these researchers pointed out the similarities between human air travel and hauling animals long distances in cattle cars; under such conditions, animals often contract "shipping fever," characterized by cough, pneumonia, and mucosal drip, all caused by a coronavirus. Perhaps, these researchers said, we are creating the perfect situation for viral spread: "When animals arrive from other locations and commingle, you see disease outbreaks," remarked Linda Saif, professor of food animal health at Ohio State University (Fox 2003b). Researchers in Hong Kong partially confirmed the animal origins of the virus on May 24, when they announced they had found evidence of the virus in three small mammals, including the civet cat. It was still too early at this point to determine whether the animals gave the virus to humans or caught it from them. One of the study's leaders, microbiologist Yuen Kwok-yung, strongly believed it was the former. Regardless of the remaining uncertainties, WHO expert Dr. Francois Meslin still declared the findings "quite exciting" ("Cat Delicacy Could Be SARS Key" 2003).

WEEK 17 (MAY 25–31)

On May 26, three days after Canada had been shoved back into the spotlight, Toronto health officials located the source of their new outbreak in the form of a ninety-six-year-old man who had died on May 1 after two attacks of pneumonia. Hospital staff did not isolate the man from other patients at the time of his admittance because they did not associate his pneumonia with SARS; they made the association only after the second outbreak. In response to these revelations, as well as the disclosing of 8 more probable cases and 3 new deaths, the WHO placed Toronto back on its list of SARS hot spots ("Toronto Reveals SARS Source" 2003). Toronto officials investigating the matter acknowledged that there could have been some 30 to 40 cases that had gone undetected during the "dry" period between outbreaks (Huang 2003a).

The last week in May revealed a Toronto once again under worldwide scrutiny. The Scarborough Hospital housed 20 SARS patients, 10 of whom were medical staff, while other members were under home quarantine. Hundreds of staff under working quarantine spent their days wearing N-95 masks, under orders to change them every four hours and take their temperature twice daily, all while interacting with patients. Staff members were also advised not to sit close together in the nurses' lounge and to keep an empty seat between them in the cafeteria (Gardner 2003).

At Toronto's Rouge Valley Centenary hospital, 4 patients died during the week, all suspected as SARS-related, though autopsies hadn't yet revealed the cause. The city's urban and suburban areas had not seen direct evidence of infection, but many hospitals bore SARS warning signs and taped shut their main doors, allowing entrance only through their emergency wards. The Canadian Federation of Nurses Unions moved its annual meeting to St. John's, Newfoundland (Wroughton 2003). Province-wide, the number of probable cases in Ontario rose dramatically: from 12 on Wednesday to 29 on Thursday, to 43 on Friday, to 46 on Saturday. Over 150 additional people were monitored closely as possible victims. Canada's thirtieth victim died on May 28; by this time in Toronto, more than 7,000 people had been quarantined, including 440 health care workers and 1,500 people associated with a high school. Still, Canadian Health Minister Anne McLellan reassured the public, "It is not getting worse . . . This second cluster has probably peaked and we are on the way out of this" ("Canada Fears New SARS Outbreak" 2003).

Halfway around the world, and despite the continuing direness of its situation, on May 25, Taiwan rejected an offer from China to help control the outbreak, claiming that they had everything under control. In its official rejection, Taiwan criticized China for interfering with international attempts to help, as well as blocking Taiwan from becoming a member of the WHO. The rejection came on the same day as health officers announced 22 new cases and 12 fatalities, bringing the island's death toll to 72 (Huang 2003b). These cases, however, did not include several hospital patients who had not passed the ten-day incubation period, raising the possibility of dozens of unreported infections ("New SARS Deaths a Blow for Taiwan" 2003). On May 26, Taiwan announced no deaths but 15 new cases, and Taipei's health bureau chief Chiou Shu-ti resigned over a major outbreak in a city hospital. Chiou's departure marked the third official to resign over SARS ("Toronto Traces SARS Cases to 96-Year-Old Patient" 2003). It did appear, however, that a turning point had passed; the number of cases per day was dropping.

In China, Yahoo! News reported that provincial officials in Guangzhou, Guangdong, had ordered sellers at markets to remove civet cats from their caged wares, as well as snakes, bats, badgers and pangolins, all of which had been identified as possible carriers of the virus. Farms that raised exotic species were told to quarantine their livestock. Violators were threatened with fines of up to $12,000. Such measures seemed effective; Guangdong had not reported a single new case of SARS in a week. China as a whole showed signs of improving as well: on the last day of the month, only a single new case was reported, along with 4 deaths—all in Beijing. The number of new cases had thus dropped by over 90 percent since the beginning of May, prompting Beijing to cut from its list nine of the sixteen hospitals set aside exclusively to treat SARS. Although it was still too early to make definite conclusions, China appeared to be containing the epidemic (Bodeen 2003b).

More good news arrived when the WHO lifted its travel advisory over Hong Kong on May 31, though 30 more deaths had been registered since the seventeenth of the month. In an odd turn of events, the virus proved a boon for businesses here: managers at restaurants reported that open-air dining patios operated at capacity and some restaurants had to hire additional staff to keep up with demand. According to one news article, this could be traced to locals seeking fresh air and open spaces, two commodities seen as healthful and lacking in the overcrowded cities. Locals seeking less crowded areas also meant that bike rental shops often rented out their entire stock, and park attendance surged by 75 percent. At least one business that rented out plots of land for people to try their hand at organic farming said business was up by 700 percent (M. Wong 2003a).

At the end of May, the government in Hong Kong passed laws designed to promote hygienic practices, and thus ward off SARS, among public housing tenants by punishing them for failing to keep their residences clean. Under these laws, which would come into effect in August 2003, tenants would face eviction if they received sixteen penalty points in a two-year period. Point-inducing violations included drying clothes in public areas, spitting, littering, throwing objects out of windows, and keeping pets. The Hong Kong Society for the Prevention of Cruelty to Animals viewed the latter of these offenses as dangerous—especially since having a pet warranted a five-point penalty—and warned that such laws would lead to a surge in animal abandonment ("HK Government Defends Points System to Evict Unruly Public Housing Tenants" 2003).

On the scientific front, researchers added further evidence regarding the possible animal origins of the virus when SARS antibodies were found in five wild animal traders who had not developed symptoms of the disease, meaning (1) they had contracted the disease some time ago and (2) the virus appeared to have mutated into a more lethal form since the traders had contracted it, based on genetic studies ("SARS Antibodies Found in Wild Animal Traders in Southern China" 2003). By May 28, researchers in Hong Kong openly declared that the virus had jumped from animals to humans because of these antibodies. Their findings "indicate workers caught the virus from the animals, developed a mild form of the disease, but then the virus mutated into a more virulent form before it was passed to other people," according to Shenzhen microbiologist He Jianfan ("Evidence SARS 'Jumped from Animals'" 2003).

The *BMJ* has not been mentioned for some time in this timeline. The last issue published in April 2003 contained no less than seven pieces on SARS, all of which opened the sections in which they were published. But such proliferation would prove aberrant. Only twelve SARS-related pieces appeared among all five issues of the *BMJ* published in May: nine news articles, two reviews, and one short blurb that appeared in the journal's "Filler" section. Few of these pieces offered any key insights into SARS. Even the May 3 edition of the journal, published just a week after the SARS-heavy edition of late April, contained only news articles about the epidemic. One noted that SARS may have peaked in Canada, Hong Kong, and Vietnam (Parry 2003e); one covered Canada's assurance that it was a safe place to visit (Spurgeon 2003b); and the last reported UK Health Secretary Alan Milburn's warning that SARS could still affect the United Kingdom (Eaton 2003). Two weeks later, the May 17 edition of the *BMJ* contained one news article and one review (actually a short, personal account of life in China by a senior lecturer in international health at the Institute of Child Health in London; see Hesketh 2003), and both of these pieces were located two stories from the bottom in their respective categories. The news that the United Kingdom had its first case of SARS (Parry 2003f) did appear as the second news story in the May 24 edition, but another news piece in the same edition—this one concerning Chinese scientists testing wild animals to find the host of SARS (Gottlieb 2003)—appeared near the end of its section. And the final May edition of the *BMJ* only had one SARS-related entry: a news story that detailed the resurgence of the virus in Toronto (Spurgeon 2003c).

WEEK 18 (JUNE 1–7)

June brought a breath of fresh air to many countries, as worldwide the SARS epidemic was in decline. Taiwan, after becoming the only country in the world with growing caseloads, had successfully adopted quarantine and monitoring policies that brought its numbers down drastically. One of the more stringent measures adopted there made news on June 1, when Taiwan instituted a nationwide ten-day temperature-check policy. Families everywhere—surveys showed 80 percent owned thermometers, and nearly that many said they would cooperate—were asked to monitor themselves daily and report anomalies. For those who didn't have thermometers, six thousand designated community pharmacies would provide the service. Only 4 people were diagnosed with SARS on the first day of the month—demonstrating the virus's decline—and the numbers went down from there ("Taiwan Launches National Temperature Check Campaign as SARS Wanes" 2003).

China, once the most infected nation in the world, ended May with an entire week of single-digit reports of SARS cases and began June by going twenty-four hours without a new case—the first day since April 20 it had been able to do so. No one died during the period either, and so China's figures remained at 5,328 infected and 332 dead. Life returned to normal as well, with Yahoo! News reports confirming regular traffic jams and a distinct lack of surgical masks on people riding buses and in crowded areas ("No China Sars Deaths for First Day in Six Weeks" 2003).

June's successes, however, were not equal for every area of the world. While Asia seemed to have its problems mostly under wraps, Toronto was still in the middle of its second resurgence of the disease. On June 1, 15 people were flagged as suspected cases, bringing the number of second-resurgence probable cases to 46, and 150 others were closely monitored as possible victims ("Canada Waits for SARS News as Asia Brings Disease under Control" 2003). By Monday, the number of active cases jumped to 52 and the death toll rose by one. The number of people in quarantine did drop by 2,000 people, bringing that total down to 5,300, but Ontario's public health commissioner, Dr. Colin D'Cunha, said that the province was still in a state of "hypervigilance"; earlier he had acknowledged that at least some of those quarantined had violated their isolation orders ("Another SARS Death in Toronto" 2003).

June also began ominously in Hong Kong, with 3 new infections and 3 new deaths reported on the first day of the month. One of the fatalities was a female ward attendant involved in treating some of the city's first victims. These new numbers brought Hong Kong's total to 281 deaths from 1,743 cases; 1,318 of those patients had been released from the hospital, leaving 83 still in treatment, 27 of those in intensive care ("Hong Kong Reports Three More SARS Cases, Three Deaths" 2003).

WEEK 19 (JUNE 8–14)

In mid-June, while not officially removing China from the list of SARS-infected countries, WHO members said that China appeared to have SARS under control. This did not mean that there had been no reported cases since the first of the month; indeed, there was one reported case the day before the

WHO statement surfaced, and roughly one person had died every day in China from SARS since the beginning of the month. The WHO based its statement on data that suggested that China was no longer exporting SARS; its borders had been made impermeable to the disease. The WHO did state that work still remained in China, however. Many questions lingered as to the disease's origin, and contagion vectors—that is, who gave the virus to whom— were murkier in China than anywhere else. Some 70 percent of patients diagnosed with SARS in Beijing since May 1 did not know from whom they had contracted the virus ("SARS under Control in China: WHO" 2003).

But encouraging discoveries emerged in the investigations into the origins and developments of SARS. Chinese animals were already strongly suspected as having passed the virus to humans, and in mid-June Yahoo! News covered the WHO's launch of a new series of studies designed to test the connection between SARS and other animal species. The civet cat was strongly suspected as the antagonist in the equation ("WHO to Conduct Fresh Studies on SARS Link to Other Animal Species" 2003). The same day also brought an announcement from Chinese researchers that a potential test for SARS, using antibodies to diagnose the virus, had been created. Until this point, doctors had been forced to rely on signs of the disease, such as high white blood cell counts and damaged lungs—signs that could be misleading (D. Young 2003b).

Another scene that pleased the WHO concerned Singapore, which was removed from the list of SARS-affected countries on the last day of May. Singapore had only tallied 206 cases and 31 deaths before controlling the epidemic, and June was mostly given over to planning contingencies for future epidemics. Singapore was especially proactive in attempting to stymie future reoccurrences of SARS and planned on implementing mandatory temperature checks for workers at shipyards, factories, and construction sites in mid-June as well as revamping health forms to include recent travel itineraries, possible contact with SARS-infected people, and current health states. Providing false information on such forms could result in fines of up to $5,797 and six months' jail time ("Singapore May Jail Patients for Dishonesty on SARS" 2003).

So successful were the attempts in Asia to control the epidemic that on June 12 the WHO stated that SARS was potentially coming to an end. Worldwide, only 7 new cases were reported on June 11, and though there were still a few places in the world where the disease remained uncontrolled, the general consensus felt the end was near (Grauwels 2003).

Canada remained one place where the disease remained uncontrolled; problems with quarantine violators continued, bringing the constant threat of public exposure to the virus. Ontario's health minister Tony Clement became so frustrated that at one point in early June he threatened to chain people to their beds if they didn't follow their isolation orders. He wasn't serious, but his concerns highlighted Toronto's problems in controlling the epidemic—and new laws did provide for fines of up to $3,650 for violators. By June 10 the number of active cases had risen to over 60 and some 6,800 people—an additional 1,500 since the first of the month—were in quarantine. These figures did not, however, include the 5,000 health care employees under working quarantine who were required to wear masks, gowns, and gloves in public and remain isolated during off-hours ("Penalize Quarantine Violators" 2003).

Unbelievably, given this increasing caseload, the Ontario Ministry of Health and Long-Term Care issued a warning to Toronto hospitals in early June reminding them to comply with provincial anti-SARS directives. Officials in the ministry had received reports from nurses at Mount Sinai Hospital complaining that they had been ordered not to comply with directives that required them to wear masks, gowns, and gloves—contradictions that meant the possible exposure to and quarantining of infants, new mothers, and at least 100 health care employees. At North York General, nurses complained that their concerns over the possible reemergence of SARS had been largely ignored by senior staff, and a nursing association official additionally reported that staff had been ordered to tell callers that facilities were SARS-free, even if they believed otherwise ("Editorial: Eves Needs to Call SARS Review Soon" 2003).

More bad news arrived on June 10, when provincial officials reported that they had been investigating a new possible SARS cluster in Whitby, located roughly fifty kilometers east of Toronto. If positive, this would have been the third cluster in Ontario—the first two being the primary and secondary Toronto outbreaks. This new group of suspected victims consisted of 15 people at the Lakeridge Health Corporation dialysis unit, all of who had developed fevers and respiratory problems. Adding to the severity of this news was the report that a North Carolina man had developed SARS-like symptoms after visiting a Toronto hospital in mid-May, making this the first possible case of SARS exported from Canada. All total, Canada now had 75 active SARS cases, 66 of which were probable, and an additional 260 people were under observation ("Health Officials Concerned over New SARS Cluster, Exported Case to US" 2003).

Over the next few days, the investigation into the Whitby cluster continued, and officials discovered that, for at least a few cases, SARS was not the infecting agent. Eight of the 15 suspects were cleared late on June 11.

Good news also came from investigations into the North Carolina SARS victim: although confirming the man as SARS-positive, doctors traced his infector to a known case, at least easing fears that the man had contracted the virus from a previously unknown victim (Sekhri 2003).

WEEK 20 (JUNE 15–21)

By the middle of the month, the WHO had lifted the travel advisory against Taiwan, commending the country for its recent proactive stance, a large difference from the widespread condemnation of Taiwanese infection control systems that had been handed down only five weeks earlier ("WHO Lifts Taiwan SARS Advisory" 2003). Serving as almost a coda to Taiwan's struggle with SARS, on June 18, two doctors were charged with "covering up SARS cases that allowed the deadly virus to spread through a Taipei hospital, leading to the island's first and worst outbreak" ("Two Taiwan Doctors Charged with SARS Cover-up" 2003). Prosecutors sought an eight-year sentence for both Wu Kang-wen, former superintendent of the Taipei Municipal Ho-Ping Hospital, and Lin Jung-ti, the same hospital's head of infectious diseases. According to Taipei District Court prosecutor Chen Hon-da, "The investigation shows the defendants neglected their duties and failed to take necessary infection control measures, causing the deaths of several medical workers and allowing the epidemic to spread" ("Two Taiwan Doctors Charged with SARS Cover-up" 2003).

June 18 also marked the third day in a row Taiwan had not reported any new SARS infections. There would be three more cases and one more death before Taiwan received the all clear on July 5, but for now the tally stood at 697 infected and 83 dead, making the island the third-worst hit area behind Mainland China and Hong Kong ("Two Taiwan Doctors Charged with SARS Cover-up" 2003).

By June 20, Hong Kong was also only days away from receiving the WHO's twenty-day "all clear" stamp of approval. The date additionally marked the day Hong Kong and Chinese health officials met to discuss a system wherein the former would receive prompt health reports from the mainland, thus hopefully avoiding future epidemics ("HK, China Discuss SARS Warning System" 2003).

It also appeared that Toronto was gaining control of its second outbreak. The number of cases declined daily: the city reported only 37 probable cases on June 17—down from 64 a week earlier. Thirty-six of those active cases were hospitalized patients, 18 of whom were in critical condition. June 17 also marked the SARS-related death of a sixty-seven-year-old man from the

Toronto area—the first SARS death in Canada in ten days. The toll now stood at 34 (Hodgson 2003).

In China, the hypothesized connections between SARS and animals had greatly affected wild game markets and associated restaurants. Shenzhen restaurants had been virtually empty for two weeks, some of them despite entirely new menus that did not feature their standard exotic fare. The markets themselves had faced similar fortunes: Xinyuan, Guangzhou's largest wild game market, now featured empty cages and uneager buyers, a scene that pleased those who monitored and attempted to halt the wildlife trade (D. Young 2003a).

Mid-June also marked a two-day gathering of health officials from around the world to discuss how to deal with future viral epidemics. Studies of worldwide reactions to SARS had produced valuable information about controlling outbreaks, but delegates were quick to point out that things could have gone better. Shigeru Omi, WHO regional director for the Western Pacific Region, said, "The SARS epidemic is now coming under control but the fight is by no means over. SARS is not defeated, other new diseases will threaten us in the future, we must be better prepared next time" ("Health Officials Ponder What Next after SARS" 2003). The success of this gathering was mixed, as the one thousand-plus attendees left with few new ideas on the origin of the virus or how it should be eradicated (Krishnan 2003).

What did come of the studies taking place around the world were warnings that future outbreaks of SARS were conceivable, and possibly only months away. Some theories suggested that a large reservoir of the SARS virus in China's animal population could cross over into the human population at any given time. Other theories echoed earlier statements that the disease was now so widespread as to be impossible to entirely contain and that it might prove to be perennial. Many researchers also pointed to the recent increases in the global trade of animals and plants and the problems caused by cross-contamination that result when species are unintentionally let loose in foreign countries (Chinoy 2003; Lodge 2003).

Whether or not such theories were valid, SARS had clearly changed the way the world thought about disease. One example of this lay in attempts to network thousands of personal computers around the world to form a massive supercomputer that could be put to the task of looking for novel drug molecules. Under such a volunteer-based program, the computers in people's homes and offices could, during spare cycles, be downloaded with software that would allow them to look for drug molecules that would bind with disease-associated proteins—in essence, to look for vaccines and cures. Such networking was projected to cut the time needed to find promising drugs from one and a half years down to a few months (Buckler 2003).

It should come as no surprise that few SARS-related articles appeared in the *BMJ* in June, and July brought only a single entry: a news story in the July 12 edition covering the WHO's announcement about the end of SARS (Fleck 2003). There was one major discrepancy to these statements. The June 21 edition of the *BMJ* was SARS-themed, the cover sporting magnified photographs of the virus and bearing the headline "SARS: understanding the coronavirus." The journal carried only a single news article relating to the disease—evidence of the waning epidemic—but it did bear two peer-reviewed papers, nine letters, and two reviews. The papers and letters, all clinical in nature and tone, discussed the positive and negative strategies adopted by various organizations in dealing with the epidemic and the lessons that could be applied to future diseases in light of what had been learned on a global level. This SARS-themed edition, however, seems out of place when viewed in the context of the surrounding editions, few of which mentioned the disease—in fact, only one out of the five subsequent issues referenced it at all: the aforementioned July 12 news entry.

WEEK 21 (JUNE 22–28)

By June 22, another 4 people had died in Canada, but the number of cases continued to decline: only 28 active cases remained ("SARS Kills Two More in Canada" 2003). Most of the week's news, however, focused on Hong Kong. On June 23, the WHO removed the region from its list of SARS-infected areas at the same time it warned Hong Kong's health officials of the possible reoccurrence of SARS if they dropped safeguards too early, drawing a direct comparison to Toronto's resurgence (M. Wong 2003b). All that remained now was for the region to revamp and restimulate its damaged economy, since Hong Kong's unemployment levels had recently reached a record 8.3 percent and businesses all over the city were feeling the impact of the diminished tourism industry. To combat the fear still present among locals and tourists, Hong Kong's government installed dispensers of anti-bacterial sprays in government buildings and busy areas and carted high-tech temperature-scanning devices to major areas of activity, such as jewelry trade fairs, airports, and border crossings (Allen 2003).

WEEK 22 (JUNE 29–JULY 5)

One more person would perish in Canada by the end of June, but cases were so few—and no new cases had been reported in some time—that the WHO removed Toronto from its list of SARS-infected areas on July 2 ("WHO Gives Toronto SARS All-Clear" 2003), leaving Taiwan as the only country still under watch.

In Singapore, a popular television character named Phua Chu Kang released, with the support of the health ministry, an anti-SARS rap CD. Songs encouraged locals to maintain good hygiene to stop the spread of viral agents through lyrics such as "SARS is the virus that I just want to minus" and "Don't 'kak-pui' [spit] all over the place, you might as well 'kak-pui' on my face" ("Singapore's Hip-Hop SARS Hope" 2003). Rarely, if ever, had governments used such methods to spread knowledge. The CD was released just after a series of crackdowns on public spitting, which had long been a fineable offense in Singapore—one CNN.com news story detailed a man who was fined $290 for spitting in a shopping district (Szep 2003a).

Public efforts to increase awareness and hygiene didn't stop at spitting. In Singapore, workers at food stalls and construction sites received twice-daily temperature readings, as was staff at more than one hundred of the city's hotels. Widespread public leaflets encouraged people to wash their hands. The government also launched a "Happy Toilet" program that gave starred ratings to all public toilets, informing people of those facilities that did not meet cleanliness standards. Singapore's health officials also announced that they would continue a program that had begun the previous month, and which had brought mass criticism, in culling the city's eighty thousand-plus stray cats in response to studies linking China's civet cat to SARS (Szep 2003a).

Global efforts at enforcing preventative measures such as these finally worked. On July 5, the WHO declared the global SARS epidemic over after removing Taiwan from its list. But WHO Director-General Gro Harlem Brundtland quickly reminded the public that the virus could resurge if people were not careful; there were still some 200 SARS patients in hospitals around the world, any one of whom could infect a visitor or staff member ("WHO: Global SARS Outbreak Over" 2003). These warnings were underscored by a health scare in Taiwan later that month when a twelve-year-old girl returned from a trip to China complaining of SARS-like symptoms. She was swiftly ruled out as carrying the virus, but not before 20 people were sent into precautionary quarantine ("Taiwanese Girl Ruled out as SARS Infection" 2003).

The Lancet did continue to print SARS-related articles throughout June and July, though in increasingly smaller numbers. The first two issues in June had four articles each, though two of these eight articles were "News In

Brief" blurbs. But the last two issues only had three articles between them, and one of those merely mentioned SARS in the context of a recent series of attacks on the WHO's health system performance since 2000 (Brundtland, Frenk, and Murray 2003). July's first two issues seemed to revamp interest in SARS, with five articles written directly on the disease, one news brief, and two other articles that mentioned SARS—though it was not the focus of those articles. The third issue of the month lacked even a single article on the subject. While the last issue in July did contain two articles, one of them was a full-length, peer-reviewed research paper confirming the coronavirus as the source of the epidemic—old news by this point, but it had not been published earlier due to the considerable legwork involved in creating it. Aside from the news brief, every article that focused on SARS during June and July was scientific in nature, summarizing the various attempts that had been made to unravel the virus's genome, prevent it from spreading via various biochemical efforts, etc. Once again, none of these articles mentioned rumor or legend, and few of them—including the news briefs—gave more than the most cursory summarization of the epidemic.

THE AFTERMATH

Worldwide, SARS had killed 774 people.[2] Toronto would claim another fatality on July 14—a seventy-six-year-old woman ("Toronto SARS Death Toll Reaches 40" 2003)—but the road to recovery seemed clear, and even more likely after Roche Holding AG, the world's biggest diagnostic firm, developed a long-sought-after test for SARS in mid-July (Shields 2003). Fast-forward to mid-August, and articles bore headlines such as "The Vanished Virus," a piece in *The Guardian* that came out the same day that China released its last two SARS patients from the hospital ("The Vanished Virus" 2003). Warnings of viral resurgence still abounded, but for many, life had returned to normal.

The effects of SARS would be felt for months in areas and countries all over the world. Even businesses thousands of miles away from the epidemic's epicenter suffered losses, such as Finland's Nokia, which forecasted that 2003's second-quarter sales could be weaker than expected due in part to SARS ("Nokia Sinks on Latest Warning" 2003). In Nokia's case, such low sales directly related to a 20–30 percent drop in cell phone sales in Hong Kong and parts of China, but company representatives were confident in a strong third quarter with the worldwide decline in cases ("SARS Hits Nokia Sales in Asia" 2003). Texas Instruments suffered similarly, its stock shares plummeting roughly 10 percent after it reported troubles selling stockpiled wireless semiconductors in Asian markets. Motorola also reported problems moving wares in Asia, noting that cell phone and semiconductor sales were at new lows ("Global Tech Giants Take a Hit from SARS" 2003). In Singapore, consumer prices as a whole fell .7 percent in June, despite retailers offering massive sales to lure customers ("Singapore Prices Fall on SARS" 2003).

In Canada, the WHO's travel advisories against Toronto heavily shook the $52 billion tourism industry. But Toronto was not the only city affected, nor was Ontario the only province to suffer. Prince Edward Island, New Brunswick, Manitoba, Alberta, and British Columbia also saw a decline in tourism, and hotels, restaurants, and tourist attractions in all five provinces showed lower profits. Even the Formula One race in Montreal—an event that normally filled all twenty thousand of Montreal's hotel rooms with fans—wasn't able to draw its regular crowd. Altogether, Canadian Tourism Commission spokeswoman Isabelle Des Chenes estimated nationwide losses at $300–$500 million over the short term, with larger losses probable over the following year ("Canadian Tourist Industry Nervous as SARS Stigma Lingers" 2003).

Air Canada may have been able to claim the largest Canadian losses from the epidemic and was definitely the hardest-hit airline in the world, filing for bankruptcy protection in April after reporting $150 million in losses due to flight cancellations. May brought a further $200 million drop in gross receipts, with similar losses expected for June. Summer bookings were also weak, leading many to believe that the damage would continue for some months ("SARS Fears Continue to Exacerbate Air Canada Losses" 2003).

Business may have been bad, but the world was recovering. Despite many warnings, there were no new SARS cases for the rest of 2003. One apparently exceptional case was announced in Singapore on September 9, involving a postdoctoral student who worked as a laboratory technician on the West Nile virus ("Timeline: Sars virus" 2003). Health officials in Singapore initially confirmed the case as SARS-related but simultaneously stated their uncertainty over whether this new case signaled a return of SARS or was merely an isolated incident resulting from a laboratory accident (Szep 2003b). Reaction to this possible new infection was immediate, with the WHO quickly launching an official investigation. But just as quickly, the WHO announced its uncertainty of not only how the man contracted the virus—since his work did not include contact with SARS—but whether he actually had the disease, as his symptoms did not include lung infections or respiratory problems ("Q&A: Sars" 2003). Because of these uncertainties and the lack of classic symptoms, the WHO refused to classify the man's illness as SARS, contradicting the earlier diagnosis made by Singapore's health officials. Instead of reassuring the public, however, this action in some ways only served to increase tension, drawing worldwide attention toward the difficulties of diagnosing the disease. It did not help that Singapore reacted by affirming the accuracy of their positive diagnosis, citing the two rounds of polymerase chain reaction and serology tests conducted on the patient. The WHO, countering such claims, then pointed to the small margin of error endemic to such tests. Singapore's Minister of State for Health further added to the confusion by referencing studies demonstrating that 5 percent of SARS patients during the last outbreak had developed a fever but did not go on to develop the disease (Szep 2003b).

A local investigation into the two laboratories in which the postdoctoral student worked revealed that one of them did conduct research on SARS, and thus it was possible that the student had come into contact with the virus. Logs showed that the student had visited this lab three days before becoming ill. Both labs were closed in response and 41 people were quarantined. The WHO, however, still maintained its position, declaring the case "not an international public health concern" and that travel to Singapore was safe (Szep 2003c). Their position seemed validated when the student continued to recover from his illness. He'd had no fever for five days, and the hospital had slated him to be released within a few days—a rapid recovery that only further confirmed the WHO's suspicions that the man did not have full-blown SARS (Szep 2003d).

In response to the case—and despite the WHO's declarations—a team of eleven international experts arrived in Singapore on September 15 to investigate the matter. A WHO biosafety expert chaired the team that included members of the CDC ("Singapore, Foreign Experts Start Probe in SARS Case" 2003). The results of their study, released a week later, found that the case resulted from a lab accident and verified that the student had contracted the virus while on the job. Genome sequencing confirmed the similarities between the lab sample and the strain that infected the researcher. The student himself had fully recovered by this point and had been discharged from the hospital, but the lab where he had contracted the disease was shut down, and the SARS virus samples contained therein ordered destroyed (Another SARS Death in Toronto 2003).

The study also pointed to a few troubling details. The accident that had caused the student's infection resulted from a cross-contamination between West Nile and SARS viral samples, indicating a lack of compliance regarding appropriate procedures for handling samples. Antony Della-Porta, the WHO biosafety expert, stated, "It's obvious the labs put in enormous effort and did a fantastic job during the SARS outbreak, but it led to some inconsistencies where labs were not really prepared to handle organisms at that level," and he recommended stricter guidelines for lab researchers (J. Wong 2003). At roughly the same time that Singapore was dealing with these problems, the Chinese University of Hong Kong announced it would finance a top-level SARS laboratory, designed to be fully mobile and available for use within a few months. Such a lab would hopefully make dealing with future outbreaks far easier, and the planned Level 3 status—the highest international safety grade—would prevent such occurrences as Singapore's leak ("Hong Kong University to Finance Top-Level SARS Lab" 2003). Additional safety measures taken by Hong Kong included an alert system and increased numbers of staff at border checkpoints to screen travelers, in addition to building a center for disease control to "speed up laboratory tests, strengthen contact tracing and disease investigations," all of which was planned to be built by year's end. Hospitals were also taking precautionary measures against future outbreaks, making sure there were at least three hundred rooms with isolation facilities, and an extra 1,290 beds (Luk 2003).

Hong Kong added to the good news on September 25, when CNN.com announced that local researchers had determined that the HIV drug Kaletra, when used in combination with ribavirin, had been shown to significantly reduce mortality rates among SARS victims. These announcements came in the wake of a series of criticisms of Hong Kong's earlier methods of treatment, which centered on a drug cocktail of steroids and ribavirin—not including Kaletra—many experts had deemed ineffective. In response to the news, Hong Kong hospitals immediately announced that all future SARS patients would be treated with the Kaletra-ribavirin cocktail for this reason as well as because the combination reduced the need for steroid use ("Hong Kong to Use HIV Drug to Treat SARS" 2003).

Such a development was no doubt welcome after a fresh round of reports declared that SARS would likely resurface in the future (Walsh 2003). The WHO only added fuel to this fire by announcing the likelihood of many SARS-like diseases cropping up in the next century for which mankind needed to prepare (Kataria 2003). As if proving this statement true, Hong Kong had a small scare in the last few days of September, quarantining 7 men after they developed high fevers and upper respiratory tract infections. Although all 7 were soon cleared—their symptoms were not SARS-related—the incident underscored the real possibility of this situation (Sisci 2003).

One of the immediately noticeable themes in post-SARS media reports concerned the assignation of fault and blame. One example came after

Canada's nurses declared Ontario unprepared to deal with future outbreaks due to lack of governmental direction ("Nurses Say Toronto Not Prepared If SARS Reappears" 2003). Such directed blame was not isolated to North America. A report released in early October 2003 chided Hong Kong for "significant shortcomings" in the early phases of SARS, implying that had Hong Kong's airports been better controlled, the virus would not have escaped as it did to more than thirty nations worldwide. Hong Kong residents had long specifically criticized their government and Chief Executive Tung Chee-hwa for their slow responses, but the report—put together by "an outside panel of experts"—avoided giving specific names, listing instead Hong Kong's "poor links between the health department and private and public hospitals, ineffective chains of command, a lack of contingency plans, poor infection control in hospitals and staff that were not properly trained"; at the same time, it recognized that China's secrecy concerning the virus played a large part in these shortcomings (Bray 2003; "SARS Report Faults Government" 2003).

Other reports faulted the treatments given to patients. By the second week in October—barely three months after the WHO declared the epidemic contained—dozens of former SARS patients in Hong Kong and China were found to be suffering from avascular necrosis, a form of bone degeneration caused by the ribavirin/steroid cocktail administered to all infected victims (Lyn 2003b).

Still other reports pointed to China's wildlife trade. Banned in May by the Chinese government after reports that the SARS virus may have come from wild animals, the markets and concomitant animal trade industry were legalized again in August after Chinese experts failed to verify the animal-origin theory. In post-SARS China, the markets were as large as ever. Even the civet cat, which was almost singled out as the source of the virus earlier in the year, reappeared on restaurant menus in Guangdong, though restaurant managers did report that requests for the delicacy had decreased greatly. Such regression led many outsiders to fear that the virus could make the cross-species jump again ("Bloody Animal Trade Thrives in Post-SARS China" 2003; Lynch 2003).

A second common theme in media reports was one of hope, specifically as it related to medical advances. This theme was not new to the post-SARS period, however; it began weeks earlier with the preliminary studies on the origins of SARS. Reports in October 2003 merely continued the trend, though they were even more positive now than in earlier months. Singapore, for example, announced in early October that it was developing an electronic chip that, using sputum or nasal fluid, could tell almost instantly whether a patient had SARS, as well as flu, dengue fever, and other respiratory illnesses. The chip was expected to be available in early 2004 and would completely negate the long waiting periods doctors experienced in receiving laboratory results (Aglionby 2003).

Other breakthroughs in October dealt with the infection rates and transmission vectors of the virus. In a report released on October 20, the WHO declared that no evidence supported the theory that SARS was an airborne virus. Instead, the disease was transmitted via direct contact with infectious respiratory droplets, usually through the eyes, nose, and mouth. The same report stated that those infected were at the greatest risk of infecting others around day 10, when viral loads excreted through the respiratory tract were at their greatest. Interesting, though unexplained, were statistics that showed only 2 reported cases of children transmitting the virus to adults, no evidence of infected mothers transmitting the virus to their unborn children, and no incidences of children infecting other children ("Report: SARS Not Airborne Virus" 2003).

The last two days of October brought a flurry of news, the most optimistic of which came from the CDC, which stated that the chances of containing a new outbreak of SARS were greatly improved, thanks largely to improved global alert systems ("Chances of Containing SARS Much Improved—Expert" 2003). At the same time, it cautioned others not to relax their vigilance, reemphasizing the possibility that the virus could return in the winter months. Additional warnings took the form of cautionary reminders that no test would positively identify SARS in the first days of infection ("Keep up the Guard on SARS, Health Experts Say at Paris Conference" 2003).

A second series of reports had a decidedly pessimistic tone. First came a study from the CDC that stated China had unnecessarily quarantined thousands of people in its efforts to prevent the spread of SARS. According to the study, it had been unnecessary to quarantine some two-thirds of the 30,000 people ultimately isolated in Beijing alone ("China Quarantined Too Many in SARS Outbreak—Study" 2003). A second study found that house cats and ferrets could become infected and pass the disease on to other animals. No evidence was found in the study to prove or disprove that the virus could be transmitted to humans from these animals, and researchers argued publicly for both sides (Kahn 2003).

The final cautionary tales for the month came from Taiwan, where doctors worried that SARS could easily return among the 3 million people expected to fall ill during the upcoming flu season. Su Ih-jen, the director general of Taiwan's Center for Disease Control, stated that the peak of the season was December 15, and Taiwan would resume temperature checks in public places by that date to watch for early signs of an outbreak ("Taiwan Says SARS May Lurk among 3 Mln Flu Patients" 2003). At the same time, Health Minister Chen Chien-jen decided to retract earlier laws requiring compulsory surgical masks and blanket quarantines. Such measures had earlier proved so frightening that one man committed suicide after learning that his family had been diagnosed with SARS, and a woman had threatened to jump out of her hospital window when faced with Taiwan's mandatory ten-day quarantine (Wu 2003). October seemed to end in ambivalence, the number of positive and cautionary articles roughly balancing.

Considering this, the rest of 2003 seemed mild, news reports lessening considerably in November and December. The only major report during these months concerned a SARS vaccine trial in China. Announced in late November, the human trials, scheduled to commence in 2004, came after weeks of studying the effects of weakened coronaviruses on animals—studies that had shown the vaccine effective on monkeys ("China Plans SARS Vaccine Trial" 2003). In the first phases of animal testing, the six rhesus macaques that were infected all showed "a detectable immune system response" against the SARS coronaviruses—a result promising enough to warrant testing the vaccine on animals more susceptible to the virus, such as ferrets. The vaccine could also be produced cheaply. Dr. Andrea Gambotto, head of the research team charged with developing the vaccine, said, "it can be produced in a million vaccine doses easily at very low cost" ("SARS Trials Lift Vaccine Hope" 2003). If October had ended in ambivalence, December ended in victory.

January 2004, however, began in fear. By the twelfth day of the month, three new cases of SARS in China—all in Guangdong—and two scientists researching the disease in Taiwan and Singapore had contracted the disease. The first Chinese case appeared on January 5, when a thirty-two-year-old male television producer fell ill. His case puzzled doctors, as he had no regular contact with wild animals. The second case—though it was still only suspected as SARS—involved a twenty-year-old waitress who worked at a restaurant that served dishes containing exotic foods such as the civet cat. By the time the third case arrived—a thirty-five-year-old male suspected of contracting the virus—the TV producer had been discharged from the hospital, but the fear of a new outbreak had spread. Guangdong officials had begun a mass culling of civet cats—an effort started in late 2003 with the revelation of a possible link between the animals and SARS—but the exterminations redoubled in effort to the point that one official at the Guangzhou Anti-SARS Office told a CNN.com reporter, "Basically, most of the civet cats in Guangdong have been slaughtered" ("Third Suspected SARS Case in China" 2004).

Mass culling of civet cats was not the only precautionary measure taken in light of the new human cases: city cleaners made regular street-sweeping excursions and exterminators targeted rats, cockroaches, flies, and mosquitoes as potential disease spreaders. The Guangzhou newspaper *Yangcheng Evening News* reported that a citywide effort to eliminate rats involved over ten thousand people and warned that more than 10 tons of poison-laced grain had been deployed in "millions of places" throughout Guangzhou. Anyone encountering a rat carcass was told to "exercise caution" to avoid becoming infected. The city government also banned the breeding, sale, distribution, and consumption of civet cat, raccoon dog, and badger ("Third Suspected SARS Case in China" 2004).

In mid-January, the WHO investigators who had visited China in 2003 to search for the origins of SARS returned to Guangdong. One of their first stops included a live-animal market, where they examined chickens, ducks, and other "edible creatures" to better determine the source of SARS, though they were quick to point out that no evidence linked poultry to the virus— a statement no doubt influenced greatly by the recent problems with avian influenza that had been cropping up throughout the area (Anthony 2004). On the same day, a SARS expert at the University of Hong Kong stated that the current strain infecting the three victims in Guangdong was not only *not* a descendent of the virus that had caused the 774 deaths in 2003, but it also appeared to be far less contagious and deadly. This new strain of coronavirus appeared to be maladapted to the human body, which explained why no one who had come into contact with the three victims had yet exhibited SARS-like symptoms: the virus was too weak to create a "superspreader." But Dr. Robert Breiman, head of the WHO team in Guangzhou, retorted, "Last year, among the thousands of cases of SARS, they included many, many people who didn't transmit and many, many people who had a reasonably mild disease. And so it may just be a mathematical thing" (Ansfield 2004).

The uncertainty surrounding this new series of infections did little to curtail public consternation. In a new mass culling, officials gathered and exterminated thousands of raccoon dogs to prevent future outbreaks. The WHO team, having barely arrived in the province, had yet to determine any connections between the three extant cases, and Breiman did little to assuage fear when he said, "There is certainly no smoking gun at the moment with any of the three cases that would enable us to say precisely where they got it . . . It's still a little bit of a mystery, a bit of what you might call a jigsaw puzzle and at some point I have a feeling this will all come together and maybe be fairly obvious, but at the moment it's not clear" ("Origin of New SARS Outbreak in China a Mystery, Raccoon Dogs Culled" 2004).

Public perception of this new strain of coronavirus was only exacerbated when two China Southern Airline flight attendants were quarantined in a Sydney hospital after returning from China with sore throats and fevers ("Australia Probes Two Suspect SARS Cases" 2004). Their story quickly turned positive, as they were released two days later, on January 16. Also on that day, Breiman announced the WHO team's initial findings, which pointed strongly toward an animal origin for this new strain of coronavirus. Their virologic forays uncovered traces of the virus in the restaurant where the twenty-year-old waitress worked, and animal cages known to contain civet cats in the back of the restaurant all tested positive for SARS. Breiman also countered his own earlier public statement in the same interview, stating that the one confirmed case of SARS in 2004—the TV producer—seemed "milder" than the 2003 strain (McDonald 2004; "SARS Virus Uncovered at Restaurant" 2004).

More good news quickly followed. On January 19, China approved the first human trials of its experimental SARS vaccine—though WHO officials rapidly pointed out that surveillance, early diagnosis, quarantines, and free exchange of information were still the best ways to combat the virus. Some thirty people immediately volunteered to be test subjects for the first phase of the study, which would determine whether the vaccine was safe for humans. It would still, however, be months before any vaccine could be mass-produced (Hoo 2004).

Additional promise in the fight against SARS arrived in late March, when researchers at the National Institute of Allergy and Infectious Diseases announced that they had developed a gene-based vaccine that had proven effective in mice. Although they cautioned that it would be some time before this new approach was determined to work in humans, it had significantly reduced the level of coronaviruses in the lungs of mice exposed to the disease. In the same article, however, researchers not connected with the study noted that such results should not be overstated; no DNA vaccine such as this had been shown to effectively treat any viral disease, and the approach was still considered unconventional ("Study: SARS Vaccine Shows Promise in Mice" 2004).

All was quiet on the SARS front for over three months following January's series of outbreaks. But on April 23, China admitted to two new SARS patients: a twenty-year-old female nurse at a Beijing disease research laboratory and her mother. Response was immediate upon confirmation of the presence of the coronavirus: 171 people were quarantined in Beijing and placed under close observation, including 5 of the nurse's coworkers (only one of whom would become infected). Another 88 were quarantined in Anhui province, where the mother lived. By the time this news became public knowledge, however, both cases were actually weeks old: the nurse had contracted SARS on April 5 and the mother had died of SARS-related complications on April 19—a death the Chinese Ministry of Health didn't even confirm until April 30. Once again, China had kept its outbreak secret for a period of time, and news reports were quick to point out the conse-quences of such secrecy in the earlier epidemic ("China Admits First 2004 SARS Death" 2004; "Two SARS Cases Confirmed in China" 2004).

These new cases would prove to be the last. There was little SARS-related news in May, save one report that the Chinese human vaccine tri-als had been successful, the study's four volunteers in good condition four days after inoculation ("SARS: Human Vaccine Trials Begin" 2004), and a second report on Toronto's rapidly recovering tourism industry ("Toronto Is Back a Year after SARS" 2004).

June's news was equally light. On the first day of the month, China announced it would discontinue its daily SARS report, as there had been no new cases since the April outbreaks and the last SARS-related patient was dis-charged from the hospital on May 31 ("China to Stop Daily SARS Report" 2004). Beijing shut down its anti-SARS office the same day ("Beijing Shuts Anti-SARS Headquarters" 2004).

The rest of the month's reports were congratulatory in nature: a review of Toronto's 2003 measures to control the epidemic that applauded the city on its efforts (Doheny 2004); an announcement welcomed by the scientific world that scientists had developed a new method of detecting SARS using a chip that would reduce the length of time for molecular testing from one week to three days ("Scientists Say Develop New SARS Tracing Method" 2004); and a cheery report by an Associated Press writer that the Hong Kong apartment block so heavily infected in 2003 because of sewage leaks had almost entirely recovered (M. Wong 2004).

The final two articles in this timeline come from early July 2004. The first detailed a report released in Hong Kong on July 5 that found severe fault with the government's handling of the 2003 epidemic. Released only days after hundreds of thousands of protestors marched on the capital to demand democratic reforms, the report put immediate pressure on the administration, specifically criticizing Secretary for Health, Welfare and Food Dr. Yeoh Eng-Kiong, former Director of Health Dr. Margaret Chan, and Hospital Authority Chairman Dr. Leong Che-hung for their inaction. Yeoh was singled out among these three, the report stating he "did not show sufficient alertness" when atypical pneumonia was reported in Guangdong province and gave the public "confusing and misleading" messages concerning the virus's spread. All three, as well as other authorities, were given blanket criticisms for permitting the admittance of SARS-infected patients into otherwise uncontaminated hospital rooms, effectively creating an epicenter from which the disease would eventually spread ("Report Blasts HK Chiefs over SARS" 2004). The second, and last, news article detailed Yeoh's official resignation two days later ("HK Health Chief Quits over SARS" 2004).

This is not, of course, a declaration that no additional news reports concerning SARS were released after this point in 2004. But they were few and far between, and at least for the purposes of this study, bore little relevance, mainly detailing scientific and medical advances. But there is one final aspect to consider in the examination of the sources used to construct the preceding timeline, and that pertains to the differences between the media and medical timelines. Although this chapter only examined the articles that comprised the medical timeline between late March 2003 and the end of July, some four months later, it should be obvious that the pages of the *British Medical Journal* and *The Lancet* were almost entirely absent of the rumors, legends, and gossip that so permeated newspapers and televised news reports. This is to be expected. These journals are scientific in nature, their articles peer reviewed and carefully selected. Still, it is odd that even the news reports that appeared in these journals were free of disease narratives, focusing instead on an unbiased, accurate representation of facts as expressed through raw data and summarizations of key events. Such reporting stands in sharp contrast to the news stories published by Yahoo! News, MSNBC.com, and CNN.com, all of which relayed vernacular narratives. While the media's timeline obviously draws in part on the medical establishment's telling of the epidemic, the medical establishment did not reciprocate. These differences in focus coincide with what Peter Washer has noted: "beyond the *realist* global epidemic of (the disease) SARS lies the globalization of the *phenomenon* of the SARS panic, where the saturation and speed of the world news media's coverage leads to the (supposed) risk posed by SARS being *socially constructed* on a global scale" (Washer 2004, 2570, emphasis in original). This is not to say that the medical timeline is the "realist" version, but it does point out that the media's construction of events contributed far more to the social construction of the disease than did its medical counterpart.

If media sources had not existed, or had been severely weakened in influence, and the public had been forced to turn to the pages of academic journals to retrieve news on SARS, would there have been as many rumors? The answers to a question such as this can only be speculative and would no doubt vary widely and be argued over vehemently. But the fact that a question such as this could be asked points to the correlation between media sources and rumors.

NOTES

1. Creating a timeline for an epidemic is difficult, more so with SARS because of, among other details, the secrecy maintained by the Chinese government, which occluded a large portion of the available information. For the purposes of the timeline constructed in this chapter, the entirety of February 2003 will be used to mark the initial weeks of the outbreak, since that is when the virus crossed international borders and attracted the public's attention.

2. The National Institutes of Health, in the July–August 2003 issue of The NIH *Catalyst*, placed the number of SARS-related deaths at 812, and the WHO's July 11, 2003, update listed 813 fatalities. But in its official 2004 report, the WHO revised the number down to 774 (see "Summary of Probable SARS Cases with Onset of Illness from 1 November 2002 to 31 July 2003" 2004).

2

SARS and AIDS
A Comparison of Etiological Legends

FROM AESOP'S FABLES TO NAVAJO TRICKSTER STORIES, from Serbo-Croatian epic poems to the works of Homer, humankind has always been interested in the concepts of "how," "why," and "where": "How did the sun get up in the sky?" "Why does the fox have a white-tipped tail?" "Where do we come from?" In the field of medicine, questions of origin are not only critical but can mean the difference between life and death: Where did the patient contract this disease? How did the patient contract the disease—from an animal, a human, a rusty nail? How long ago? Where was (s)he? Questions such as these occupied central theses in the 2003 SARS epidemic, as World Health Organization (WHO) researchers put forth considerable effort to trace the source of the virus back to the Chinese civet cat.

As intelligent as humans are to ask these questions, however, we sometimes fall short in patiently waiting for the responses. We want our answers, and we want them now. And if no answer is immediately forthcoming, we sometimes create our own hypotheses to fill the vacuum. At times these hypotheses prove ultimately correct: researchers suspected the animal-human SARS link as early as March 24, 2003, though they did not prove it until May 28, 2003. At other times, hypotheses ultimately fall far short of the mark, such as the conspiracy theory that Saddam Hussein had released SARS as part of a biological warfare campaign.

Questions of etiology are found in almost every type of disease narrative—rumor, legend, gossip, joke—and are so distinct and varied that they merit their own study. Furthermore, most every modern disease has its origin story. For example, AIDS etiological narratives have focused on "government conspiracies, African or Haitian AIDS, 'patient zero' type characteristics, superbugs transmitting the virus through bites, [and] hundred-year-old AIDS cases" (Goldstein 2004, 77), and arguments over where AIDS came

DOI: 10.7330/9780874219296.c002

from and who to blame for it parallel similar speculations concerning "the bubonic plague, smallpox, syphilis, and . . . influenza" (78). This chapter will explore the similarities between these narratives—primarily between AIDS and SARS, though other diseases will not be ignored—pointing out how, in many cases, the narratives are so analogous as to make it seem that the differences lie *only* in the name of the disease.

AIDS is arguably the disease that has spawned the greatest number of origin stories. A disease that has made newspaper headlines for a quarter of a century, it should come as no surprise that AIDS has spawned more narratives than would comfortably fit in even a sizable book—and dozens of such books have been published. Diane E. Goldstein's *Once Upon a Virus: AIDS Legends and Vernacular Risk Perception* contains a litany of etiological legends, and the bibliographic entries to chapter 4 of that book alone constitute a panoply of sources. Ultimately, however, Goldstein states that all of these stories can be grouped into three main theories concerning the origins of AIDS:

> 1. that AIDS has developed from a natural disease previously existing only in some other species of animal, which has recently managed to infect humans thus triggering the epidemic . . . ; 2. that AIDS has developed from a much older human disease not previously noted by science, either because it has always been confined to a small group with an acquired immunity or because it has only recently become virulent . . . ; [and] 3. that AIDS is a man-made virus manufactured either accidentally or deliberately in a laboratory. (Goldstein 2004, 80)

Bonnie Blair O'Connor's *Healing Traditions: Alternative Medicine and the Health Professions*, while primarily focusing on the alternative medical responses of the public to AIDS, still mentions the beliefs that (1) the disease came from God, whether as a test of faith or as a punishment (as in smote upon the gay community as penalty for the licentiousness of their lifestyle), and (2) the disease is the result of witchcraft practiced against the inflicted, including actions of "evil spirits, demons, the Devil and witches" (O'Connor 1995, 152). Paula A. Treichler, in *How to Have Theory in an Epidemic: Cultural Chronicles of AIDS*, notes humankind's continued attempts to blame AIDS on someone else: African countries blaming other African countries; the United States blaming Africa; Russia considering the disease a foreign problem attributable to the CIA or Africa; Caribbean and American peoples believing the disease came from US biological testing; and the French saying it originated from an American pollutant (Treichler 1999, 29–30). Patricia A. Turner's (1993) *I Heard It through the Grapevine: Rumor in African American Culture* discusses the beliefs held by African Americans that the CIA created AIDS as a bioweapon (mirroring the Russian belief

noted in Treichler), and Gary Alan Fine has extensively discussed "the alle-
gations that government conspiracies exist to create or spread the HIV virus"
(Fine 2005, 5). So numerous are AIDS "origins" that early categorizations
of the narratives often referred to them simply as the "4 Hs": homosexuals (especially men), hypodermic needles, hemophiliacs, and Haitians (see
Bennett 2005a, 128–29).

Many of these narratives share threads of conspiratorial paranoia.
Numerous examples of stories revolve around notions of purposeful germ
warfare, where man-made bioweapons have been unleashed upon certain
ethnicities, countries, and even age groups. Paul Smith, in "'AIDS—Don't
Die of Ignorance': Exploring the Cultural Complex of a Pandemic," summarizes what he calls a "whole belief system which focuses on how AIDS
developed," examples of which include that it "is an out-of-control germ
warfare virus . . . it has been put in the fluoride in our water . . . [and] in
the U.S.A., the Centre for Disease Control put it in K-Y Jell to get at all the
homosexuals" (Smith 1990, 74). Another example of this line of thought
can be found in Vanessa N. Gamble's "Under the Shadow of Tuskegee:
African Americans and Health Care," in which she states,

> Beliefs about the connection between AIDS and the purposeful destruction of
> African Americans should not be cavalierly dismissed as bizarre and paranoid.
> They are held by a significant number of Black people. For example, a 1990
> survey conducted by the Southern Christian Leadership Conference found that
> 35% of the 1056 Black church members who responded believed that AIDS was
> a form of genocide. (Gamble 1997, 1775)

The beliefs of these respondents are in large part justified by history. One
of the more infamous experiments of the twentieth century was the 1932–
1972 Tuskegee Syphilis Study, "in which [400] African American men who
had syphilis were studied to follow the natural course of the disease, without
being given any information about it nor any treatment even after antibiotics became available" (Whatley and Henken 2000, 83). Thus, for some
African Americans, believing in AIDS as a bioweapon could be seen as little
more than a shift in terminology.

But AIDS is not the only disease to boast etiological legends, nor are
such legends confined to modern epidemics. Yves Bercé (2003) has noted
that Pre-Revolutionary France's bouts with plague, and the nineteenth century's cholera problems generated many accusations of "voluntary spreaders
of the illness, poisoners of fountains, greasers of door knobs, perverse doctors, nurses or grave diggers, [and] killing vaccines" (quoted in Campion-
Vincent 2005, 109), many of which bear strong resemblances to claims
made about AIDS. The distrust of other, lower classes, as seen here, was

echoed during the polio epidemic, when the healthy and rich blamed the impoverished for spreading the disease. It had to come from the poor, so the logic went, because the healthy and rich lived clean, honorable lives.

Although many diseases have warranted warnings not to touch or come close to those infected (bubonic plague, polio, influenza, etc.), none is arguably more infamous than Hansen's disease.[1] Laurie C. Stanley-Blackwell's article on Acadian Good Samaritan legends and the New Brunswick epidemic of Hansen's disease in the 1840s deals in part with the narratives locals created to deal with this disease; they reveal a strong emphasis toward othering—emphasizing the disease as having come from somewhere else. In this case, New Brunswick residents created the narratives to temper harsher, outside claims that the disease was somehow merited by or born of those infected. The narratives created a distance between the origins and victims of the disease, stating that the "poisonous virus was not the growth of this spot, but was brought here by some traveler" (Stanley-Blackwell 1993, 39). In doing so, these stories "demystified the disease, mitigated its harshness, and combated the pervasive notion that the disease was an hereditary scourge among the Acadian population" (Stanley-Blackwell 1993, 33) and helped explain the presence of Hansen's disease.

Central to all of these narratives, regardless of the disease they refer to, are the concepts of race and racialization. Margaret Humphreys, in "No Safe Place: Disease and Panic in American History," states that panic over diseases with foreign origins begets racism and xenophobia, since those diseases are blamed upon the people who inhabit the country of the disease's origin. When we find ourselves surrounded by the very people who are "responsible" for the disease, erecting boundaries around our own homes is an "inevitable response" (Humphreys 2002, 850). But such actions also result in the formation of psychological boundaries between "us" and "them." The quarantining and avoidance of other races and ethnicities is the consequence of such boundaries; numerous historical examples include the quarantining of San Francisco's Chinatown during the bubonic plague epidemic of 1904 and various fears associated with immigrating Jews in 1892 (who were tied to typhus) and Italians in 1916 (who were blamed for polio) (Humphreys 2002, 852).

The racial comments present in Humphreys's work correspond with what Charles L. Briggs has noted: that "narratives about epidemics make racial and sexual inequalities seem natural—as if bacteria and viruses gravitate toward populations and respect social boundaries" (2005, 272). This "racialization," defined by Michael Omi and Howard Winant as "the extension of racial meaning to a previously racially unclassified relationship, social practice, or group" (Omi and Winant 1986, 64), can be seen as a consequence of living in the modern world where, as described by Jesús Martín-Barbero, we do not have societies with media but media constructs that shape society (Martín-Barbero 1987). In this sense, the narratives that appear in the media influence the way professionals and laypersons perceive the health system, both in terms of its practitioners and how it relates to the nonmedical sections of the population. The same could be said of how the population perceives disease. Any new virus or bacterium that originates in a foreign country is immediately and irrevocably tied to that place and the people who live there, and thus AIDS becomes synonymous with Africa, SARS with China, etc. At the same time that these diseases become synonymous with race, they can also reshape racial boundaries, changing the way laypersons and professionals within an ethnicity perceive each other. Such changes are not necessarily irrevocable—few people today would still associate Jewish people with typhus—but they can provide ruts in the road, as it were, into which future discussions of the connections between disease and race can slip. As Briggs says, "Producing narratives of race, disease, and space involves the collaboration of biomedical professionals, public health officials, politicians, reporters, and, often, anthropologists. Such narratives can be firmly in place before an epidemic has begun, thereby shaping epidemiological investigations, prevention and treatment regimes, and long-term effects" (Briggs 2005, 277).

Alan M. Kraut's (1995) *Silent Travelers: Germs, Genes, and the "Immigrant Menace"* provides a second look at issues of race and disease, strongly demonstrating the historically assumed links between immigrants and epidemics, especially regarding tuberculosis, cholera, and the bubonic plague. The reality of the situation, Kraut argues, is not that immigrants necessarily carried diseases but that the conditions they were forced to live in—many of them exploited for cheap labor—were of such poor quality and sanitation that disease often resulted. American citizens were thus largely to blame for the outbreaks for their negligence in creating decent living situations for these immigrants. Despite this—or rather, because of a lack of understanding of this—immigrants continued to be blamed as carriers and spreaders of disease. This stigma has proven impossible to eradicate, as evidenced by Haitian nationals accused of propagating the AIDS virus in the 1980s (Kraut 1995, but see also Fairchild 2003; Markel 1999; and Marks and Worboys 1997). Racialization such as this finds an easy scapegoat in the form of people who are already stigmatized in some way or another, whether as prostitute, criminal, foreigner, or some other illegal and/or immoral label: "in many of the deliberate-infector narratives, the aggressor is portrayed as a member of a threatening ethnicity or social group—a group already thought to have eroded morals" (Goldstein 2004, 48).

Disease narratives are, in other words, widespread and are often rife with racism and paranoia. Illustrations of these narratives, such as those above, could be continued for some time, but it is not the intention here to give an example of every type of etiological legend found in the history of disease, nor is it to rehash what numerous authors have discussed at length. The aim is to demonstrate that SARS is also bursting with story and shares many of the same tales told of other diseases. It should be made clear that this is not to claim that a SARS-related narrative corresponds to any given narrative from any given disease. It is a statement that SARS, in its short life, gained a number of etiological legends, all of which bear striking resemblances to those narratives found in other diseases.

The origin narratives in this chapter were collected from the Internet, published news sources, and personal interviews. Few of these narratives are similar at the sentence level—meaning that individual details vary widely and little resemble those found in other narratives—but at the story level they share such similarities that every narrative falls into one of three categories: conspiracy theories, experiments gone wrong (recognizing the oft-times thin line that can separate these two categories), and animal origins.

In fact, of the narratives gathered for this chapter, so few concrete examples did not fit into these categories that only one seems discussable: that SARS is extraterrestrial in origin. This theory comes from Cardiff University's Chandra Wickramasinghe and the late astronomer Fred Hoyle. The story—reported in the British tabloid *The Sun*—is that SARS is an outer space microbe that entered Earth's atmosphere via a comet or meteorite. This is an extension of a long-debated and nonmainstream scientific theory known as panspermia, or the hypothesis that life on Earth began from an extrasolar source. Interestingly, this origin theory did gain some credit in the scientific community: microbiologist Milton Wainwright, from the University of Sheffield, has stated that the expansion of the SARS virus appears to follow general schemes laid down by panspermic theorists. In an e-mail to MSNBC.com's Cosmic Log, Brig Klyce of the Cosmic Ancestry website furthers his belief in Wickramasinghe and Hoyle's hypothesis, writing that the two scientists "proposed that the link between new flus and China was caused by the jet stream's bump over the Himalayas a long time ago . … I think it's quite plausible, and could account for the SARS epidemic as well" (Boyle 2003). Klyce likens the spread of SARS to that of the Spanish flu, which "first struck soldiers in outdoor training camps in the Midwest. Later, it struck around the world almost simultaneously, but took weeks to travel from N.Y. to Boston . . . And it spread to isolated individuals who never came into contact with any infected person" (Boyle 2003).

Francis A. Plummer, director of Canada's National Microbiology Laboratory, added unintended credibility to panspermic theories by voicing his doubts concerning the coronavirus origin of SARS. Plummer's statements, made in April 2003, revealed that laboratory work had only been able to find evidence of the SARS microbe in 40 percent of Canada's SARS patients and that some who tested positive for SARS showed no symptoms (Boyle 2003). Plummer's work was later proven incorrect, with more advanced testing resulting from better knowledge of the disease, but such statements seemed only to fuel the "SARS from the stars" movement for a short time.

When it comes to conspiracy theories and experiments gone wrong, however, SARS bulges at the seams. Even its acronym has been appropriated in the popular medium to fit in with conspiratorial musings, the letters said to stand for "Saddam's Awesome Retaliation Strategy" instead of "Severe Acute Respiratory Syndrome" (Glazer 2003). While this appropriation seems to be done mostly for humorous reasons—as an SMS, or Short Message Service, joke—it still demonstrates the possibilities inherent in conspiracy. AIDS, too, has such acronymic examples. In 1986 young men in Zaire rewrote *SIDA*, the French word for AIDS, to stand for " 'Syndrome Imaginaire pour Decourager l'Amour' (Imaginary Syndrome to Discourage Love)." The motivation behind this was twofold, some believing "that Europeans were using stories of an imaginary disease to discourage Africans from being lovers and that [their] motivation stemmed from jealousy" while in the United States, African American communities used the same redefinition process to discuss a belief that they were purposely given misinformation that would prevent them from reproducing (Whatley and Henken 2000, 82).

The appropriation of the SARS acronym does not seem to be the result of any real fear of Middle Eastern retaliation—even the direct reference to Saddam Hussein is more humorous than fearful—but there are other conspiracy theories that do appear to stem from genuine concern, ranging from concerns over governmental control to fears of bioweapons. An excellent example of the former comes from the website *Educate-Yourself*, which contains a section on "Emerging Diseases." Its author, who identifies himself only as "Montalk," specifically states that SARS is "simply part of a hostile agenda implemented by the world's political and military elite to keep earth's population locked down and under control" (Montalk

2003). Discussions of the methodologies implemented by the government to enable such an outcome center around the extreme measures taken by health officials to prevent outbreaks in Toronto in 2003. Montalk's view, however, is that SARS was not dangerous at all but was promoted as such by the government—with the help of the WHO—to "tenderize" the public into "accepting increasingly restrictive curbs upon their freedoms." This SARS "test run," as Montalk refers to it, was a means by which the US government could pass laws that would allow them to quarantine anyone suspected of infection, as well as lockdown entire cities—laws that could be reinforced at any time with only the slightest "clever media hype of any manufactured disease." The entire Toronto epidemic is furthermore claimed to be nothing more than an exercise in economic destruction—though the webpage does not state why the US government would target a Canadian city for this purpose.

This webpage also contains other SARS conspiracy theories. One of the other two examples relates to a larger concept of disease as the possible result of "vibrational frequencies" broadcast to a target population via "audio or microwave subliminals" (Montalk 2003). This theory does fit the "fear of bioweapon" theme, Montalk stating at length that

> Because one's mental and emotional states play a large part in immunity, these subliminal programming techniques would merely have **to implant negative thoughts and emotions** in order to pry open a gap in a person's awareness for viruses to then successfully invade the physical body. Also, through sheer hysteria psychosomatic illness can result, a phenomenon which I don't doubt has played a hand in Asian SARS cases. (emphasis in original)

The website does not clarify who is broadcasting these signals, or their purpose in doing so. The only hint comes from Montalk's suggestion that we are all "supporting the medical society" by watching television—the primary tool used to broadcast these vibrational frequencies.

The second conspiracy theory forwarded by Montalk entails "chemtrails," or chemicals that the theory claims the military has been spraying in our skies since 1998. Visible as vapor-trail streaks of white in the sky, Montalk claims these chemtrails contain many harmful substances purposely placed there by the military, including "immune suppressing chemicals, such as ethylene dibromide . . . radar and microwave reflective metallic substance like barium or aluminum . . . dielectric hollow polymer fibers . . . [and] viral and bacterial vectors remnants of genetic engineering and replication procedures used to construct the pathogenic vectors," the ultimate purpose of which is to "suppress human evolution on a physical, mental, and spiritual level" by performing " 'gene therapy' upon targeted populations by spraying them with viral vectors capable of shutting down the DNA activation process in those infected." SARS is not specifically stated in this section as a consequence of chemtrails, but it seems clear that the author does link the two in terms of the immune-suppressing effects of the chemtrail chemicals: we contract SARS because our immune systems have been artificially lowered to substandard levels.

Not all SARS-related conspiracy theories exhibit the same level of organization-specific blame and paranoia as do those of Montalk. In fact, concern over the vague nature of the virus was so widespread in the early stage of the disease that one high-profile Australian newspaper noted that "health officials were initially forced to quell conspiracy theories about SARS being an act of terrorism" or biological warfare ("SARS Outbreak a Medical Version of Bio-Terror?" 2003). And while some of these rumors did place the blame for the virus on a specific source, others left the question open-ended or merely pointed fingers in the general direction of a geographical region, such as the Middle East or Asian continents.

An excellent example of this latter form of nonspecific blaming comes from the blog *SARS Paranoia*, wherein the author refutes rumors of the virus being man-made and a biological weapon. The rumor in question quotes Nikolai Filatov, head of Moscow's epidemiological services, who gives the following as grounds for the man-made nature of SARS: "the composition of SARS is unkown . . . there is no vaccine available for SARS . . . 'The virus, according to Academy of Medicine member Sergei Kolesnikov, is a cocktail of mumps and measles, whose mix could never appear in nature'" (Cindy 2003). This legend does not mention which person or organization could have masterminded such a fusion of diseases; it simply announces that it couldn't have been done without man's help.

Astutely, the author of this article—"Cindy"—first points out that the composition of SARS *is* known, presenting the reader with a link to a PDF document of the virus's genome, then makes a direct comparison of this conspiracy theory to a mid-1980s rumor that the government had released a "gay" virus (i.e., AIDS) into bathhouses to rid the world of homosexuals. "Of course," she says, "that wasn't the case. If HIV had gotten as much publicity in it's first six months of known infection, we might have a cure by now. Personally, I have a greater fear of coming down with a plain old cold then of contracting the SARS virus." Regardless of the dubious nature of the HIV-publicity claims, it is apparent that by the time this blog was published—May 9, 2003—SARS-as-conspiracy was entrenched in the public consciousness, and at least a few people were noticing similarities between these new narratives and those they'd heard about other diseases.

A second example of this nonspecific blaming comes from *The Rumor Mill News Reading Room*. In an article titled "SARS Kills 50% Patients over 65—A Perfect Age-Specific Weapon," the author—"Izakovic"—begins by quoting legitimate WHO data showing that the SARS death rate was higher than originally estimated and mortality rates varied by age: "50% for patients of 65 years or older, 15% for people from 45–64, 6% for patients from 25–44, and below 1% for patients old 25 years or younger" (Izakovic 2003). He presents further legitimate data in the form of summarizations of studies published in the UK medical journal *The Lancet*, which found that the SARS "corona virus samples collected from patients do not show the mutations and are remarkably stable," though Izakovic does not make the nature of these mutations clear. What he does clearly summarize are the journal's findings that the stability of the virus points to the strong possibility of a viable vaccine.

From this point in Izakovic's thread, speculation takes over, as is evident in his three-paragraph conclusion:

> From this report it is clear that SARS is not a Chinese bioweapon designed to target enemy forces because it, practically, does not affect population below 25 which makes bulk of any armed forces. Even commanding structure that is made mostly of people under 44 is safe without any special measures.
>
> On the other hand, stability of virus shows that it is not a natural mutation and allows for secure vaccine for those in targeted age group that must not become victims.
>
> Stability and age specific death rate, an perfect weapon for age selective culling of older population world-wide.

Again, there is no specific mention of the origin of the virus—simply that it could not have been naturally formed. In addition, Izakovic's website, www.deepspace4.com, mentions not only the "chemtrails cause disease" origin theory Montalk spoke about but the theory that the US government developed AIDS as a method of thinning the black population—another example of a single author using roughly the same narrative to describe multiple disease origins.

So far, the examples in this chapter implement nonspecific blame— that is, they say that while someone somewhere is clearly responsible, the authors either do not know whom to blame or decline to speculate. There are, however, equally as many examples of conspiracy theories that do point a figurative finger at a specific group.

One example comes from *The Rumor Mill News Reading Room* in response to Montalk's discussions of chemtrails. On December 29, 2003, "Hobie" posted an article declaring that viruses are in fact solvents: that man-made chemicals in our environment are causing disease. Hobie's information comes from an article by "Aajunos [actually Aajonus] Vonderplanitz," in which Vonderplanitz claims that viruses don't destroy cells, they merely show up when cells are destroyed and exist primarily as solvents that "carry toxins into the bloodstream for disposal." Hobie further quotes an article by Jim West: "The orthodox SARS paradigm completely omits and avoids toxicology for good reason: SARS disease symptoms are identical to pesticide and air pollution disease symptoms. And these poisons correlate in time and place with SARS epidemics."

The pointed finger in Hobie's article is found in an extensive quote he borrows from West: airlines are responsible for the outbreak. The reason? "Airlines routinely apply pesticides to airplanes, especially those on Asian routes," and these pesticides are causing people to become ill (Hobie 2003). Demonstrating the often thin line that separates fact from rumor, at least part of this claim can be confirmed: a CDC health guide to international travel does state that many countries require disinfection of inbound flights, and that the acceptable methods of disinfecting planes are to "either spray the aircraft cabin with an aerosolized insecticide (usually 2% phenothrin) while passengers are on board, or treat the aircraft-s interior surfaces with a residual insecticide while the aircraft is empty." This guide does note that some flight crew members have reported reactions to the spraying—rashes, lung irritations, tingling and numbness of extremities—but is quick to note "there are no data to support a cause-and-effect relationship," and that the WHO declared this method of disinfection safe in 1995 (CDC Health Information for International Travel, 2005–2006, 2006).

A second example of a blame-specific conspiracy theory—again from *The Rumor Mill News Reading Room*—was posted by author "Rayelan," whose chosen title for his April 28, 2003, article details many of the underlying issues: "Is SARS the Bio-Weapon I Was Told About in the Early 90s?" Rayelan begins by quoting from legitimate news sources such as the *Birmingham Post-Herald*: "It may be that some individuals have a genetic quirk that makes them more efficient spreaders of the virus, some have said. Others speculate that some ethnic or environmental difference may account for the hot spots" (Rayelan 2003). A second quote from a legitimate source comes from a detailed paper that ran in the March 1997 edition of the journal *Science* concerning a successful genetic reconstruction of the virus responsible for the 1918 flu epidemic that killed between 20 and 40 million people worldwide. Using information such as this, Rayelan then moves away from his legitimate sources to build a hypothesis that SARS is, in fact, the newly cultured 1918 flu virus and has been genetically altered to infect people of primarily Asian descent.

From here, Rayelan reminds us that many North Americans could in fact have Asian DNA, as a Discovery Channel program he watched suggested that North, Central, and South America were settled by Asian peoples crossing the "Alutian Islands" during the last Ice Age. Thus, it is entirely possible that many North Americans who do not appear to contain any Asian blood would be affected by the virus, and so SARS could be part of what Rayelan terms "The Great Dying": an Armageddon-like scenario in which four-fifths of the world's population perish. Under this scenario, SARS might only be the first in a series of viral waves sent crashing against the shores of humanity.

Those Rayelan claims as responsible for these viral waves varies, depending largely on the affected population: if the virus stays mainly within China's borders, it was released there by the United States in an attempt to slow the progression of China's economic and political importance. But if the virus spreads to other nations and proves fatal for millions, it was created and released by a group Rayelan calls the "NWO"—New World Order—whose purpose is to weaken the world's population to the point where no nation will be able to withstand the installment of a "One World Government." For reasons not fully fleshed out in this article, Rayelan claims that China and the former Soviet Union are the NWO's primary members, and their main target is the United States—the only nation strong enough to withstand their geopolitical advances.

A conspiracy theory that in many ways echoes the cataclysmic suspicion present in Rayelan's narrative comes from Dr. Leonard Horowitz, DMD, MA, MPH. Horowitz's contributions to these proceedings are in many ways singular, for he brings to the table not only an impressive list of degrees but is a Harvard graduate in public health, an "expert in the fields of medical sociology, behavioral science, and emerging diseases" (Horowitz 2004), and claims ten best-selling books on the subjects of conspiracy. In one of these, *Emerging Viruses: AIDS & Ebola—Nature, Accident or Intentional?*, he claims to have reprinted for the first time US government documents that prove that a branch of the US Army bioengineered AIDS- and Ebola-like viruses. Conspiracy theorists probably don't take lightly the weight of such arguments.

Horowitz's theories concerning SARS are just as controversial as his arguments regarding AIDS and follow the same suit: SARS has been bioengineered and is being used to control the global population. The culprit behind these viral attacks is not specifically named—that is, no company or business name enters the discussions—but Horowitz does mention that the only suspect with the means and methods to execute such an attack is the "global military-medical-petrochemical-pharmaceutical cartel" (Horowitz 2004). What Horowitz sees as the purpose behind these attacks shares similarities with Rayelan's hypothesis: that their "likeliest purpose is in facilitating evolving economic and political agendas that ultimately include targeting approximately half the world's current population for elimination." This is a required step in achieving global domination because a smaller, more frightened population is easier to control. As Horowitz points out, we have already learned via the Homeland Security Act that populations under duress are more likely to agree to limitations in freedom in exchange for greater protection (i.e., governmental power and control).

Not all blame-specific conspiracy theories exhibit this level of cataclysmic paranoia. The last two examples in this section are rather mild in comparison to Rayelan's and Horowitz's narratives, as neither of them involve global attempts at world domination. The first comes from the Association for Asian Research, which published an article in late May 2003 concerning a rumor created by Beijing officials that SARS was not Chinese in origin but had in fact appeared in the United States in February 2002. The rumor appeared in at least four major Hong Kong newspapers in early May 2003, at least one of which—the *Wen Wei Po*—is a recognized mouthpiece for the Chinese Communist Party. According to the rumor, an American woman in either New Jersey or Philadelphia (depending on the newspaper) fell ill with flu-like symptoms, developed acute pneumonia, and expired within hours of hospitalization. The *Wen Wei Po* was the chief source for the transmission of this rumor, which persisted among Communist Party officials in Hong Kong despite repeated denials by the United States and other Hong Kong newspapers, some of which accurately reported that the US case was not SARS but meningitis. Still, the rumor lasted long enough that it made its way to Guangdong province, where Governor Huang Huahua mentioned the 2002 American-based case of SARS during a governmental meeting in early May 2003 (Lin 2003).

The last example of a blame-specific conspiracy theory comes from an interview conducted with Angel in July 2005:

> I had a friend, we used to get together during Saturday, and he used to tell me, told me once that SARS originated from the States, the U.S. The reason is because Canada is not a friend of U.S. Like, when they go to war in Iraq, Canada didn't go to war to Iraq with the U.S. So that's why the U.S. hates Canadian. So they produce this SARS to kill some people in Canada . . . He also told me that the Philippines is very close to China, and also very close to Hong Kong. And, I think there's only two people died during the SARS outbreak, right? And again,

the reason is only two people has died is because the Philippines and the U.S. are friends. (Angel and Rosita 2005)

Angel's narrative echoes many of the concerns that have fueled the conspiracy theories examined in this chapter: distrust of governments and overly powerful organizations, fear of the unknown, concern over one's own mortality (as well as that of friends and family), and apprehension at the loss of personal privacy, all intermingled with points of blame and counterblame.

The final category of etiological legends is animal origins. Goldstein gives us a succinct summary of the types of beasts that have been associated with the spread of the AIDS virus: "monkeys of various types, regional origins, and colors (African green monkeys, blue monkeys, red monkeys, green-eyes monkeys, chimpanzees, baboons, tree monkeys, and rhesus monkeys); insects of various types (fleas, flies, mosquitoes, and cockroaches); and finally sheep, lambs, and even the [colo-] rectal gerbil" (Goldstein 2004, 81). The task of tracking and summarizing the animal origins of SARS is no less interesting. The disease was formally introduced on February 26, 2003, and by March 24 researchers who discovered a coronavirus as the potential cause of the disease had begun to consider the possibilities of an animal origin for the epidemic, since coronaviruses were known to affect both animals and humans. By May 23 the virus was traced back to the civet cat.[2] Thus, little time passed in the development of the SARS story for animal origin legends to have arisen.

Still, in that short time numerous animals were blamed. Summarizing only those relevant points from the previous chapter, we quickly come up with a list of suspects. The cockroach appears to have been one of the first nominees for disease-carrier, suspected as early as April 8 as the prime candidate for explaining the migration of the virus between residences in Hong Kong. On May 7, residents of Beijing either killed or abandoned hundreds of dogs and cats, fearing them to be spreaders of disease. On May 12, a newspaper reported that some scientists believed that a bird could be the cause. The civet cat was named as the prime suspect on May 23, but that didn't stop provincial officials from banning other animals from sale in Southern China, including snakes, bats, badgers and pangolins. In late October, house cats and ferrets were named as potential spreaders. And still the list grew. In January 2004, in response to the threat of a new outbreak, Guangzhou officials ordered exterminators to sweep clean the city's streets, focusing especially on rats, cockroaches, flies, and mosquitoes. At the same time, government officials also banned the breeding, sale, distribution, and consumption of civet cat, raccoon dog, and badger.

Of the people interviewed for this book, however, only four recollected any SARS origin stories that involved animals, and they were surprisingly unified: all four narratives circulated around China's exotic animal markets. Three of those four interviewees—Angel, Rosita, and Seny—even specifically mentioned the civet cat as the animal associated with the spread of the virus.[3] The fourth interviewee, Jennifer, had this to say: "I think the one that stayed with me, with regards to the origin, was that it came from animals, that it had to do with the . . . close contact with exotic animals in China, like monkeys or geese or something like that. Just exotic animals, that they were being eaten, or that they were being kept as pets, or for medicinal uses" (Jennifer 2005). Later in the same interview, Jennifer defended her belief in these narratives by comparing their veracity to established fact concerning the origins of other diseases:

> Just because . . . I guess Ebola I think has been sort of linked with monkeys, if I'm correct, and that I think I sort of also know that there are certain viruses or diseases that run through animals and don't affect them, but then due to the sort of increasingly, increasing contact between humans and animals, that we're all of a sudden being exposed to things that have, that might lay dormant in animals, but somehow affect us differently.

These interviewees thus present a distinctive lack of variance in their efforts to name the source of SARS—a condition likely brought about by their exposure to local media, which focused on the civet cat narrative to the exclusion of others. Still, the similarity among their answers does demonstrate the power of an etiological legend, especially one attached to a disease that could have affected their lives. That at least one of those informants further recognizes that her narrative had been shaped by her exposure to similar narratives told about other diseases further demonstrates this power, revealing that even members of the public who do not encounter disease as a part of their day-to-day lives are still shaped and affected by the narratives associated with disease, to the extent that the narratives can be fairly clearly recalled some years after the disease has ceased to make headlines.

The purpose of this chapter has been to point out the similarities between these etiological legends, both within a single epidemic such as SARS and across the disease spectrum. It should be clear after these investigations that disease-related conspiracy theories and animal origin legends share common foundations, and that many of the narratives found within a single epidemic closely resemble narratives that have sprung from other infectious outbreaks.

One final point can be made concerning the narratives examined here. While SARS and AIDS legends do present numerous commonalities, at least one critical difference exists. While the conspiracy theories surrounding other diseases are relevant and similar to the ones that are found with

SARS, SARS does have specific characteristics that shape those theories in specific ways—namely, that it waxed and waned with such rapidity that it became difficult to identify a potential target group. SARS was never present on a global scale long enough to be directly linked to one group of people, a fact reflected in the ever-shifting targets mentioned in conspiracy theories: SARS was created to kill the elderly; SARS was created to kill the Chinese; SARS was created to kill Canadians; SARS was created to kill everyone. In contrast, AIDS, in its early stages, was linked almost exclusively to the homosexual population, creating a direct target, if not creator (though this, too, could be argued as definite, considering the number of legends surrounding the divine origin of AIDS). The amorphousness of the legends present in SARS may be due to the sense that the disease never had a chance to run its full course. Even into summer 2004, newspapers were still warning of the big outbreaks of SARS expected during the upcoming winter—outbreaks that never came. Whatever the cause, the effect was definite: a series of conspiracy theories that stumble over each other—and sometimes themselves, as with Rayelan's narrative—in attempts to place blame and merit. The consequent multiplicity of potentially targeted peoples, while confusing, does by itself reveal an interesting underlying facet of conspiracy theories: that even if there is no clear sense of who is being targeted, there is always a passion for the conspiracy itself.

NOTES

1 Hansen's disease is the preferred term for leprosy, since the terms leprosy and leper are considered offensive and politically incorrect.

2 Although in October 2005, one Chinese health expert claimed that a horseshoe bat originally infected the civet cat—another animal that is a delicacy in southern Chinese cuisine (see "Bats Passed SARS to Civet Cats: Expert" 2005).

3 Angel and Rosita actually said "civet rats" and Seny said "cavot cat," but it seems obvious that they all meant civet cat, the errors in nomenclature no doubt due to asking them in 2005 to recollect the name of an animal they likely hadn't recalled in over a year.

3

We Gather Together
SARS and Public Space

THE COMMON THREADS BETWEEN SARS NARRATIVES and the genre of contemporary legend as a whole are not limited to AIDS, nor to diseases in general. While the previous chapter focused on etiological legends and the commonalities between those related to SARS and other diseases, this chapter focuses on issues of physical locations where large numbers of people congregate. These gathering places, especially those pertaining to and involving people of Asian descent, were the nexus of many SARS narratives, providing a feeding ground for public rumors. Especially relevant are Asian food establishments, such as Toronto's Ruby Chinese Restaurant, which collapsed financially following rumors of a SARS-infected chef.

For the purposes of this chapter, a gathering place is defined as any stable business, organization, or conglomerate of smaller businesses that are fixed in space. Restaurants, marketplaces, bars, and malls fit under this definition, as do schools and hospitals, all of which feature spaces where people can meet and discuss ideas. Meaghan Morris has noted the usage of gathering spaces in businesses such as these in "Things to Do with Shopping Centres": "The use of centres as meeting places (and sometimes for free warmth and shelter) by young people, pensioners, the unemployed and the homeless is a familiar part of the social function [of those locales]—often planned for, now, by centre management (distribution of benches, video games, security guards)" (Morris 1999, 397). Left aside for the moment are discussions of mobile locations and businesses such as airplanes, buses, and taxicabs, as those will be a central focus of the following chapter. Also temporarily set aside are those buildings that constitute integral parts of these motile businesses, such as airports and bus terminals. A nonmotile gathering place may thus be thought of as a largely immobile or temporally stable building or collection of businesses; they are located at the same physical space at any

DOI: 10.7330/9780874219296.c003

point in time (assuming the businesses are still viable) and do not, as a critical part of their operations, offer transportation services to the public.

Many specific legends—such as those involving the discovery of various parts of rodents or domestic pets in the refrigerators or meals at Chinese restaurants—center around persons of Asian descent. Just as one of the underlying concerns present in the Chinese Restaurant legend (and its variants) is the contraction of disease, SARS resulted in the creation of dozens, if not hundreds, of rumors concerning the dangerous potential juxtaposition of large numbers of people—Asian or otherwise—and the coronavirus. These SARS legends bear striking resemblances to sometimes decades-old versions found in other disease outbreaks and carry the same basic warning: beware of other people.

As seen in the previous chapter, numerous legends concern the contraction of AIDS by an unwitting victim. One of the key differences between AIDS and SARS is that while the former is almost exclusively contracted through bodily fluid exchange—mainly blood and semen—the latter virus can be contracted via airborne respiratory droplets, and so it is possible for a person to become infected just by being in the same physical location as a carrier. Although the chances of this happening are remote, the possibility is there, resulting in a mutation of the structures underlying the gathering place narratives that SARS appropriated from the contemporary legend genre. [1]

First, however, we take a look at non-SARS gathering place legends as a whole, examining the key features and stories that make up these narratives. An easy way to start such an examination is through this example, from an 1888 poem titled "My Other Chinee Cook," by James Brunton Stephens:

> "Go, do as you are bid," I cried, "we wait for no reply;
> Go! let us have tea early, and another rabbit pie!"
> Oh, that I had stopped his answer! But it came out with a run;
> "Last-a week-a plenty puppy; this-a week-a puppy done!"
> Just then my wife, my love, my life, the apple of mine eye,
> Was seized with what seemed "mal-de-mer,"—"sick transit" rabbit pie!
>
> (Brunvand 1986, 102)

This poem is admittedly problematic as an opening example for several reasons—namely, that the action does not occur in a gathering place and there is not an explicit mention of disease as a consequence of action—though the wife's becoming ill after learning the species of animal she has been eating hints in that direction. But the overt stereotyping and racism present here does closely resemble what might be found in a more modern version of the legend, and it does contain the basic theme of Asian people serving forbidden (by Western standards) foods to unsuspecting patrons.

An example that more closely resembles the gathering place narratives outlined above comes from Mark Twain, who related in *Roughing It* a near-encounter with rodents at the grocery store of Ah Sing in Virginia City, Nevada. After sampling and enjoying Sing's brandies, Twain and his companions were offered "a mess of birds'-nests; also, small, neat sausages, of which we could have swallowed several yards if we had chosen to try, but we suspected that each link contained the corpse of a mouse, and therefore refrained" (Twain [1872] 2003, 353). J. A. G. Roberts, in *China to Chinatown: Chinese Food in the West*, offers an even more modern and exemplary narrative, gathered from the pages of *Saga Magazine*, where a reader recalls her husband craving Chinese takeout despite stories "rife of people who ate Chinese food getting bones stuck in their throats which were later identified not as chicken bones, but cats' or even rats' bones" (2002, 178).

These last two narratives adequately summarize the more common versions of the Chinese restaurant legend, but neither quite strikes all of the available chords. Paul Smith, in *The Book of Nasty Legends*, gives what is possibly the ideal, platonic form of the narrative. A group of friends are at a Chinese restaurant enjoying their food when one of them begins to choke. The victim is rushed to a local hospital where a surgeon removes a small bone from his or her throat. The bone is sent for analysis, and the returned report states that it came from a rat. As Smith concludes the story, "The public health department immediately visited the restaurant to inspect the kitchens and in the fridge they found numerous tins of cat food, half an Alsatian dog and several rats all waiting to be served up" (Smith 1984, 54).

The ending to this version of the story neatly connects the mystery of the rat bone's origin with the distrust of foreigners that plagues contemporary legends—or what Smith calls "our irrational fear of the unknown and exotic impinging on our traditional way of life" (Smith 1984, 54). Even better, Smith's ending gives the reader a sense of the "true" disgusting nature of Chinese restaurants: that they serve not only rats, but also dogs and cat food. This legend, as Smith states, has been circulating in the British Isles since the 1950s and is well known throughout Europe—though the ethnicity of the offending restaurateurs does vary, as does the denouement; sometimes the meat served to the patrons is in fact their own pet dog, cooked up for them as the result of a language barrier with a foreign waiter who interpreted "feed my dog" as "feed me my dog."

In these examples, the connection between gathering place and disease has for the most part been inferred; the closest any victim has gotten to being ill involved choking or vomiting, both of which are conditions that can be easily and quickly remedied. Other legends are not so timorous about the dangers of gathering places. A search in July 2007 of Snopes.com's index using only the word AIDS turned up at least five examples. The first involved legends detailing AIDS-infected needles stuck into the seats at movie theaters at just the precise angle so as to penetrate into unsuspecting patrons' derrieres. Variants of this legend that involve needles in pay phone coin slots or taped to gas pump handles would also apply, if telephone booths and gas stations are considered temporally displaced gathering places (i.e., while at any given time only one person may be occupying the space, over the course of a day several dozen people will have occupied it).[2] A fourth example (counting the pay phone slot and gas pump handle variants as separate narratives) involves HIV-positive blood slipped into ketchup dispensers at restaurants, and a fifth involves HIV-positive semen turning up in the garlic sauce at a local pizza joint. Clearly, gathering places and AIDS go hand in hand: What better way for the antagonist to infect others but to place the virus in a location where dozens of people come into contact with it every day? This same logic is found in legends surrounding Church's Chicken, as detailed by Patricia A. Turner in *I Heard It through the Grapevine: Rumor in African American Culture*: that the Ku Klux Klan had put either spices or drugs into the chicken "that would cause sterility in black male eaters" (Turner 1993, 139).

Legend-based negative consequences of being in a gathering place are, of course, not always intended. Many legends do involve victims coming to intentional harm at the hands of an antagonist (i.e., AIDS-infected needles left in public places), but others involve victims suffering unintended misfortune. Chinese restaurant stories might fall under this category, depending on how the story is told and where it is set. Rats, cats, and dogs all have long and recognized histories as foodstuffs in China—especially in the southern provinces (c.f. J. A. G. Roberts 2002, 20)—and some restaurants in Asia continue to serve rats in modern times, as reported in the *Wall Street Journal* in 2008 (cf. Hookway 2008). It is conceivable for a Westerner to wander into a restaurant and order a dish without knowing its nature, and the logical reverse of this happens in some legends: that a Chinese cook in North America, not knowing that rats are *not* eaten here, perhaps because he does not speak English, simply continues to use them in his meals as he has always done.

It is also entirely possible that the relevancy of the danger in the gathering place has little to do with disease. Many contemporary legends detail public-space harm that is devoid of mention, or even inference, of viruses or bacteria but specifically acknowledge dangerous animals; two examples are "The Hapless Water Skier" and "The Incautious Swimmer," both of which involve water sports participants at local lakes or swimming holes who dive or fall into a bed of Water Moccasins or some other species of poisonous water snake. Also included in this category are the multiple variants of animal-in-store-merchandise legends: "The Snake in the Blanket," "The Spider in the Yucca," "Spiders in Cacti," "Snakes in Dry Goods," "The Creeping Comforter," and "Snakes Alive!," to name a few (c.f. Brunvand 1986; Brunvand 2004).

Contemporary legend is also full of narratives that involve non-disease-related public-space harm caused by other humans. Because of the numerous legends that fall under this category, the examples presented here are limited to those that occur in shopping malls. Outside of the workplace, malls are one of the most commonly visited public gathering places for the general populace. The larger malls in North America are designed to easily accommodate several thousand people at any given point in time, and even small-scale malls can comfortably fit a hundred patrons. Such spots are rife for legend. It is human nature to be suspicious of those we don't know (de Vos 1996), and in malls, we are surrounded by scores upon scores of unfamiliar souls, any of whom may—at least in legend—turn out to have ulterior motives. So it should come as no surprise that narratives such as this one have been making the rounds:

> I just heard on the radio about a lady that was asked to sniff a bottle of perfume that another woman was selling for $8.00 (In a mall parking lot). She told the story that it was her last bottle of perfume that sells for $49.00 but she was getting rid of it for only $8.00, sound legitimate?
>
> That's what the victim thought, but when she awoke she found out that her car had been moved to another parking area and she was missing all her money that was in her wallet (total of $800.00). Pretty steep for a sniff of perfume!
>
> Anyway, the perfume wasn't perfume at all, it was some kind of ether or strong substance to cause anyone who breathes the fumes to black out. (Brunvand 2004, 245)

The protagonist's ultimate motive in this story—robbery—is fairly benign when compared to some of the other fates that befall people in shopping malls. Take, for example, the following plots of legends: women getting abducted after being lured into the parking lot with promises of cash and fame if they'll appear in a commercial being filmed outside; ankle-slashers hiding under people's cars; the man who helps fix a woman's flat tire turns out to be a would-be kidnapper with a knife and length of rope in his briefcase; small girls go missing and are found a half-hour later drugged, disguised, and being smuggled out of the mall to be sold into white slavery rings; and a small boy goes missing and is found minutes later in the bathroom, surrounded by black gang members who have kidnapped him in order to castrate him as part of a gang initiation ceremony. The list could extend for pages and pages.

What is clear, however, is that gathering places are commonly equated with danger in contemporary legends. Nowhere is this more present than with SARS, though it should be immediately noted that the narratives that follow are not limited to the legend genre but include hoaxes, rumor, and gossip. The critical commonality is the gathering place. One crucial difference between the legends previously discussed in this chapter and those that follow is that while the link between gathering places and danger in contemporary legend may be either overt or merely suggested—and while the nature of that danger may be human, animal, or viral in origin—SARS narratives are marked by a *lack* of ambivalence: the danger is definite, the danger is here, and the danger is other people.

Widespread public knowledge of the existence of SARS can be definitively traced to February 26, 2003, when an emerging Chinese disease was given its now-infamous name. The earliest any citizen of Canada could have come into personal contact with the disease inside that country was roughly two weeks later, after the first reports of SARS came out of Toronto on March 14. Two weeks after that, Chinese businesses in that city were feeling the effects. An article in the *Toronto Star* on March 29 noted that the city's Pacific Mall—North America's largest indoor Asian shopping mall—was virtually empty, with some stores claiming sales drops of 70 percent (Oliveira 2003). This is a precipitous decline for a 400-store-strong complex—and that within a larger complex containing an additional 500 stores. Moreover, the article in the *Star* noted that mall staff had been reporting decreased sales for "about two weeks" (Oliveira 2003). In other words, business at the mall began to drop within *hours* of the first cases of SARS appearing in Toronto. The connection in the public mind between Asians, gathering places, and danger was immediate, as was public reaction.

But the numbers at that point in time did not justify such a response. By March 29 only three Canadians had died from the disease, two of who were Chinese—a mother and son (Oliveira 2003). What seems to have created the panic that caused the mall's business to plummet were the official efforts to stop the spread of SARS before it could do any further damage. By late March thousands of Ontarians had been ordered into self-quarantine and the WHO had asked Canada to begin screening airline passengers for SARS. Despite the low numbers of Canadian cases and deaths, the public had learned of the massive potential for SARS from local and worldwide governmental warnings and responded in kind. Part of this response included the dissemination of rumors, and according to merchants at the Pacific Mall, the Internet was the single largest source of rumors (Oliveira 2003).

Also affected was Toronto's Ruby Chinese Restaurant, where the staff pointed toward e-mail as the source of their problems. "Some lawless people spread rumours through the Internet that a staff member from our restaurant contracted the virus," said Frankie Lee, a spokesperson for the restaurant. "In addition to attacking our business' image, they caused unnecessary public panic and affected the whole community . . . Not many Chinese people want to go out to eat and many people are staying at home" (Oliveira 2003). Lee estimated that business at the restaurant had dropped by 80 percent in two weeks, for a total loss of revenue in the $15,000–$20,000 range. Rumors such as this would ultimately lead Canadian Prime Ministers Paul Martin and Jean Chrétien, along with several liberal members of Parliament, to dine at Chinese restaurants in Toronto in mid-April, inviting members of the press along to witness the lack of danger in visiting such establishments ("PM Hopes Meal Helps Debunk SARS Myth" 2003).

This was only the beginning of global SARS rumors. On April 1, a teenager in Hong Kong placed a prank message on his website stating that the SARS virus was sweeping through the city, forcing the government to declare the entire municipality, along with its 7 million inhabitants, "an infected place" that would be placed under immediate quarantine. The hoax triggered massive and widespread panic. Already frightened by the March 31 news that an entire apartment complex had been placed under quarantine, residents emptied grocery store shelves of canned and preserved goods, and financial and stock markets plummeted—including the Hong Kong dollar. Local authorities were forced into immediate action to counter the rumors; Director of Health Margaret Chan made a public statement that there was "no plan to declare Hong Kong an infected area. We have adequate supplies to provide the needs of Hong Kong citizens and there is no need for any panic run on food" (Lyn 2003c).

The same day, a reporter for CNN who resided in Hong Kong noted drastic changes in public behavior within the last week. The presence of surgical face masks, he noted, had increased from near zero to near ubiquitous; he had even taken to wearing one despite his initial skepticism of their usefulness. Just as revealing was an account from a Hong Kong friend of his who had traveled to his company's Singapore offices for business. Upon arriving, he was "politely requested" not to enter the offices, as news of his arrival had frightened local employees (Havely 2003). In the desire to provide for the safety of those forced to gather in groups because of business, even the most remote possibility of infection had to be countered.

Back in North America, an apparent April Fools' joke posted on a Massachusetts Institute of Technology website in Boston caused an uproar similar in nature—though not in scope—to the one in Hong Kong. The website claimed that an employee of Boston's China Pearl restaurant had been infected with SARS and advised against visiting Chinatown in general. Again, those who read the warning heeded its advice and passed it on to others—though it is unclear whether that was out of belief or a simple better-safe-than-sorry mind-set. The effect on the Chinese community was immediate: the restaurant's business dropped by 70 percent overnight, and other businesses in the area reported similar damage. As one article put it, "There can actually be legal parking spaces found in Chinatown throughout the day, a clear sign that the April Fool's joke has damaged the normally bustling business community" ("Chinatown Businesses Hurt by SARS Hoax" 2003). Local business leaders were, after a few weeks, able to correct the situation, thanks in part to a seminar conducted at the China Pearl to denounce the rumors and fact sheets printed by health officials and disseminated through Boston's businesses and schools.

Only one state away, New York's Chinatowns reported similar rumors, some of which were also attributed to April Fools' jokes. Although the affected business owners considered none of the jokes humorous, one in particular was immediately damaging:

> For those of you who eat in chinatown, please be advised for that SARS has hit that area. As of today I heard that the owner's son(s) & the entire staff of the restaurant BO KY located on Bayard st. b/t Mott & Mulberry Sts. has been infected with the SARS. The owner was infected & has passed away recently due to what have seemed to be flu like symptoms. I think its best that you either stay away from that area or eat in.
> Please pass this along for those who I might have missed. (D. Emery 2003)

This rumor was circulated on the Internet and in New York's Chinese press, which picked it up off the Web. The news came as quite a shock to Chivy Ngo, owner of the Bo Ky, who received condolence calls and flowers, even from close friends. Although all of the rumors were quickly squelched, the damage had been done: the public stopped coming. Even store owners fell prey to the fear. Kay Cheng, the manager of the city's Excellent Pork Chop House, admitted to a reporter that he stayed in his house on his days off, too afraid to leave lest he catch the bug (Saulny 2003).

Businesses continued to falter around the globe as April marched on. On the third day of the month, *The Age*, an Australian newspaper, picked up a Reuters story that carefully detailed the Hong Kong scenario. It painted a grim picture. Businesses of all types were forced to drastically alter their daily routines because of customer losses. California Red, one of Hong Kong's largest karaoke bars, normally bustling with activity, had recently temporarily closed three of its twelve outlets—and this *after* spending HK $1 million (US $128,200) to disinfect the bars, buy disposable paper caps for microphones, and publicize cleanup efforts. Sparse mask-wearing and fast-moving groups now populated normally crowded marketplaces like Causeway Bay. Local gyms were nearly empty, and the few clients who still exercised wore masks while doing so. Receipts at bars and restaurants in the trendy Lan Kwai Fong district were down by 40 percent or more from the same period a year earlier, during what was normally one of the busiest tourist seasons, as overseas visitors came to watch the Hong Kong Sevens rugby tournament. Restaurants of all types reported so few customers that many establishments closed down their buffets to stem food spoilage. Citywide, employees worked half shifts or took unpaid leaves of absence to avoid being laid off. Yu Pang Chun, chairman of the Hong Kong Retail Management Association, called it "the worst crisis we've had, worse than the Asian financial crisis, the bursting of the dotcom bubble and the 9/11 attacks in the US" ("Hong Kongers Shun Karaoke Amid Virus Fears" 2003).

On April 8, ABC News reported on the economic losses in Boston, New York, and San Francisco, revisiting many of the businesses affected by the previous week's April Fools' jokes. Their investigations still showed widespread fear of public places, as evidenced by mostly-empty stores across the nation. Chinatowns in many major cities were especially hard hit. Boston's China Pearl estimated their business continued to suffer a loss of 70 percent. Surrounding stores experienced a similar backlash by association. In San Francisco, sales of surgical masks, rubbing alcohol swabs, and latex gloves were brisk, but restaurants, grocery stores and tourist shops weren't faring well. The only positive note was that the Bo Ky restaurant in New York had rebounded from its initial losses, thanks to community leaders and news reports exposing the hoax (T. Emery 2003).

April's news also brought reports of other Asian markets in California suffering losses. The first rumor, in Sacramento County, focused on Welco's Fruitridge Road and Del Rio Avenue stores, both owned by brothers Jimmy and Tommy Phong. Spread initially and predominantly by e-mail, the hoax claimed that Tommy had died of SARS, his wife was in critical condition in the hospital, all employees at both stores were infected, and police had been forced to shut down the businesses. Public Health Officer Glennah Trochet was quick to stymie the rumor in an interview, noting that the county as a whole had only a single case of SARS. That case was unrelated to any Asian market and had been handled efficiently, with the patient recovering well. Nevertheless, locals began avoiding not only the stores owned by the Phong brothers—both of whom were alive and well—but the surrounding establishments. Hoang Van Nguyen, a resident of the area, said that he had stopped shopping in local stores because the message frightened him: "Since this stuff is going on, I have been reluctant to go there as much as I used to" (Griffith 2003).

A second rumor in California sprung up several hundred miles south in the city of San Gabriel, located in Los Angeles County. An e-mail version closely matches that written about New York's Bo Ky restaurant, though with different details and a longer plea for action:

> The SARS disease has spread to our neighbor. Today 4–3–2003, the police has shut down Hawaii and San Gabriel Supermarket due to the employee somehow got hit by this virus. Also one of the chief at Capital restaurant in Alhambra also got this virus. The Sam Woo restaurant in the FOCUS plaza was close early today to avoid getting it.
>
> Friends, please take care of yourself and your family. Avoid going to ASIAN areas!!! This is very serious about life and death and spreading them to the love one. Pay close attention to the Chinese newspaper and be alert about this deadly virus. Please pass this message to all of your friends so they can protect their love one too. (D. Emery 2003)

The article that covered this story—gathered from the website About.com—opened its comments section with a quote from an Agence France-Presse dispatch: "Fear of the SARS virus is becoming a more dangerous epidemic than the disease itself." Confirming the accuracy of this statement, the article then notes that, as of mid-April, not only had all of the rumors been found wanting for truth, but "no cases of SARS [had] been found in any Chinatown in the United States" (D. Emery 2003). Despite this, versions of SARS-in-Chinatown rumors were collected in San Francisco, Las Vegas, Sacramento, and Boston (D. Emery 2003), as well as Honolulu (New Milford Visiting Nurse Association 2003). Canada had also been hit by rumor e-mails at this point, and the narrative arose across the Atlantic only a few days later, when Britain's Chinese restaurants began losing customers, prompting at least one establishment to place an advertisement in a Chinese newspaper denying that staff members had contracted the virus (Vasagar 2003).

This wasn't the end of the SARS rumor mill's run. Possibly the worst of the individual scenarios happened at the end of April 2003, when a man at the Taipei Municipal Hoping Hospital (TMHH)—already beleaguered by rumors of SARS deaths—hanged himself after hearing a story that his wife had contracted SARS. TMHH staff, reacting to both the untrue SARS rumors and the true suicide rumor, attempted to force their way out of the hospital when authorities sealed it off to investigate the man's death. Within a matter of hours the incident was brought to the attention of a US CDC official staying in Taiwan, who immediately reported back to his headquarters that the entire city was "out of order." It took the intervention of Lee Lung-teng, deputy director-general of the Department of Health in Taipei, to set matters straight, though that only happened after two CDC officials visited the TMHH to assess the situation (Chen 2003).

Rumors such as these spread throughout Asia, but affected China most heavily. Hospitals in Beijing were quarantined on what seemed a weekly basis in April, and workers refused to show up for shifts. Restaurants, theaters, and shopping malls stood empty. Elementary and middle schools closed for up to two weeks. Some universities confined students to campus to prevent anyone from bringing in the disease. Many left the city, and possibly the country. Fear of Beijing's rumored SARS crisis even caused a few nearby villages to blockade their borders entirely, refusing to allow outsiders to enter. So devastating were the rumors and concomitant fear that by early May, Citigroup had lowered its estimate of China's 2003 economic growth from 8 percent to 6.5 percent (Beech 2003). Nowhere in the world was the link between gathering places and fear so omnipresent.

The SARS narratives used in this chapter so far have been gathered from media sources and the Internet and were placed in a rough chronological order. It should be obvious by now that many SARS narratives do exhibit a correlation between danger and gathering places. In addition, most of the narratives that appeared after early May 2003 follow the same basic formula of empty shopping malls, grocery stores, and restaurants, most of which were located in predominantly Asian sections of large cities.

One group of narratives, gathered from oral interviews, remains to be examined. Some follow the same basic format as those previously discussed, but a few merit special attention. One informant, Mike, was working as an emergency medical technician in Toronto during the epidemic. Mike mentioned the abandoned nature of Toronto's Chinatown, though he could not recall avoiding it himself, nor could he remember any of his friends purposely not going to those areas. More pressing are his experiences as a paramedic during this time and how the public perceived him. Some of Mike's narratives came secondhand from other medical personnel and concerned patients in hospitals and nursing homes whose families did not visit them during the epidemic. But the larger number of his stories involved personal experiences, especially in his capacity as a paramedic.

Mike was quarantined in mid-March because he had entered Scarborough Grace hospital without wearing a mask and gown. He had been authorized to do this but was informed a few days later that all personnel who had not been protected, despite the authorization, were to be quarantined. When he returned to work "about seven-and-a-half days" later, his working environment "progressed sort of from wearing masks in all calls to wearing a mask and gown; up to mask, gown, gloves; then double-gowning, double-gloving, face shields, hoods; and then other calls we wore full Tyvek suits, so full head-to-toe, sort of like the fellows in the *E. T.* movie" (Mike 2005). Aside from the hot and stifling nature of such protection, Mike commented that the suits dramatically affected public reaction to medical personnel: "There was sort of an air of apprehension, there was an 'I don't know' to it, and of course media, all the footage, the transfer footage, the response footage, we're the guys outside, so we're the easiest ones to videotape, to record in our big hoods and gowns and masks, and so there's the association there." Mike also recalled "people . . . walking towards me, and crossing the street, even though I was by myself and there were no patients around, there was no one ill. Or people covering their face in their elbow, sort of the pit of their elbow, or holding their jacket sleeves and whatnot over their face, sort of to prevent themselves from breathing in near me." Mike's mother, by simple dint of association, was also treated differently at work, encountering constant questions from coworkers and managers regarding the last time she had seen Mike, as her answer could mean possible endangerment for people in her office building.

But interviewees Angel and Rosita expressed the most extreme fears. Angel freely reported that his fears of contracting SARS were intense enough that they went well beyond mere gathering places and included quite literally any public space outside of his house. For "around six or seven months," Angel and Rosita "basically . . . stayed home. Like even Saturday we never [went] out." They "tried to avoid people coming to the house" as well (Angel and Rosita 2005). Angel seems to have been the main source of these actions, as described by his wife: "For me, I'm not a worrier, but it affected me because it affected [Angel], pretty much, because he . . . so he, we didn't go out anymore. He stocked up on water. He had this great big sign posted on the house: 'Wash your hands.' [laughs] Even the children's friends, if they came, please wash their hands." Rosita, however, was not without her own sources of concern, admitting that she would have been wary to enter funeral parlors during the epidemic.

Angel, on the other hand, offered a large list of places he avoided, including malls, movie houses, restaurants, and medical facilities: "So one thing, you know, I'm afraid to go to the clinic, like if you are sick, like if you have colds, you would avoid going to see the doctors, because who knows, somebody before you has seen the doctors and left something, and then you go to see the doctors and you might have SARS." Angel's avoidance of public places was aided by the fact that he had retired by this point, a fact he used to his advantage when grocery shopping—the one activity he could not avoid: "I go to [get] groceries, but during not the rush hour. I try to avoid when there are times that there are lots of people." Angel did recall a friend of his—also retired—whose fear even outstripped his own: "A good friend, he didn't go to see his barber, and he was, his hair was long and he had so many, because he was afraid."

So great was public fear of SARS that even sneezing in a gathering place was likely to cause a reaction, as related by interviewee Jonathan:

> I was studying at Robart's Library at the University of Toronto, and it was a packed room, and I sneezed, and I heard a girl under her breath at the table say, "SARS," this panic everyone had. And it was hard to tell how much it was just a pure joke on her part, if she was just goofing around, or if she really . . . I mean, when you're in this enclosed space, I can imagine that there is that kernel of fear, you know, you're kidding but . . . who knows what's around? (Jonathan 2005)

Jonathan's narrative is exemplary for its revelation of the nature of fear. As Jeannie B. Thomas remarks in *Featherless Chickens, Laughing Women, and Serious Stories*, laughter can be caused by "the broaching of the taboo and emotionally charged topic of death" (Thomas 1997, 46). Joking behavior can come from the same wellspring of emotion, and Jonathan's remarks make this clear. Was the girl who said "SARS" really joking, or was she serious? Or was it a little of both?

Another relevant issue to many of the narratives presented in this chapter is that of "popular epidemiology," defined by Phil Brown as "the process by which laypersons gather scientific data and other information, and also direct and marshal the knowledge and resources of experts in order to understand the epidemiology of disease" (Brown 1992, 269). Brown points out that a key difference in interpreting disease between "professionals" and "laypeople" is that the former focus on disease processes while the latter are more concerned with personal experiences of the illness. These divergent approaches to disease often result in considerable discord between the two parties, where neither is entirely willing to meet the other at that group's worldview. Professionals are proclaimed as too clinical and detached in their focus, and laypeople are charged with relying on unscientific and overly subjective opinions. Laypeople, however, can be extremely aggressive in their demands for data, and in situations where the scientific world fails to meet those needs, they will search for data from other groups, and even create their own groups—sometimes comprised at least partially of sympathetic professionals—to conduct studies appropriate to their demands.

Brown even presents a set of stages common to popular epidemiology. These stages reflect processes that occur during investigations of correlations between pollutants and health effects—not diseases and health effects—but many of the stages still apply. They are as follows:

1) A group of people in a contaminated community notice separately both health effects and pollutants.

2) These residents hypothesize something out of the ordinary, typically a connection between health effects and pollutants.

3) Community residents share information, creating a common perspective.

4) Community residents, now a more cohesive group, read about, ask around, and talk to government officials and scientific experts about the health effects and the putative contaminants.

5) Residents organize groups to pursue their investigation.

6) Government agencies conduct official studies in response to community groups' pressure. These studies usually find no association between contaminants and health effects.

7) Community groups bring in their own experts to conduct a health study and to investigate pollutant sources and pathways.

8) Community groups engage in litigation and confrontation.

9) Community groups press for corroboration of their findings by official experts and agencies. (Brown 1992, 269–70)

In the SARS narratives presented in this chapter, many of these stages appear—especially if, in addition to "government officials" and "scientific experts," media sources are added to the list of groups consulted and brought in by laypersons. What also needs to be made explicit is that, in many cases, there is only the need for a *perceived* correlation between cause and effect. Under these criteria, the stages may be applied to SARS narratives as follows:

1) A group of people notices separately a set of well-publicized health data associating SARS with people living in China, and the existence of local people of Asian ethnicity.

2) These people hypothesize something out of the ordinary—namely, a connection between SARS and any person of Asian ethnicity.

3) People share this information via oral and electronic means, creating a common connection and a community based around fear.

4) This new community, now a more cohesive group, reads about, asks around, and talks to media sources, local officials, and other group members about the correlation between Asian peoples and SARS.

5) The community reorganizes the media, via supply and demand eco-
    nomics, into an entity dedicated to providing information about Asian
    peoples and SARS.

6) Government agencies, in response to waxing xenophobic pressure, issue
    official denials of the presence of SARS in local Chinatowns and Asian
    neighborhoods.

7) Community groups bring in further examples from their own experts
    (i.e., media sources and firsthand and/or friend-of-a-friend testimony) to
    respond to the denials.

8) Community groups continue to engage in confrontations with Asian
    peoples, even if only by avoiding them, their businesses, and their
    neighborhoods.

9) Community groups may press for corroboration of their findings by offi-
    cial experts and agencies but may also simply see deserted Asian restau-
    rants and neighborhoods as ample evidence of the veracity of the link
    between Asian peoples and SARS.

The comparison of SARS narratives to the rubric created by Brown is perhaps forced, and the resulting schema doesn't function as linearly as does the
original. Many of the SARS stages may be happening simultaneously, while
Brown stated that his stages usually occurred sequentially. This is largely
because he is detailing a situation where the perceived connection between
health effects and pollutants turned out, on official examination, to be an
actual connection. As such, Brown does not consider the ramifications to
his set of stages that would come if the connection were proven false. In
other words, his stance does not deal with false-positive narratives, and thus
he is never forced into a situation where his theories must take into account
why disease narratives can exist despite their incorrectness. What comes
from considering such factors is a realization that disease narratives can form
their own authoritative gravity. That is, the existence of a rumor stating that
SARS has been located in an Asian neighborhood or business can be seen as
providing its own proof: the narrative wouldn't exist if it weren't true—or, at
least, if it weren't true *somewhere*. Brown does concede that "lay investigators
may pursue specific inquiries with their own agenda in mind . . . [empha-
sizing] certain health data and [minimizing] other reports" (Brown 1992,
278). But he never considers the ramifications to his theories that would
come from the collected data being incorrect but not recognized as such.
Popular epidemiology *can* be based on the gathering of accurate, provable
data, but it does not have to be.

    This is not to say that Brown's conclusions and theories are without
merit, for he does present rubrics that are valuable in studying disease narratives. Especially relevant are his comments on the question of how it is
possible to know whether lay investigations provide accurate information.

Although even in this section Brown limits his comments to defending the layperson's findings, rather than discussing what would happen if they were proven incorrect, he still offers a positive message concerning the importance of paying attention to lay investigations:

> Public health officials worry that some communities might exaggerate the risks of a hazard, or be wrong about the effects of a substance. Yet if this occurs, it must be seen in context: community fears are too often brushed aside and data has been withheld. Given the increasing cases (or at least recognition of those cases) of technological disasters, drug side effects, and scientific fraud, public sentiment has become more critical of science. In response, lay claims may be erroneous. But this is the price paid for past failures and problems, and is a countervailing force in democratic participation . . . Exaggerated fears may be understood as signs of the need to expand public health protection, rather than justifications to oppose lay involvement. Even if a community makes incorrect conclusions, their database may still remain useful for different analyses. (Brown 1992, 278)

Relating these comments back to SARS, Brown might be of the opinion that it is necessary to study disease narratives because (1) they offer a glimpse into lay understandings of disease and (2) the study of such narratives can reveal to medical professionals methods of better interacting with the public. What should not happen is official scorn or debasement of those rumors, since such efforts tend to only reinforce the belief systems that made the rumors possible in the first place.

Although the full scope of narratives that arose during the SARS epidemic contains many entries that do not involve fear of gathering places, a significant number does. The nature of SARS facilitated and exacerbated the creation of these stories, being a virus that was, even early in its existence, humming with real stories of the deceased, who had done nothing more endangering than occupy elevator space with a contagious individual. Many interviewees reported feeling "trapped" by fear, a sentiment that runs throughout the narratives collected from the Internet and media sources. Public reaction was immediate and widespread—to the extent that less than a month after the word SARS made its first newspaper headline, rumors and hoaxes concerning infected individuals working in restaurants, malls, and other gathering places arose in places as distant and different from each other as Beijing and New York. Fear of gathering places was ubiquitous and, for many, paralyzing. Interviewee Luis is given the final word here:

> It was a really scary time for everybody. It limits your movement, and you're not free. You feel you're not free when you go outside the door. You want to go here and then you think, "Oh, because of SARS let's avoid this." If somebody put the chain on you that you are [on] the leash, you know, you can only go so far and so much, that's how you feel. (Luis 2005)

NOTES

1 One newsletter proclaimed that the average person had a better chance of winning the Powerball lottery than of contracting SARS from standing next to a coughing stranger—see New Milford Visiting Nurse Association 2003.

2 For an examination of this phenomenon as recognized and utilized in traditional practice, see Lynne S. McNeill's article "Portable Places: Serial Collaboration and the Creation of a New Sense of Place" in *Western Folklore* 66, no. 3/4, 281–300.

4

Private Actions in Public Spaces
SARS and Paradigm Violations

ACCORDING TO LINDA C. GARRO, "to understand the impact of illness . . . on a person's life, it is necessary to develop an understanding of
the narrative context" (Garro 1992, 133). In other words, any true study of
the actions undertaken by a group suffering from an illness must take into
account "the meaning that they place on these actions" (Calnan 1987, 8). In
the SARS epidemic of 2003, public transportation became anathema, with
airports in Toronto, Singapore, Australia, and numerous other countries
showing marked decreases in passenger numbers. Many narratives expressed
fear and concern over long-distance and intercontinental travel. Plane-,
train-, and bus-related services suffered as a result. But the flow of information between countries, due largely to the Internet and media sources,
increased greatly. This led to a counterintuitive reaction wherein, though
informational globalization waxed prolific, cultural and social globalization
was stilted. The widespread diffusion of technology that enabled public
knowledge of foreign affairs only served to make people wary of other cultures at best. At its worst, this technology made possible the circulation of
narratives that proved entirely counterproductive to cultural globalization
through the rapid diffusion of inaccurate information regarding ethnicity.
Many of these erroneous narratives ultimately dealt with the concept of
private actions performed in public spaces as sources of endangerment. The
antiglobalization narratives present in SARS were intricately and insepa-
rably linked with incorrect cultural stereotypes, and these were ultimately
the result of widespread incompetence in determining the meanings other
ethnicities placed on actions.

As James L. Watson notes, "Globalization is a process that is replete
with ironies. One of those ironies hides behind the SARS crisis: a premodern agricultural system—based on pigs, ducks, chickens, and centuries-old

DOI: 10.7330/9780874219296.c004

technology—could well turn out to be the greatest threat to the postmodern global system" (Watson 2005, 202)[1]. A second discrepancy is that the ultimate tally of SARS—the 774 fatalities—is in hindsight highly disproportionate to the reactions and conspiracy theories; similar reactions occur in response to most diseases. Our conceptions of global security are thus largely skewed. Jeanne Guillemin, in discussions on the nature and realities of bioterrorism, notes that biological warfare "by humans against humans has been rare and historically inconsequential" (quoted in Watson 2005, 202), and that by far the larger number of disease-related deaths come from nature.

Given these discrepancies, it can quickly be established that diseases such as SARS, and public reactions to them, are a consequence of globalization and should be expected because of it. Many of the largest novel epidemics of the last one hundred years, (AIDS, SARS, avian influenza, Ebola) and still more of the most common historical and modern diseases (malaria, rabies, salmonellosis, trichinosis, typhus), are all zoonotic in nature, resulting from human-animal microbial transfer. Such transfers will most likely take place in areas in the developing world—"premodern," as Watson calls them—places like China's Guangdong province or Africa's Congo. Historically, these places were isolated from other parts of the world, and thus non-airborne infectious diseases had far fewer chances to spread. Today it takes little more than a plane ride for these diseases to spread halfway around the globe. So while globalization theorists in the 1990s spent their time analyzing the border-and-nation-shattering nature of the Internet (c.f. Kelly 1998; Rosecrance 1999), it now seems that they should have focused less on the spread of bits of information and more on the spread of bits of viral DNA. Globalization has not resulted in a utopia, but a worldwide hot zone. As Ann Marie Kimball succinctly states, "More remarkable than the recent emergence of SARS and the H5N1 virus [in China], perhaps, is the fact that we have not seen more of such events in this region" (Kimball 2006, 62).

The harsh realities of globalization—that it is not the cure-all many assumed it would be—come as no surprise. Ralph Peters states, somewhat cynically, "Those who imagine that greater understanding, courtesy of the Internet, will deliver an idyllic peace don't know humanity . . . Just as hippie communes fell apart because somebody had to do the dishes, predictions that war will become 'unthinkable' fail because they embrace a dream and ignore human reality" (Peters 2005). Even within the field of globalization theory there is discord as to the ultimate benefits and drawbacks of the shrinking of the sociocultural world. But there is little argument that SARS is definitely a marker of the dangers that can come of it. Those theorists who have studied the disease unanimously point at the unpreparedness of the global community to deal with such an epidemic.

Many of the examples supporting such arguments within the academic community are the same narratives that circulated so widely among the general population while SARS was waxing and waning: contaminated flights, buses, airports, hotels, etc. If one of the markers of globalization is the increased ability to travel quickly to distant places, businesses and modes of transportation that support this ability cannot help but be inexorably intertwined with the narratives—both good and bad—that surround globalization.

A consequence of placing these businesses at the center of the problem is that their employees are also placed there. Rumors and realities involving so-called SARS superspreaders who worked for the airline industry were common in newspapers and circulated widely in oral forms among the lay population. One such case involved a single airline attendant named Esther Mok, who is believed to be the index case for more than 160 of Singapore's infections in April 2003. Infected herself by a man who caught the disease in Hong Kong, she is known to have unsuspectingly passed on the virus to dozens of passengers, including one man whose general poor health, including diabetes and kidney disease, masked his symptoms, making it possible for him to infect at least 40 doctors, nurses, patients, and guests in two wards of the Singapore General Hospital before his SARS-positive status was discovered ("Are Some Better SARS Transmitters" 2003).[2]

Mok's direct relationship to the high number of Singapore cases parallels an earlier Hong Kong case involving an unnamed airport worker admitted to the Prince of Wales Hospital in early March. This patient quickly became the biggest superspreader of the time—replaced only by Mok a month later—infecting 112 people, including every doctor and nurse assigned to him. The man's highly infectious nature was ultimately traced back to a jet nebulizer, which sprays medicated mist directly into the lungs, expanding the phlegm-filled passages to allow for easier breathing. While this does help the patient, the larger lung passages and improved breathing capacity result in the increased exhalation of viral materials (McNeil and Altman 2003). From the perspective of rumor, however, in both his and Mok's cases, the superspreader worked for the airline industry, and together these two people infected almost 300 others within a matter of days.

Employees of these businesses constitute only a small part of the larger body of narratives. Many stories involve passengers on flights who spread the virus. An airline passenger brought SARS to Canada—itself a damning piece of evidence for antiglobalization theorists. Other established infection vectors include Air China Flight 112 on March 15, which included a 72-year-old male passenger who infected 21 of the flight's patrons, directly resulting in the presence of SARS in both Inner Mongolia and Thailand (Lakshmanan 2003). Even scares that ultimately turned out to be false alarms pointed their figurative fingers directly at the airline industry—such as the New York-to-Singapore flight on March 15, which was grounded and quarantined in Frankfurt, Germany, after officials learned that one of the passengers was a doctor who had been treating SARS patients in Singapore only days earlier. Ultimately, none of the flight's 400 passengers tested positive for SARS, but the story still made headlines (Cohen, Naik, and Pottinger 2003). Looking at the history of SARS, it may easily be said that if the airline industry had not existed, the disease would not have had the impact that it did.

Moving away from the airline industry, many narratives concern the negative effects of globalization on ethnic identities and disease panic. Several interviewees mentioned general fears of traveling by bus, plane, and train, but two interviews in particular stand out as exemplary. The first was conducted in late September 2005 with Heather. During 2003 Heather was living in Hamilton, Ontario, attending university but making regular trips to see both her brother in Toronto (roughly an hour's drive northeast) and her parents in Ajax (an additional half-hour drive northeast).

Heather reported that Toronto's outbreak had little effect on her day-to-day life, Hamilton being far enough away that its residents only "got the tail end of the paranoia" (Heather 2005). Visiting her family was another matter, especially since her mother worked in a caretaking capacity at the time. Heather described her mother as "a little bit of a hypochondriac, I think because of her medical training . . . She works in a nursing home, so she had to go through the whole experience of gowning up, putting on [a] mask every day that she went to work." This constant reinforcement of care and precaution, as well as natural parental instincts, led Heather's mother to request that her children participate in the same level of care in their daily lives. Among other details, one care package Heather received from her mother included "socks, some barbecue sauce, some jam . . . a book I had left behind . . . a hairbrush," and a package of medical-grade filtering masks accompanied by a note that read, "I'd like you to please wear them when you go outside."

But her mother's strongest response came when Heather wanted to come home for a weekend. In Heather's words:

> To do that I'd have to take a GO bus, which is the common public transit system between Hamilton and Toronto, and I think [mother] had just been reading about how they had been tracing SARS to the initial spread being on an airplane, and so she got really paranoid about me taking any kind of public transit, and said, "No, you're not allowed to come home. If you're gonna come home, we'll come get you in the car." (Heather 2005)

In total, the drive her parents made so Heather could avoid the public transit system totaled six hours: four times the one-and-a-half-hour drive from Ajax to Hamilton. This is double the time it would have taken Heather to make the trip by bus, but the security her mother felt was deemed worth the time and effort.

This first narrative deals heavily with disease panic and the lengths to which some people went to protect themselves and their loved ones, but Heather's second narrative combines this panic with ethnic identity, revealing a disturbing series of connections in the mind-set of the general population. During 2003 Heather lived with two Chinese roommates: one male and one female. As Heather says, "it was interesting going out with them because . . . if they coughed ever they'd get some strange looks." These reactions didn't seem to bother the male roommate, whose allergies caused him to sneeze often in public, and he would immediately afterwards engage Heather in a joking banter that she recounts as beginning with "Ha ha ha: you have SARS." The situation more heavily affected her female roommate, "Rita," especially in regard to how she was perceived in public. Even though this roommate was not overly concerned about the epidemic, laughing at Heather's mother sending her surgical masks, she was still stigmatized because of her ethnic identity:

> [Rita] lived in downtown Toronto, and would go back between Hamilton and Toronto frequently. She, when she was on the subway, she'd sit, she'd describe several times sitting down beside somebody and having them get up and move over. And so I think that's . . . she started driving her car a little bit more often because that just started to make her uncomfortable. (Heather 2005)

The effects of this stigmatization were not isolated to Rita, as the rest of her family experienced similar reactions when in public. In Rita's family's case, the strong public reactions against their Asian heritage made the whole family postpone a trip to China to attend a wedding because of their concern that they would not be allowed back into Canada.

The second interview that pertains to the current discussion comes from a man named Benjamin, who worked as a bartender in San Francisco, California, in 2003. According to Benjamin (2005), the San Francisco area did not experience a great reaction against SARS, other than Chinatown experiencing "somewhat of a lull," as was common in many Chinatowns across North America. But that spring, from roughly May 15 to June 15, Benjamin was traveling through China's Hubei province and its neighbor, Chongqing municipality. Benjamin admits that many of his friends and family in the States had urged him to cancel his trip, and it had taken him quite some time to convince them that his travels would not lead him into any viral danger. His family had fallen into the general mind-set that anything Asian was dangerous, and it took Benjamin's intervention to show them how their fears were "exacerbated by their lack of knowledge of China and how big it is, and maybe the lack of preciseness about how concentrated the cases were."

Benjamin went to China as part of a personal project involving the Three Gorges Dam. Benjamin had a keen interest in the fate of the people who lived along the banks of the Yangtze River, and since December 2001 had made several trips to China to take videos for a documentary film. His 2003 trip was central to these efforts; it allowed him to witness the closing of the sluice gates at the dam on June 1, which permanently blocked the natural flow of the Yangtze and started the buildup of the reservoir behind the dam—a reservoir that didn't completely fill until late 2008 and now ultimately stretches some 375 miles, covers over 1,300 archaeological sites, and has resulted in the displacement of between 1 and 2 million people.

Benjamin's documentation of this act, and the consequences that would eventually come of it, meant that he spent May and June 2003 traveling along the length of the Yangtze, encountering dozens of villages that had rarely seen outsiders. He had read that many of these small villages were actively blockading their streets to prevent foreigners and travelers from entering because of the SARS epidemic, and the fact that "travelers were dubbed the carriers of the disease" by locals weighed heavily on his mind:

> That was something that really fueled my fears at first, because I was going to be going to a lot of small towns in rural China that don't see a lot of foreigners, and I was worried that I would see a lot of, that I would be met with fear of getting SARS, you know, from me . . . Well that was what I was worried about. I mean, because I was dubbed, I would be a traveler, coming, going from one place to another place, possibly picking something up from one place and bringing it to another. As would any traveler within China, you know, a Chinese traveler as well.

On the other hand, once inside those towns, Benjamin recalled rarely seeing anyone wearing a surgical mask. He placed the number at "maybe one out of every 10,000," and quite often the masks people were wearing were "dirty and falling off."

According to these reports, people in China evidenced the same reactions to foreigners as did people in North America: people of different ethnic identity, or strangers in general, were suspect; local, familiar people were less so. This is especially apparent in Benjamin's descriptions of traveling along the Yangtze. Villages far preferred having outsiders stay as outsiders—even to the point of openly barricading their borders—but people inside those villages were free to do as they chose and were not considered harmful.

This sharp division exists in contradiction to the realities of viruses and disease vectors, for it takes little effort for disease to cross a man-made barricade. Even blood-borne diseases may cross through the actions of insects and rodents. As in Edgar Allan Poe's "The Masque of the Red Death," no barrier is impenetrable, and disease can creep inside even the best-maintained walls. Worse, once inside that barrier, the virus can multiply quickly and easily. The common cold, for example, is hypothesized to be more present in winter because humans spend more time indoors and in contact with other people during the cold months, and this situation provides the perfect breeding ground for disease.

Yet we have to attempt to divide those who are potentially diseased from those who are "known" to be healthy. In the case of small villages in central China, the locations of these dividing lines are obvious: the town limits. These lines are seemingly independent of race, age, and sex. The only information needed is who is from the town and who is not. Even if such geographical barriers are recognized as frail, their existence still provides relief and may in fact help greatly to keep out what is not wanted. In large cities, the likelihood of such geographical barriers grows exceedingly small. It is possible to quarantine houses or apartment complexes or even whole cities, but the people living inside those cities still have their daily duties, including working, shopping, and using public transportation to access the more remote parts of the city. In these circumstances people will thus be constantly surrounded by the potentially diseased. Where geographical barriers fail or are impossible, lines are instead drawn around those who are unknown or different—or around race, sex, and age—so strangers and other ethnicities become the targets of suspicion.

The basic ideas behind these separations were recognized and laid out as early as 1959 by William Hugh Jansen, who designated his theory the "esoteric-exoteric factor in folklore." Accordingly, "the esoteric applies to what one group thinks of itself and what it supposes others think of it. The exoteric is what one group thinks of another and what it thinks that other group thinks it thinks" (Jansen 1959, 206–7). Esoteric thoughts are turned inward, pondering the self; exoteric thoughts concern others. Furthermore, esoteric thoughts stem "from the group sense of belonging and [serve] to defend and strengthen that sense" (207). As a result of this, Jansen claims that smaller groups are more likely to have stronger esoteric elements.

These arguments are visible within Heather's and Benjamin's narratives. Heather's statement—in itself a collection of smaller narratives about several people—demonstrates especially well how Jansen's theories apply to at least two different ethnicities. On the one hand, we have Heather's interactions with her mother, which demonstrate her mother's perceptions of her own family as safe and Torontonians as a whole as dangerous. Demonstrating the power of the esoteric factor, this means that Heather's mother has grouped roughly 5 million people—including Toronto's Census Metropolitan Area—into a single category, regardless of age, sex, or race. On the other hand, we have Heather's reports of what her Chinese roommates experienced during the SARS epidemic (i.e., the incidences of people avoiding them on buses and subways, which are clearly cases of Asians as a whole suffering stigmatization).

Benjamin's reports show similar flexibilities in the lines between who is considered safe and who is considered unsafe. The comments that he chose to open his story with—"I was worried . . . that I would be met with fear of getting SARS, you know, from me"—are an excellent summarization of the esoteric factor. He knew his own SARS-negative status but recognized that people would potentially see him as dangerous. Switching groups for a moment, it is perfectly clear from Benjamin's narratives what the esoteric thoughts of the small villages he encountered along the Yangtze were—namely, that other people are dangerous, regardless of whom they are. Here, as in the case of Heather's discussions with her mother, age, sex, and race are irrelevant.

In both cases involving the dissolution of racial and ethnic lines in the determination of who is possibly diseased and who is not, we find that the groups making the determinations are relatively small: Heather's family and Chinese fishing villages. The absolute determinations of Asians as potentially diseased that Heather's roommates experienced occurred in situations with a large and amorphous deciding group; not just a bus-full of people made the determination, but Torontonian society as a whole. Jansen's original esoteric-exoteric arguments did not include discussions of disease, but it does seem that they apply. Small groups have stronger esoteric elements and are more easily capable of grouping large numbers of people of varying identities into an Other category, while large groups have weaker esoteric elements (perhaps a consequence of the amorphous nature of the group, where it is more difficult for one member of the group to know what every other member is thinking or doing) and more frequently draw lines along racial and ethnic borders.

These narratives may also reflect a different kind of fear, as discussed by Mikel J. Koven in his article " 'Buzz Off!': The Killer Bee Movie as Modern Belief Narrative." Koven hypothesizes that killer bee movies, which involve swarms of genetically altered bees racing up from South America and attacking US border towns, may reflect racial undertones and anxieties. Moreover, these stories allude to at least two races of people as fearful and Other. One race is obvious, given that the bees in question are often referred to as "Africanized" or "Brazilian," and so Koven states, "Specifically with Irwin Allen's [movie] *The Swarm* . . . the Brazilian honeybee seems to act as a metaphor for white paranoia about African-Americans in the U.S." (Koven 2001, 6). But he argues that a second race may be alluded to in these stories, if certain key contextual facts are noted—specifically, that the decade that popularized many of the killer bee movies and books (the 1970s) marked the end of the Vietnam War. As such, *The Swarm* (1978) and Jack Laflin's novel *The Bees* (1976) may also reflect the nation's growing hesitation with Vietnam, as well as its embarrassment at not having secured a conclusive victory. Koven states,

> Implicit in these narratives is the idea that the United States needs a military victory to counter their defeat in South East Asia. Seen racially, the bees could even be seen to represent the Viet Cong themselves—the bees' yellow and black markings representing both the racial stereotyping of East Asians as "yellow"-skin colored and the black of the Viet Cong uniforms. These military victories over the bees [in the movie and the novel] can therefore be seen as symbolic victories against a Vietnamese that the American military machine could not defeat in reality. (Koven 2001, 10)

If SARS narratives are examined in the same vein, it becomes immediately apparent that many of Koven's conclusions can be applied. Not only are many of the narratives overtly racist in tone and message, but even in those narratives that exclude mention of race and focus specifically on transmission vectors—such as Heather's mother's concern over the virus being spread by airplane and bus—racial undertones may still be present because SARS *came from China*. In fact, it may be said that the coronavirus is a metaphor for the Chinese, or indeed anyone of Asian descent.

Such a hypothesis stands in line with many of the sentiments pervading the United States today, revealing deep-seated distrust of the Chinese. While no military battle between the two countries has taken place, several other factors influence public perception. First among these is the ever-present reminder that China is a Communist country, and as anyone who grew up during the Cold War was taught, Communist countries are evil. Frequent news stories detail China's human rights violations. Economic concerns also come into play here, such as the increasing amount of money the US government borrows from China or the outsourcing of jobs by US businesses to Asian countries. Finally, there are also the perennial concerns with immigrants—Asian or otherwise—moving into US cities and taking citizens' jobs. Other examples could be brought in to strengthen these ties but are hardly necessary. These few illustrations alone evince the strained relations between the United States and China. Like killer bee stories serving as a metaphor for US relations with Vietnam, SARS narratives reflect American opinions about the Chinese.

Examined under yet another light, these narratives reveal concern over actions performed out of place, or more specifically, private actions performed in public places. Mary Douglas, in discussing the concept of dirt and uncleanliness, notes that the beliefs society holds about hygiene are relative: "Shoes are not dirty in themselves, but it is dirty to place them on the dining table; food is not dirty in itself, but it is dirty to leave cooking utensils in the bedroom, or food bespattered on clothing; similarly, bathroom equipment in the drawing room . . . out-door things in-doors; upstairs things downstairs" (Douglas 1988, 35–36). In SARS narratives, many underlying fears involve similar matters of sanitation and objects out of proper place. What separates SARS narratives, and disease narratives in general, is the object that is considered to be out of its proper place: the infecting agent.

Although disease narratives have many forms and come in multiple varieties, they can all be ultimately traced back to this infecting agent—whether it appears on a needle or razor blade, is present in semen or saliva, or can be transmitted through the air we breathe or only through bodily fluids. But while Douglas states that food is dirty when present in the bedroom or on clothing (implying that food is sanitary when located in the kitchen and on plates), no such demarcations apply to infecting agents. The SARS virus is clearly seen as dirty in all the narratives collected for this study, but the best line that can be drawn to identify where it does and does not belong is between *anywhere else* and *me*. That is, while the "improper" location for the virus can be definitely identified as the narrator's personal space, or even the personal spaces of a small group of people surrounding the narrator, the "proper" location is rarely spoken of and is instead left as an ambiguous, amorphous location found anywhere other than where the narrator currently stands.

If the location of the narrator is sacrosanct, and is the improper location for the virus, it stands to reason that any actions that cause a virus to enter the personal space of the narrator are also improper. Sneezing and coughing, for example, are widely recognized as methods of transmitting diseases. Even small children are told to cover their mouths and noses when performing such actions. Public and widespread knowledge of scientific germ theory may be inaccurate and incomplete by medical standards, but it is sufficient to recognize that sudden expulsions of breath from the lungs can result in the airborne dispersion of disease-causing materials, which is one reason why people prefer not to shake the hand of someone who has just sneezed into that hand.

Sneezing is, in addition, a private action. It is recognized as a potential spreader of disease, and thus something that should be shielded from the rest of the world by hand or handkerchief, but it is also an involuntary action—something that cannot be controlled. Sneezing results in the temporary loss of the sneezer's hold over his or her own body. The eyes involuntarily squeeze shut and the respiratory system is subverted from its normal job of supplying the body with oxygen in order to attend to the single, uncontrollable work of expelling a large amount of air forcefully and rapidly. Sneezing leaves a person at his or her most vulnerable: sightless and powerless. To a great extent, the only action a person is capable of performing while sneezing is, in fact, sneezing. Sneezing greatly hinders speech, vision, and activities involving highly controlled muscle movements (painting, running, playing a musical instrument, typing, etc.)—perhaps making such activities outright impossible—and it may be argued that thought processes are also retarded. Sneezing leaves us naked. It should come as no surprise that we hide our faces when we sneeze, or excuse ourselves from conversations to turn around (if given sufficient warning), and sometimes apologize for our actions afterwards.

In SARS narratives, the private nature of actions such as sneezing or coughing (the latter also marked by a socially imposed covering of the mouth) are made all the more relevant because they are performed in public spaces. Heather's interactions with her male Chinese roommate upon his sneezing in public—"Ha ha ha: you have SARS"—show at least some level of awareness concerning the danger of such an action. Heather mentions that such an exchange was "trivializing" the otherwise serious nature of a sneeze in the middle of an epidemic, an action that fits three of Jeannie B. Thomas's four functions of laughter, in this case "incongruity," "superiority," and "recognition of a taboo topic" (Thomas 1997, 43). Thomas's definition of "incongruity" is especially relevant in relation to this scenario: "this thing that is out of place here" (48). The juxtaposition of private action and public space creates the same recognition of uncleanliness as is present in Douglas's quote (i.e., things that are out-of-place are dirty). While a sneeze by itself might not result in a large response, when combined with its disease-spreading potential *and* the epidemic and general panic over SARS, the action creates an immediate and noticeable reaction.

The final layer in these narratives is that of stereotyping ethnicities—or outsiders and strangers—as diseased or disease carriers. The attribution to an ethnic group of either careless or purposeful introduction of a disease into a previously safe community puts the final nail in the coffin. These people are dirty as well as different; they act inappropriately, and they are harming us. Jennifer, a Chinese-Filipino interviewee, describes the stereotypes and reactions present in SARS narratives especially well:

> There was one time I was on a bus and . . . at that point we were living in Scarborough, which is, it's made up of a lot of immigrant communities, and there are a lot of Chinese peoples who are primarily in the northern area of Scarborough, going into Markham—Markham is a huge Chinese community, I think primarily from Hong Kong and Taiwan—and I was on the bus one day, and I was sitting beside this Caucasian girl, and this black guy sitting beside her, and they, I think were teenagers, thereabouts, and I think I coughed. No, I didn't cough, the girl started, like, fake coughing beside me, and the guy beside her was kind of giggling, but in an uncomfortable way, and I felt that to be sort of a joke, like because I was Asian, and because we were in Scarborough, and because we were on a bus, they were making fun of the fact that I was Chinese, I could possibly have SARS . . . Maybe it was an opportunity to . . . a reason for their stereotypes. Like for them to have certain stereotypes, it was a perfect opportunity for them to come out with jokes about it. (Jennifer 2005)

In this particular instance, no specific action on Jennifer's part, such as a cough or sneeze, incited the response. All that was needed was simply the presence of an individual perceived to be from a dangerous group.

The ultimate causes of such narratives are many and depend on social and familial factors, but sociologist Stephen L. Muzzatti places the blame squarely on informational globalization as it is present in the media. In an examination of media reports of SARS, Muzzatti notes that many of the articles in popular newspapers were sensationalistic at best, reporting exclusively on negative occurrences such as deaths, quarantines, business failures, and masses of masked faces. He states, "this type of coverage made SARS appear far more widespread, contagious, and dangerous than it truly was. It also served to tear away the thin and flimsy veneer of 'tolerance' in America, revealing deep-seated racism and xenophobia" (Muzzatti 2005, 123). Asians as a whole became "folk devils," or what Stanley Cohen calls "unambiguously unfavorable symbols" (Cohen 2002, 41) because of their association with the disease. Thus, it may be argued that experiences such as the ones suffered by Jennifer and Rita (Heather's female roommate) are direct consequences of living in an era when a news report filed in China can appear in an American newspaper only hours later.

Terry Ann Knopf pointed out over thirty years ago that rumor often begets violence, prejudice, and discrimination, and as legend overlaps rumor (Knopf 1975), the same qualities can be said of it. In the modern era, where rumor and legend spread—for the first time in history, faster than the speed of sound—the realities of Knopf's claims become ever more apparent. Narratives such as the ones in this chapter represent the worst of legend and rumor. The ease with which information passes between disparate parts of the modern world has at times resulted in significant benefits for humankind, but it has also enabled the widespread and rapid diffusion of panic and negative stereotypes. The public reactions and revulsions experienced by Jennifer, Rita, and Benjamin were no doubt fueled, at least in part, by rumor and legend. Similar reactions occurred around the world, where only a matter of days passed before SARS became inextricably, globally linked with Asians. The resulting narratives left Asian Americans who had never set foot outside North America accused (however lightly or humorously) of being potential infectors. In these cases, informational globalization *promulgated* pejorative stereotypes. In other cases knowledge of the existence of SARS led to the labeling of large numbers of strangers and outsiders as dangerous, sometimes resulting in the literal barricading of those people from towns. By "racializing illness" (Muzzatti 2005, 125) in this manner, the world was left in the midst of a wave of racism that was not only widely practiced by "official" news sources but also publicly encouraged and tolerated.

NOTES

1 Watson's example is arguably not, by dictionary definition, an example of irony, which is usually defined as an incongruity between surface-level meaning and underlying meaning. His point, however, is quite salient.

2 Mok's story parallels that of another superspreader, Gaëtan Dugas, the so-called patient zero of the AIDS outbreak, who used his capacities as a flight attendant for Air Canada to travel the world and purposely infect people with the AIDS virus. At least one report states that 17 percent of the first 248 AIDS cases in the United States were linked to Dugas (see Goldstein 2004, 113–15). Although Mok did not purposely infect people with SARS, the consequences of her actions were just as severe, and the fact that she, like Dugas, was a flight attendant provides the two narratives with an eerie similarity.

5

"Please Receive Communion through Your Hands"

*Personal and Communal Mediation of Stigma in the
2003 SARS Epidemic*

THE 2003 SARS EPIDEMIC IN TORONTO, CANADA, resulted in the stigmatization of ethnic groups, neighborhoods, and eventually the entire city.
The effects of this stigmatization included, on a widespread level, consumer
abandonment of Asian businesses, citywide losses in tourist-generated
income, and public avoidance of hospitals. On the level of individuals, reactions ranged from mild cautiousness to self-imposed quarantine, at least
one collected instance of which lasted more than six months. As Arthur
Kleinman and Sing Lee point out, social stigma is intimately tied to health
system responses (Kleinman and Lee 2005, 173–95). Yet despite the well-
publicized narratives of loss and panic, the larger population of Toronto
made few changes in their daily schedules. People still had to buy groceries,
go to work, and attend church. Individuals from stigmatized ethnic groups
in stigmatized communities traveled every day to their offices via subway
and bus lines, nestled tightly beside people from relatively "innocent" neighborhoods. This chapter will examine closely narratives such as these, filling a
gap in stigma research by looking at the methods used by individuals in the
SARS epidemic to mediate the fears associated with stigmas. These attempts
at mediation evidence a paradigmatic need for security, as reflected in the
changing of personal actions and behaviors, and a simultaneous syntagmatic
need for stability, as the intended meanings behind the actions remain constant despite the changes.

Stigmas, archaically, were brands burned into the skin of slaves or
criminals for identification purposes. Modern definitions of the word have
branched out denotatively, referring to several types of blemishes, ranging

104

DOI: 10.7330/9780874219296.c005

from crucifixion wounds to common birthmarks. But the connotations of these modern renditions still evince many of the term's negative archaic implications. To be stigmatized—to be marked—is to be labeled as somehow wrong or impure. Stigmas—especially those referring to medicine and disease—are characterized by discrimination, negative labeling, ostracism, and exclusion (Goffman 1963; Kleinman and Lee 2005). Stigmas, in this sense, affect all levels of society and result in such varied problems as workplace productivity losses, violations of basic human rights, medical noncompliance, the scapegoating of marginal groups, familial breakdown, and individual suffering (Kleinman and Lee 2005). At best, stigmatization results in a perceived difference. At worst, it means personal and financial ruin and can lead to suicide.

Various definitions of the more modern meanings of stigma have been forwarded, some of the earliest attempts coming from Erving Goffman: first, "The term stigma . . . will be used to refer to an attribute that is deeply discrediting" (Goffman 1963, 3); and second, from the same book, "an undesired differentness from what we had anticipated" (5). Gerhard Falk expands on this by explaining the most common modern American uses of the word, where "'stigma' and 'stigmatization' refers to an invisible sign of disapproval which permits insiders to draw a line around 'outsiders' in order to demarcate the limits of inclusion in any group" (Falk 2001, 17). Although not actually providing a dictionary definition of the word, Falk's comments do clearly demonstrate the nature of what it is to be stigmatized: set apart and marked as somehow unclean or unhealthy.

Modern sociological studies of stigma are largely based on Goffman's book *Stigma: Notes on the Management of Spoiled Identity*. At the time he wrote his book, stigma studies were relatively new. The preface to *Stigma* states that much of what had been done in the field before the book's publication had come from social psychology, and even there the field was hardly "over a decade" old (Goffman 1963). The footnote on the same page that summarizes the previous decade's work on the subject references five psychologists but only one sociologist—and tellingly, Goffman specifically highlights one of the psychologists as having provided the most useful data. Goffman's efforts in many ways represented the seminal attempts to introduce the field of stigma to the discipline of sociology.

Unfortunately, Goffman's meditations on the nature and mechanisms of stigma do not, in several key ways, include discussions of the types of stigma associated with SARS. For instance, he gives the following as the three main "types" of stigma:

> First there are abominations of the body—the various physical deformities. Next there are blemishes of individual character perceived as weak will, domineering or unnatural passions, treacherous and rigid beliefs, and dishonesty, these being inferred from a known record of, for example, mental disorder, imprisonment, addiction, alcoholism, homosexuality, unemployment, suicidal attempts, and radical political behavior. Finally there are the tribal stigma of race, nation, and religion, these being stigma that can be transmitted through lineages and equally contaminate all members of a family. (Goffman 1963, 4)

Even a cursory glimpse at this list should suffice to show that Goffman does not include the stigma that is associated with many diseases.

Briefly summarized, the types of stigma above can be broken into three categories: *physical deformities, character flaws*, and *tribal association*. Polio and Hansen's disease, both of which Goffman uses as examples of the first category, are indeed diseases, but in these instances physical deformities occur as a side effect of an untreated viral or bacterial infection, respectively. In other words, Goffman included these diseases in his spectrum based not on the presence of the infecting agent—that is, the poliovirus or the *Mycobacterium leprae* that causes Hansen's disease—but on the presence of the disfigurements that result from these infecting agents. There can be little argument that those who contracted SARS in 2003 were stigmatized, but the SARS virus did not cause the kinds of physical disfigurements or deformities present in Goffman's categories. Like those infected with AIDS, SARS victims initially appeared to be no different than anyone else. It was not until late in the progression of the disease that the similarities ceased. This was not due to physical deformities, however, but high fevers and respiratory problems. SARS victims were stigmatized simply because of the presence of an invisible infecting agent. Goffman's types of stigma thus require a fourth category—*the infected*, which includes anyone who is currently (or, it could be argued, has ever been) host to any virus, bacterium, fungus, parasite, etc. deemed in some way offensive, dangerous, contagious, or disgusting by the public.

But even with the inclusion of this fourth category, at least one key form of stigma within the SARS epidemic is not adequately described: the stigmatization of perfectly healthy individuals such as health care workers and Asians. Most notably missing from Goffman's list is the *potential* of someone to belong to a stigmatized category. All of the examples he used to support his arguments come from people who *are* recognized as members of the stigmatized categories into which they have been placed and actually have the conditions for which they have been stigmatized: people with Hansen's disease and amputees for being "deformed"; suicides and drug addicts for having recognized character flaws; African Americans for belonging to a different race. None of Goffman's examples incorporate the idea of *potentiality*, or the fear or worry that someone who is not immediately recognized as a member of a stigmatized community *might* belong to a category of people who are somehow different or discredited. And so logic dictates that a fifth category of people must be added to Goffman's list: the *potentially discreditable.*

Asians especially fell into this category during the SARS epidemic. Those interviewees who appeared in any manner whatsoever to be a member of that broad category of people classified as Asian felt stigmatized despite their SARS-negative status. At least one Caucasian informant (Benjamin, the San Francisco bartender) reported the same feelings while traveling through China, and a second Caucasian informant (Mike, the Toronto EMT) felt stigmatized not because of his race but because of his profession. All of these people occupied liminal places in public perceptions of the SARS epidemic. While not identifiably sick, they were not identifiably healthy either. Their stigmatization was thus the result of their *potentially* being ill.

This is not to say that Goffman never conceived of the potential nature of stigma being associated with the non-stigmatic. He does introduce what he terms "courtesy stigma," the best explanation of which comes from Kleinman and Lee: "Traditionally, stigma extended to those who it was believed had become morally polluted by their suffering, and whose moral pollution, it was also believed, might be contagious to others, so that they and their family members also bore this kind of personal and collective loss of face" (Kleinman and Lee 2005, 180). Goffman did accept that, in this manner, stigma could affect large numbers of people, but his arguments indicate that the range of courtesy stigma extended only to the reaches of the family.

Goffman also approached the concept of the potentially discreditable in his discussions of the differences between the "discredited" and the "discreditable." According to Goffman, the discredited label can be applied to someone whose "differentness" from a "normal" person is immediately visible or known. People suffering from Hansen's disease easily fall into this category because of the disfiguring nature of the disease, as do people who are widely and publicly recognized as homosexuals, murderers, unemployed, etc. The discreditable label, in contrast, is applied to someone whose differentness "is neither known about by those present nor immediately perceivable by them" (Goffman 1963, 4)—in other words, a person with Hansen's disease who is able to hide his disfigurements under his clothes or a murderer (homosexual, unemployed person, etc.) who is not suspected of such. While this latter category of the discreditable does admit the possibilities of the unseen stigmatic, it is still based on the *presence* of a differentness. The discreditable person is only someone whose discrediting attributes have not yet been discovered. Nowhere in this two-part paradigm exists the possibility of a perfectly healthy, unsullied person being wrongly stigmatized.

The narrowness of this view has since been updated. Kleinman and Lee, for instance, state that it is not "surprising that stigma associated with SARS quickly transferred to ethnically Chinese communities in many parts of the world" (Kleinman and Lee 2005, 181) and note the historical commonness of such transferences. Among other examples, they point to a study sponsored by the American Medical Association in the late 1800s that investigated "the hypothesis that Chinese women were spreading a unique and particularly virulent strain of so-called Chinese syphilis" (181). They also note the torching and razing of Chinese neighborhoods in both Hawaii and San Francisco after the bubonic plague surfaced in those areas in 1899 and 1900, respectively, despite the lack of any evidence of an Asian origin of the disease. Gerhard Falk describes this kind of stigma as "societal deviance": "a condition widely perceived, in advance and in general, as being deviant" (Falk 2001, 22). In the two examples cited by Kleinman and Lee, this societal deviance is apparent in the automatic assumption of Chinese culpability. In these cases, the condition perceived as being deviant is simply the condition of being Chinese. Falk's descriptions of the nature and origin of stigma prove far more capable here of accounting for the widespread stigmatization of Asian peoples in the 2003 SARS epidemic, for rather than attempting to break down the roles of the stigmatized and the reasons for their placement into negative categories, Falk simply states that "stigma and stigmatization can occur whenever and wherever some people find behavior or characteristics of other people offensive and/or reprehensible" (24).

Any examination of the nature of stigmatized individuals and the reasons behind their stigmatization, however, is incomplete without a corresponding study of the reactions the public has toward them. The literature in this area is fairly consistent and reads more like an extended series of variations on a theme. As Kleinman and Lee state, the stigmatized individual can expect "discrimination, negative labeling, menacing societal responses such as ostracism and exclusion, and even violence" (Kleinman and Lee 2005, 173). In responding to the stigmatized, the public constructs a mind-set to create what Goffman calls a "stigma-theory": "an ideology to explain his inferiority and account for the danger he represents, sometimes rationalizing an animosity based on other differences, such as those of social class" (Goffman 1963, 5). In discussing this reaction, Falk notes that

Émile Durkheim claimed that the "function of creating a boundary in any human group is group solidarity" (Falk 2001, 32) and furthermore summarizes Edward Sapir's recognition of stigma and stigmatization-producing language as "'inventive thought,' which means that people who have little or even no experience will nevertheless express opinions on a subject they do not know by using language which then constructs the reality that is thereafter perceived" (Falk 2001, 22). Other literature within the field follows the same basic pathways: we react negatively to those groups that we consider dangerous or different and construct boundaries around them to separate them from ourselves (cf. Becker 2002; M. T. Berger, 2004; Berger and Luckmann 1967; Feagin and Batur 2004; Lichtenstein 2004; Loury 2002; Persell, Arum, and Seufert 2004; Reinarman and Duskin 2002; Schwartz and Skolnick 1973; Shilts 1987).

In short, the only requirement for the construction of a stigmatized identity is not even necessarily the existence of a recognized differentness but the mere notion that differentness may exist. Once that label is applied to the stigmatized group, it is self-sustaining. The language used to label that group is, through circular logic, sufficient to prove that group deserving of the label. Stigmatized individuals are labeled because they are different, and we know they are different because they are labeled. Such a self-fulfilling prophecy explains in large part the continued presence of long-standing stereotypes. We "know" that Mexicans are lazy because they are Mexicans, and all Mexicans are lazy; we "know" that the Irish are drunkards because they are Irish, and all Irish people are heavy drinkers. Obviously, it is difficult for an individual in a stigmatized community to escape such labeling, for the fact that they belong to that community "proves" the label to be correct, all evidence to the contrary notwithstanding. Similarly, the existence of a label on a stigmatized community can be used to "prove" the culpability of that community for any related offenses. If the Chinese were historically blamed for Chinese syphilis and the bubonic plague, they can also easily be blamed for other, newer diseases, since the existence of the older stories "proves" that they are dirty, disease-laden people.

Just as important as the labeling of stigmatized groups of people are the reactions that those groups of people have to being labeled, for these reactions ultimately reveal the most about the stigmatized groups. During the SARS epidemic, as with many other epidemics, the stigmatized included people who had contracted SARS as well as those who had *not* contracted the disease. While the reactions of both groups to the stigmatization might be similar, definite differences distinguish the groups on enough levels to warrant their separation. For example, while those who have and have not been infected with SARS may chafe at their inclusion into a stigmatized category, and while both groups may feel the placement and concomitant reactions of the public unwarranted, the reasons behind such reactions are different. While individuals who have been infected with SARS may feel their stigmatization as undeserved and unpleasant for a number of reasons—their having successfully fought off the disease, their rejection of the diagnosis, their rejection of or lack of understanding of the serious nature and contagiousness of the infection, general stubbornness, etc.—the individuals who have not been infected with SARS feel their stigmatization is undeserved precisely because they have *not* been infected.

Regardless of the nature of the labeling, the ultimate response to the stigmatization is to mediate the fears associated with the disease. Mediation, by dictionary definition, is an act of agreement, compromise, or reconciliation, usually conducted between two parties in an attempt to strike some accord or peace. Used in this book, the word still carries the meanings of reconciliation and peace, but the act of mediation does not necessarily occur between two physical parties. Instead, it can be an internal struggle, involving a conscious effort made to come to some inner peace. For many people stigmatized during the SARS epidemic, these efforts balanced the stresses associated with stigmatization; mediation, as it is used here, is a loose synonym of the infinitive "to cope."

The act of mediation is thus a positive act, a movement toward learning to constructively deal and live with a given situation or circumstance. During the SARS epidemic, a basic and common method of alleviating the tensions of stressful situations involved the concept of humor as relief. Take the following excerpt from interviewee Jonathan as an example:

> My cousin by marriage, his mom was coming in. He must be like thirty, his early thirties. He was picking up his mom at the train station, and when she got off the train when he met her, he was wearing a mask, and he was all serious and he quickly handed her a mask and gloves to put on, telling her how dangerous everything was. So after a while, when she was wearing the mask and the gloves, then he started laughing and told her he was just joking, it wasn't necessary. But the whole family wanted to kill him, they thought it was, he was a real jackass for scaring his sixty-year-old mother like that. (Jonathan 2005)

As Elliott Oring states, the distribution of tension in a narrative is the key to its interpretation as humorous or non-humorous. A humorous narrative requires some tension to make the topic interesting, but excessive tension or emotional involvement for either narrator or audience member cancels out the humor. Jokes about cancer can be humorous but are probably less so if your sister died of it (see Oring 1992, 12–13). Jonathan's story is a perfect example of this concept. For the cousin, the tension in the act of tricking his mother was appropriate for the determination of the act as humorous. But for the family, the tension exceeded those levels.

Humor is, of course, relative, and it should come as no surprise that a narrative such as this would be seen as humorous by some—including Jonathan, as evidenced by his laughter—but as disturbing and inappropriate by others. Jonathan himself recognized the breaking point in this equation in a separate section of his interview, when he discussed a trip he took to visit his sister in Newfoundland, Canada:

> Yeah, we joked about it, about not telling people when we'd got to Newfoundland that we had just come from Toronto, because it was in the middle of the SARS hysteria. In the cab or . . . just anywhere, like our first couple of days there, I'd forgot all about this, there was just so much fear that, we wanted to joke about it with people, but we were afraid that some people would just leave the room [laughs]. It's crazy.

A similar comparison of the tensions involved in the creation of humor came from interviewee Luis. When asked if he remembered hearing any SARS jokes, Luis's first response was, "No. Because people I deal with, people . . . everybody took it seriously. Everybody took it seriously. Because how can you make a joke when you see people dying and there's no cure? You yourself get scared, too. You just hope and pray that this will stop and there will be a cure for this particular disease" (Luis 2005). Luis later acknowledged that some people in Toronto did employ humor in their responses to the crisis and said of them,

> Well, they might have their own reason. But in my opinion, maybe some people want to . . . because everybody's too serious, they want to make a little, they want to make people relaxed or . . . they maybe make jokes like that. But I don't think inside them, whoever makes that, I don't think they have a bad intention of putting the real meaning on it, because it's a serious matter.

In fact, several interviewees related humorous stories, jokes, or anecdotes concerning their experiences with the epidemic. As noted in the previous chapter, Heather and her Chinese roommate "Rita" regularly and openly joked about contracting the disease—"Ha ha ha: you've got SARS"—in response to coughing. As well, Mike, the EMT, recalled several instances where people in the widely stigmatized health profession used humor as a coping mechanism. First, he recalled at least two instances of the SARS acronym being appropriated and recontextualized to comment on the epidemic. Although he had forgotten the new definition of one of the recontextualizations by the time of his interview in 2005, he did recall that it had something to do with "'Summer Recreation' . . . something about getting a vacation through quarantine." He did, however, quite clearly recall people joking that SARS stood for "Shitty Acute Respiratory Syndrome," in response to the quarantines and hassles.

Mike's largest contribution to this discussion was an extended narrative relating how he and his colleagues in the health profession used humor to cope with the stresses of the epidemic:

> I remember walking into a bar, this bar on [Toronto's] Yonge Street, where they call Bingo and it's offensive and it's sort of a charity game for humor. It's also a bit of a show. And walking into the bar and, "Oh, there's Mike, and he's got SARS," you know, and people would turn around. Or, one really good one that I used to do, and I still do all the time, is if we [health care practitioners] get into an elevator, let's say in a busy office downtown where you get fifteen people in the elevator, and you [would make a coughing noise], and someone [would say], "SARS." And people giggle or they cover their face. When we would get into elevators and people would cover their mouths, you know, there's no patient, it's just us going up to a call, you'd [make a coughing noise] just to sort of, you know, a ruse . . . [As well,] whenever I put the full-body white suit on, because [in] downtown Toronto we mostly wore masks and gloves and gowns, but you could put the white full-body suit on, and people in public would look at you just like you're insane, you look like the Michelin Man, so it was funny to do that. And there were times when you'd walk in some place and, just to watch, just to watch people's reaction to you order coffee, you know, white gown. There was an email that went around as well that was "SARS On Ice," versus "Stars On Ice," where someone had taken pictures of, all these still shots of the "Stars On Ice" people doing their ice dancing, and then cut-and-paste or painted on gowns and gloves and masks on these people. Just stupid things, but they're cute nonetheless.

In Mike's narrative, the active, spoken use of humor as a coping mechanism is apparent, as is the importance of learning how to interpret situations as humorous. It would be easy to react negatively to walking into a coffee shop and having the public "look at you just like you're insane," but Mike stressed in his interview that such a reaction is ultimately self-defeating. Negativity only begets negativity; stress only begets more stress. Mike comments on this later in the interview:

> It's really important not to lose sight of the fact that we've been going for thousands of years with all kinds of diseases and plagues, and there's so much hype. I don't mind, I guess, and I have a very open sense of humor. Certainly people who were losing family members to the disease might not find it funny, probably won't. But, and again, that's a matter of perspective, and from the perspective that I have, having had to deal with it, having been accused of having SARS, having people cover their face when I walk around, my neighbors in my apartment building never came by to see me, I don't mind, myself, I think that's normal. People react to any kind of stressful situation, often with extremes, and often with the extremes of nervousness, humor, laughing. They cut the stress by making a joke.

Humor is a natural reaction to stressful situations. The specific types of humor shown in these interviews fall mainly under the classification of gallows humor, defined by Antonin J. Obrdlik as "humor which arises in connection with a precarious or dangerous situation" (Obrdlik 1942, 709). Obrdlik created this definition as part of a sociological study of gallows humor as it appeared in Czechoslovakia during its World War II Nazi invasion and occupation. The correlations between this event and the SARS epidemic may be slim—though epidemics are often referred to in militaristic terms, and it is no stretch to say that SARS "invaded" Canada—but Obrdlik's comments on the nature of anti-Nazi jokes in Czechoslovakia still find purchase when applied to a modern disease crisis:

> People . . . found in anecdotes an intellectual and emotional escape from the disturbing realities. It was symptomatic that the more ominous the news coming from invaded Austria, the more numerous and pointed were these anecdotes. They became a means of social control in that they bolstered the morale of the Czech people, and, although they were so often but the expression of wishful thinking, their importance as a compensation for fear could not be overestimated. (Obrdlik 1942, 710)

These comments coincide with what James A. Thorson has said of gallows humor: that it "is both intentional (not circumstantial) and has a coping motive. It is humor that is generated for a reason. That is, it's not just a funny thing that happened, like mourners with no place to go; rather, gallows humor is created knowingly and for a purpose" (Thorson 1993, 18). And since, as Obrdlik noted, this type of humor seems to be more common the stronger the negative entity that enacts it, the proliferation of black and gallows humor in hospital settings should come as no surprise (see Bosk 1980; Kuhlman 1988; Maxwell 2003; Sayre 2001; and van Wormer and Boes 1997).

Other activities similarly evidenced the use of humor as a coping mechanism in dealing with the SARS epidemic. The animated television program *South Park*, for instance, aired an episode on April 30, 2003, titled "Red Man's Greed," in which a group of Native Americans attempts to drive out the residents of South Park to enable the destruction of the town and the subsequent construction of a superhighway connecting their reservation's casino to Denver, Colorado. The townsfolk stymies the group's first few attempts, but the casino's owner, Chief Runs With Premise, hatches a devious plot: he infects a batch of blankets with SARS by rubbing naked Chinese men against them, then gives the blankets to the residents of South Park. All of the townsfolk become ill, only to be saved in the end when Stan, one of the protagonistic children, discovers that a combination of Campbell's chicken noodle soup, DayQuil, and Sprite cures SARS.

An animated sitcom such as *South Park* can only be used as evidence that humor was used to respond to the SARS crisis; show creators Trey Parker and Matt Stone did not belong to a stigmatized community. But public efforts such as theirs were not limited to American television. As Torontonians as a whole constituted a stigmatized group, Toronto's 2005 Fringe Festival provided the ultimate example of a stigmatized community responding to their situation through the use of humor. The festival hosted, among its many productions, the musical *SARSical*, written by Brandon and Kurt Firla (aka the Rumoli Brothers) and Waylen Miki (aka the Severe Acute Repertory Theatre Company). The show's skits and songs—including "I Kissed the SARS Babies" and "Teen in Quarantine"—mocked the marketing of the SARS epidemic. Many critics, offended by the show's light-hearted stance on death and disease, scorned the original production, but strong ticket sales led the Factory Studio Theatre to pick it up for a second run in 2006, and in late 2007, the show was revamped for a full-scale production (Pedersen 2006; "SARSical" Sets Disease to Song and Dance" 2006).

The application of humor as a mediating device has not gone unnoticed in stigma literature. Michael Edelstein, discussing the Hanford Nuclear Reservation in Washington State, notes that the residents of the three towns located within the reservation—Hanford, Richland, and White Bluffs—often use humor to cope with the stigma that comes from living in an area that still boasts extremely high background radiation levels as well as a significant number of leaky belowground nuclear waste storage systems. Edelstein reports that it is not uncommon to hear locals joking about how easy it is to find their children at night since they all glow in the dark (Edelstein 2007). Susan Seizer, in an ethnography of popular theater artists in the southernmost Indian state of Tamil Nadu, examines how the artists—all of whom are lower class and stigmatized as such by their countrymen—use humor to cope with problems endemic to their status, such as being refused rental privileges by landlords (Seizer 2005). And Sharon E. Preves's study of intersexed individuals points out the ways informants dealt with social and public stigma through humor (Preves 2003).

Especially notable in its discussions of humor is Marcia Gaudet's *Carville: Remembering Leprosy in America* (Gaudet 2004). In studying the lives and narratives of individuals who contracted Hansen's disease, Gaudet found that they often used humor as a mediatory strategy. Until the 1960s, anyone in America diagnosed with Hansen's disease was sent into involuntary and supposedly lifelong quarantine at the National Hansen's Disease Center in Carville, Louisiana—a fact that only changed with the advent of medical treatments in the mid-1900s. It was thus common that patients frequently attempted to escape (or abscond, the official term used by the center), and patients quickly built a corpus of narratives concerning successful attempts at absconding and the often-humorous encounters they had with outsiders. These narratives, Gaudet notes, "[tended] to poke fun at the stupidity and prejudices of 'outsiders'" (2004, 80). More importantly, when told to outsiders, the narratives "[seemed] to be establishing a kind of bond with the listener to let him know that they had faced the adversity and overcome it" (85–86).

The last category of narratives to be studied in regard to their evidencing fear-related mediation includes narratives concerning church practices. Three interviewees recalled examples. The first comes from Heather, who briefly mentions that her mother's Anglican church, as part of its prayer section, added the phrase "We pray for all those with SARS" to its list of Prayers of Intercession. It is unclear from Heather's narrative whether any of the members of this church were themselves stigmatized, but as the church was located within an hour's drive from Toronto, it is likely that at least some of the parishioners knew someone who was. Heather does state that Prayers of Intercession are a regular part of this particular church's services, and so it "would just have seemed like a natural, normal thing" to include SARS victims in the recitation (Heather 2005).

The two remaining narratives make the fear-mediating nature of church practices quite apparent and evince the extent to which people were willing to alter basic routines to provide for their own safety. These two narratives are especially relevant because both come from the highly stigmatized Filipino-Chinese community in and surrounding Scarborough, near Toronto. Luis for example, recalled the following:

> When the SARS was at its peak, meaning you see people die here and there, you try to [avoid] restaurants . . . public places as much as possible you avoid. Even in the church, the priests always say, normally you shake hands when you say "Peace be with you," even the priest was telling people just to be cautious, we just greet each other, "Peace be with you," instead of shaking hands. Those are the precautions that even in church was good practice. That was at the height of the SARS crisis. (Luis 2005)

A second narrative, which both encapsulates and expands upon Luis's entry, comes from Seny, who related the following story about her church, showing how even holy ground can become tainted by fear:

> So it's like, if you have [SARS], almost you feel that you're doomed. People recover, but because it was so contagious, that they can spread it by, say, air, coughing, sneezing and everything, right? So whatever you hold, right? So

you're being paranoid, wash your hands, "Happy Birthday!" washing of the hands . . . [laughs] People don't even want to shake hands even [in] church, right? In the Catholic, I've been pure Catholic, I don't know, but when we have the mass you go around, you turn and you shake hands, right? People, the priest would say, "Okay, because of the SARS, you just bow your head." [laughs] So people bow their head. And also you're going to the church, you have the holy water and the "T" on your forehead and you make the sign of the cross. They took out the holy water! [laughs] . . . Because it contaminates the quickest. They're saying that SARS is spread by holding, like the hands, so you always need to wash your hands after contact, physical contact, so nobody shook hands . . . I [also] think they stopped, yeah, because the priest had . . . usually sometimes people sip communion through the mouth, right? So the priest made this announcement, "Please receive communion through your hands." [laughs] . . . They [still] passed out the wafers, but through the hands. But not, not . . . to get at the priest holding it, because the saliva would cause the SARS, right? So if you stopped putting communion and the host into the mouth, right, but just done it through the hand, right? So everything was like that . . . The wine disappeared [as well]. They didn't . . . well, the wine was there, but then some people, there were some churches that they offered wine for the communion guys to drink, but that stopped for a while. 'Cause when you go to communion, some churches offer wine separately from the wafers and the bread. (Seny 2005)

Seny's comments evidence a metaphorical line in the sand in relation to danger and gathering places. The desertedness of businesses and large areas of Toronto—such as Chinatown—is indicative of high levels of concern and fear, but many of the establishments left largely empty during the SARS crisis were of an ultimately entertaining, dispensable nature. People do not immediately *need* to eat at restaurants, nor do they immediately *need* to go to the movies or shop for clothes. These activities can safely and easily be at least temporarily set aside, and their absence provides minimal disruption to the basic, day-to-day workings of the household. But some activities need to be performed on a regular basis, and for the religiously devout, Sunday morning church is as critical to the soul as bread is to the belly. Many of Seny's congregation continued to attend mass during the 2003 epidemic because of this, but that church exhibited the potential of a dangerous juxtaposition between large numbers of people and a contagious, deadly virus. Since ceasing to attend church was not an option, official services were altered to reduce the possible avenues of disease transmission. Physical contact with other human beings was either eliminated altogether or, where that was not possible (as in the passing of communion wafers), kept to a minimum and performed in such a manner as to reduce possible contact with "dangerous" body fluids like saliva. The methods that churchgoers and church officials chose to deal with this problem highlight the extents to which they willingly endangered themselves for the sake of perceived basic needs.

Such changes in church activities evidence a paradigmatic need for security, as reflected in the alterations of personal actions and behaviors and, simultaneously, a syntagmatic need for stability, as the intended meanings behind the actions remained constant despite the changes. Scarborough's Filipino-Chinese community was heavily stigmatized during the SARS epidemic, and the members of that community were aware of their stigmatization. Furthermore, that stigmatization affected the members of that community, and many of them attempted to avoid contact even with members of their own community. Luis's narrative detailing how parishioners were asked not to shake hands while saying "Peace be with you" is a perfect example of how members of a stigmatized community dealt with the fear that encapsulated their lives. The churchgoing sentiments of brotherly love and well wishing were still present, as the members of the community recognized the importance of group solidarity, but they altered their actions in response to the threat of disease and contamination to ensure the safety of individuals. Seny's narrative evidenced similar reactions: the recognition of others was still present, but the act changed from a handshake to a bow of the head. Similarly, the reception of communion and the concomitant religious experience and importance were still present, but parishioners received the wafers in their hands rather than in their mouths. Seny's comments do evince at least one alteration that falls outside of this category—the complete removal of holy water from the fonts, with no apparent attempt to replace it with a different action or gesture—but even then the overall meaning of the religious nature of church participation has not changed. Her comments do not demonstrate that the absence of holy water changed her churchgoing experiences on any fundamental level, especially as she continued to attend church during the epidemic. Nowhere in her narrative is the alteration of these actions and behaviors announced as a negative experience. Instead, the alterations simply seem to be acts that parishioners accepted as a consequence of the epidemic—acts that only changed the physical ways church was conducted, not the religious way they experienced it.

The 2003 SARS epidemic brought about the stigmatization of large groups of people, some of them demarcated by race, some of them simply because they lived on a certain block or in a certain neighborhood. It most certainly brought about the stigmatization of thousands, perhaps millions, of people who did not deserve the label. Humor often mediated the emotional responses these people had to being given such a label, and the examples in this chapter often demonstrate a lighthearted, almost flippant response. This does not, however, mean that the existence of jokes is a sign that SARS was not taken seriously. For when it comes to jokes about disease, the underlying reality—indeed, perhaps the message—is always more serious, and often far darker, than the punch line.

6

The Cause and the Cure
Folk Medicine and SARS

WHEN CONFRONTED WITH A DISEASE, it is a natural human reaction to want to escape. Self-preservation is deeply ingrained in our psyche. Barring this possibility, the next logical step is to find a way to prevent the disease from affecting us. And if those attempts fail, we begin to search for ways to heal ourselves and rid our bodies of the invading forces. The SARS epidemic provides a unique opportunity for examining all three of these approaches, because the border-crossing nature of the virus led to situations in which individuals found themselves suddenly confronted with a disease that only a few hours earlier had not existed in their neighborhoods, or even their countries. Under such conditions, especially early in the epidemic, when official medicine had not yet been able to provide an explanation for the infecting agent, many people turned to folk medicine.

The escapist reactions of the public in response to the epidemic have already been covered in the examinations of deserted restaurants, airports, and neighborhoods. This chapter opens a new forum in looking at the ways people responded to the encroaching cornonavirus when escape was not an option, whether for economic, personal, political, or other reasons. The result of these studies is proof that SARS is unique in the types of cures the layperson created in response to the threat of disease.

Let us begin with a look at the history of the study of cures and remedies in medicine. Examining previous work on the subject will provide useful background information in demonstrating why SARS is unique and show how the study of folk remedies has changed over the past 120 years. This data will frame the theoretical approaches taken in this chapter.

Discussions of the natures of cures and remedies present in folk medicine are numerous, occupying volumes of scholarship and covering areas as diverse as philosophy, psychology, and ethnopharmacology. Early texts in

DOI: 10.7330/9780874219296.c006

folk medicine were predominantly text-oriented, in keeping with the philosophies present in the field of folklore at the time, and consisted largely of long lists of remedies for various problems. William George Black's (1967) *Folk-Medicine: A Chapter in the History of Culture*, the preface of which dates the work to 1883, is an excellent example of such an approach. His work contains chapters on both "Personal" and "Animal" cures, as well as the importance of charms, saints, colors, numbers, the sun and the moon, magic writings, rings, and various forms of "domestic folk-medicine," that altogether constitute some 130 pages of a 220-page book. Producing such voluminous lists required impressive scholarship, and the categories Black formed to organize his collections are useful. But from a modern perspective, the work as a whole lacks such critical contextual information as the beliefs and values of the practitioners of these cures and remedies. A typical passage from Black's work, chosen at random, reads:

> To avert the destruction of an entire drove it is still known that the burial of one cow alive may be useful. More cruelly, there are instances of a cow being rubbed over with tar, and driven forth from the stricken herd. The tar is set on fire, and the poor animal is allowed to run till death puts an end to its sufferings. To burn to death a pig has been recommended by a wise woman of Banffshire as a cure for cattle disease. The ashes were to be sprinkled over the byre and other farm buildings. ([1883] 1967, 74)

While Black does list the source for his information—William Edward Hartpole Lecky's *A History of England in the Eighteenth Century*, which itself cites Arthur Mitchell's *On Various Superstitions in the North-West Highlands and Islands of Scotland, Especially in Relation to Lunacy*—no further information concerning the practitioners of such traditions is forthcoming. Pessimistically, Black's work at times reads as little more than a list of curious or barbaric and outmoded trains of thought in folk medicine, such as the paragraph after the one quoted above, which is devoted entirely to examples of human sacrifice-as-cure from history and begins with the subjective sentence "Human sacrifices are, happily, now rare" (74).

Black's work did further the study of folk medicine in its own way, for his textual studies of cures and remedies contradicted earlier sociological thought that "all primitive theories attribute disease and death to the spirits of the dead" (Black [1883] 1967, 205). Instead, he advanced the theory of three main "primitive explanations" of disease, presented in order of greatest frequency and importance: "(1) the anger of an offended external spirit; (2) the supernatural powers of a human enemy; and (3) the displeasure of the dead" (205), the studies of which can lead mankind to a greater understanding of itself. While these theories may no longer be considered correct, they still evidence a progression in analytic thought. But in terms of contextual analyses, Black's work falls short of current standards.

Fast-forward almost a century, and the textual analyses practiced almost to exclusivity by Black were slowly giving way to more context-based approaches. Text-based studies do still appear in print (cf. Brandon 1976; Emboden 1976; Fox-Baker 1981; Guerra 1976; Lacourcière 1976; Radbill 1976; T. Smith 1981; Stallings and Tilton 1981; Sullivan 1981; Vogel 1976), and one of the more prominent late twentieth-century textualists was Wayland D. Hand. His *Magical Medicine: The Folkloric Component of Medicine in the Folk Belief, Custom, and Ritual of the Peoples of Europe and America* (1980), a collection of twenty-three of his articles on folk medicine, consists almost entirely of text-based studies. Like Black, Hand meticulously cited the sources of his data, but rarely does the reader get a look into the lives of the people who practiced these medicines. For all of its excellent research, *Magical Medicine* offers three hundred pages of various cures and remedies and virtually no discussion of the practitioners.

This is not to say that Hand's work did not significantly advance the field. What Black did in terms of codifying and organizing folk medicine in the latter part of the nineteenth century, Hand did for the middle third of the twentieth. His essays detail how folk medicine can be broken into distinct categories of cures and remedies, and he provides examples for each of his groupings. Hand does claim in an essay written in 1975 that "the magical element in folk curing is a somewhat neglected field in folk medicine" (Hand 1980, 1), a statement that seems exaggerated given the lengthy tracts devoted to it by Black, but his other theories provide interesting insights into the field as a whole. For example, in his discussions of the "conditions and circumstances that may enhance the [magical] folk medical act or insure its success," Hand chooses to categorize his entries by "the adverbs of time, manner, and place" (2). Within these discussions, Hand avoids the normal pattern of naming a malady and listing possible cures for it, instead choosing to look at, for example, cures that take place at crossroads, regardless of the malady they are designed to treat. A reshuffling of categories such as this illuminates similarities between widely dispersed items, allowing researchers to make connections that were previously hidden. And so Hand provides lists of cures categorized not by disease but by how, when, and where cures are administered.

Hand's work was also useful in expanding the field of study to all areas of humankind rather than just focusing on third world or impoverished peoples. In an article on disease etiology, he states,

[Forrest E.] Clement's seminal paper on the causes of disease deals largely with ideas held within the primitive community in various parts of the world, yet for almost all of his five main theories of the cause of disease (sorcery, breach of taboo, disease-object intrusion, spirit intrusion, soul loss) parallels can be adduced from medical and folk medical aetiologies that derive from people of high culture, modern as well as ancient. (1980, 251)

This quote presents a more modern and inclusive version of Black's "primitive explanations" of disease along with the idea that it is not only the "primitive community" that continues using such explanations. Instead, he correctly points out that humankind as a whole maintains these beliefs; thus, limiting research in the manner evidenced by Clement only impoverishes folkloristic understanding of the topic.

Within Hand's lifetime, a critical shift in the field of folklore came with the insistence that context-based studies would provide even greater understanding of a given area. The presence of this context-based approach is evident in Bruno Gebhard's 1976 article "The Interrelationship of Scientific and Folk Medicine in the United States of America since 1850," wherein he states,

The division of folk medicine into a natural, rational science and a magico-religious healing art is generally accepted, but I would not limit the first aspect to herbal healing, as Don Yoder does. There is more to it than purging, bloodletting, fasting, sweating, and so on. I prefer to speak of both parts together as *lay medicine*, identical to what in the last century was called domestic medicine . . . I like to define lay medicine as the patient's—not the doctor's—concept of health and disease and the cures applied in case of illness or accident. (Gebhard 1976, 90)

Although Gebhard's article does spend most of its length discussing the history of folk medicine and giving itemized, textual lists of common "folk medicine items," it is still noteworthy in two ways. First, it marks one of the early uses of the term *lay medicine*, and second, it ends by stating that folk medicine has one critical advantage over scientific medicine: "it has no doubt; it believes" (97). Gebhard never goes so far in this article as to conduct a context-based study, but he does hint at its importance. To say that there is "more to" folk medicine than the cures is a definite move toward contextualism, as is mentioning that the patient's concept of health and disease is at least as important as the doctor's. And the mention of the importance of "belief" in lay medicine is directly indicative of the changes that would be made in the field in the following years.

The shift from text to context resulted in an explosion of articles in the 1970s and 1980s centered on the *reasons* patients used cures rather than just the cures used by patients. Attempting to examine the field of folk medicine from the viewpoint of practitioners and consumers forced academics to look at the "why" of the situation: Why are people still using folk or "unofficial" remedies in an era dominated by the success of scientific, "official" medicine? After all, by 1980 scientific medicine eradicated smallpox; drastically reduced through vaccines the number of yearly deaths from disease; transplanted human hearts, kidneys, and lungs; and delivered the first test-tube baby. In light of such astounding achievements, why would people still turn to magic and religion for medical help, much less the weeds growing in their backyards?

Some of the earliest efforts to answer this question came in the form of scientific studies of folk medicines themselves. George G. Meyer's 1981 article "The Art of Healing: Folk Medicine, Religion and Science" devotes part of its length to a summary of the studies that have tested the pharmacologic properties of various plants. Specifically mentioned is Ortiz de Montellano, whose work in the mid-1970s found that of twenty-five plants commonly used in Aztec folk medicine, sixteen had been proven in laboratory studies to produce the claimed effects and four more had possible activity. In addition, Meyer notes J. L. Diaz's study of plants used by *curanderos*, which concludes that most of the remedies make "pharmacologic sense" (Meyer 1981, 10). The ultimate goal of studies such as these is stated to be proving that folk medicine does often make "scientific sense," and that many of the plants are specifically chosen after long periods of investigation by *curanderos* and their global counterparts. As such, folk medicine ought to be taken more seriously by scientific medicine.

Pharmacologic efforts such as these were relatively common throughout the 1970s and 1980s. Social scientist Virgil J. Vogel, for instance, devoted his work to studying of the efficacies of Native American medicines. His magnum opus in this respect is *American Indian Medicine*, a 1990 publication that approaches six hundred pages in length, almost all of it devoted to the pharmacologic studies of various plants (Vogel 1990). Ralph W. Moss's *Cancer Therapy: The Independent Consumer's Guide to Non-Toxic Treatment & Prevention* (Moss 1992) and *Herbs Against Cancer* (Moss 1998) performed the same analyses, though for the more tightly focused field of herbal cancer therapies.

But the strengths of Meyer's article lay not in the summaries of other authors' works but in the statement that "elements of folk medicine, religious healing, and scientific medicine need to be incorporated into all healing practices. Indeed, when integration has not occurred, the patient will seek separate care in all these areas" (1981, 7). While pharmacologic studies that prove the ultimate scientific effectiveness of remedies are a step in the right direction, the ultimate goal of folk medicine research should be patient-oriented, and Meyer's statement directly reflects this philosophy. Researchers and medical practitioners need to take into account the beliefs and attitudes of patients because disregarding them only leads to situations where patients seek additional help elsewhere. The problem with this approach occurs when the types of help sought prove harmful or contradictory, such as in the case of herbs that counteract or prove toxic in conjunction with hospital-based treatments and medications. For example, many patients begin taking antioxidant-rich vitamin pills after a cancer diagnosis because they believe such efforts will prove beneficial. But patients receiving radiation therapy for cancer are supposed to *avoid* ingesting antioxidants, since such compounds inhibit or negate the effectiveness of the radiation. If for no other reason than safety, the beliefs and attitudes of the patient must be taken into account, and medical practitioners need to learn to address such issues with tact and open-mindedness.

Further steps in building the patient-oriented approach examined the similarities between folk and scientific medical systems and the structure and nature of folk medicine as a whole. Sometimes these approaches were used simultaneously, or within the same article, to build an extended series of bridges between the fields. The Nordic Research Symposium of 1981, held in Kuopio, Finland, resulted in several published articles central to these points. Tuula Vaskilampi, working out of the University of Kuopio, looked at both scientific and folk medical systems in his article "Culture and Folk Medicine." Vaskilampi's sociological analysis, according to Carol P. MacCormack:

> suggests two fundamental elements in all medical systems: (1) a cognitive and ideological sub-system, and (2) an organizational sub-system. The former encompasses perceptions of disease etiology, explanations of illness, the natural course of illness, and treatment. The organizational sub-system includes social relations, especially between patients and healers, as well as legal entitlements and constraints. (MacCormack 1982, II)

In stating that both folk and scientific medical systems contain these elements, Vaskilampi points out the rationality and complexity of such systems, stating—in the same way as do proponents of the pharmacological approach—that folk medical systems are far from the simpleminded and illogical bits of quackery that they are so frequently assumed to be. Instead, folk systems can boast the same levels of complexity and ingenuity as scientific systems and their treatments are just as hardily researched.

The remainder of Vaskilampi's article specifically attempts to organize and define common ideas within the field, despite the differences in values that come with cross-cultural philosophies. Nature is stated to be a highly valued idea within folk medicine, especially in the sense of the wholeness and liveliness of natural things. As noted by Brian Inglis (1980), such a value is present within such diverse medicines as "vegetarism, homeopathy, herbalism, naturopathy, osteopathy and spiritual healing" (Inglis, quoted in Vaskilampi 1982, 4), but despite the variety of such medicines, the ultimate meaning and importance of nature, as noted by Julia Twigg (1979), is that it is "seen as containing messages and truths of deep emotional impact" (Twigg, quoted in Vaskilampi 1982, 4).

"Wholeness" is another concept common to folk medicines, the study of which reveals many of the reasons folk medicines remain popular in the modern era. Wholeness is "expressed in the emphasis of the balance of the body and the mind. The aim of care is to treat the whole person and not only symptoms of the disease. We find health in the harmony between individual and nature and universe" (Inglis, quoted in Vaskilampi 1982, 4–5). Where scientific medicine is often criticized for treating the disease and caring little for the patient—or perhaps better stated, focusing on the singular disease to the exclusion of all other possible and multiple health-related issues—folk medicine examines the person as a whole. Still present in these examinations is the importance of treating the body, but folk medicines are also willing to examine the spirit and soul.

In total, Vaskilampi states, "The cultural content of belief systems involves several positively valued ideas: nature, wholeness, purity, humanity and individualism . . . These ideas are becoming salient in other spheres of life, too. They form countertrends to the reductionistic technological development which many people reject as unsatisfactory" (Vaskilampi 1982, 12). Folk medicine provides more than the simple extirpation of virus and bacterium offered by hospitals. Instead of treating people as anonymous broken and empty vessels that must be quickly and all-too-often surgically repaired, practitioners of folk medicines treat them as full and vital bearers of life who must be slowly and carefully mended from the inside out using a variety of largely noninvasive strategies.

Bente Gullveig Alver, another participant in the Nordic Research Symposium, carried this idea to a clearer conclusion in "Folk Medicine as an Open Medical System," wherein she states, "The reason so many people seek treatment by alternative means is that folk medicine is an open system capable of responding to human needs as they arise in space and time in contrast to official medicine which is locked into a system of a priori assumptions" (Alver 1982, 124–25). Alver specifically lists four types of illnesses that most frequently result in the consultation of folk healers:

"chronic illnesses . . . fatal illnesses . . . various psychological disorders . . . [,] and conditions which according to the physicians are not illnesses at all" (130). In each of these cases the official medical system is seen as failing the sick and inflicted by either not effectively treating the disease or rejecting the patient's claim of disease. Alver's list may actually be too restrictive, for it does not include the various folk medicines used to treat such everyday problems as upset stomachs and hangnails, but it does illuminate the under-lying issues of cold and clinical distance that frequently accompany stories of hospital visits.

Two more articles are necessary to fully demonstrate the transition from the text-based to context-based approach. The first is another of Alver's articles, "The Bearing of Folk Belief on Cure and Healing," published in 1995 in the *Journal of Folklore Research*. Alver's discussions in this article constitute a fuller and more extended version of arguments made in her earlier article regarding the patient-centered nature of folk medicine. Early on, she outlines the importance of folk medicine as a whole as well as the importance of beliefs inherent to folk medicine as they apply to the broader concept of culture:

> In all cultures, people's perceptions and belief systems regarding health are closely tied to fundamental values, such as those concerned with the maintenance of life and the loss of life and to certain conceptions of "the good life." Therefore, the research domain within which one deals with people's beliefs relating to disease and treatment is highly important for our understanding of culture seen as a totality. (Alver 1995, 22)

Thus, folk medicine ontogenetically recapitulates the phylogenetic development of the larger culture, the former encapsulating and mimicking the latter, but on a smaller scale. Alver's statements on this matter are given as unidirectional, but they can be reversed, and thus an understanding of a culture can result in a strong prediction of what a researcher might find upon first encountering that culture's folk medicine. Cultures that, as a whole, emphasize the quality of life over the quantity of it will carry those attitudes over to their folk medicines.

The importance of such a statement lies in the differences between folk and scientific medicines, as Alver hints in her earlier work but restates in this later article:

> Many people feel they are being helped within the folk sector. They report that they lead more functional lives than they had before treatment, have greater success in what they do, and are happier. On the whole, they describe an improved general condition. However, their doctors seldom feel convinced. The doctors, whose judgment stems from a biological perspective, usually conclude that the

patient is as sick as before, though sometimes they will concede that the patient is experiencing a good period, especially in the case of the chronically ill or those with life-threatening sicknesses. (1995, 26)

Ultimately, both folk medicine and scientific medicine attempt to treat the various maladies that plague humanity, but their approaches differ vastly concerning what constitutes "health" and "cure." Folk medicine mimics culture as a whole, and thus concepts found in culture are likely to also be found within the domains of folk medicine. It is partly because of such similarities that folk medicine is the easier form of treatment to slip into; its concepts are familiar and friendly. Scientific medicine, on the other hand, precisely because it is based on reason and logic, hypothesis and laboratory-based proof, and emotional suppression in favor of cold, hard facts, is not seen as reflecting culture as a whole. Its concepts are alien and clinical and its practitioners stereotyped as prone to disregard anything that does not coincide with their school-learned worldview.

Alver, in describing such differences, uses the work of Peter Elsass, Kirsten Hastrup, Arthur Kleinman, and Allan Young to supplement her own theories:

> Health disorders have a biophysical as well as a socio-cultural aspect. In medical anthropology these two features are designated *disease* and *illness*. Disease is viewed as the biological disturbance in the body, while illness refers to the cultural and social meaning attributed to the disorder (Young 1982). One may visualize the two aspects graphically as partly overlapping one another and jointly constituting the total health field with a particular culture (Hastrup 1984; Elsass and Hastrup 1986, 10–11). On the whole, professional medicine is oriented toward disease, while the folk (lay) sector has its orientation toward illness. The medical strategies in relation to disease are designated *curing*, while those in relation to illness are termed *healing* (Hastrup 1984; Kleinman 1980, 82). (1995, 25)

Such a radical difference in philosophy frequently serves to alienate the layperson from official medicine because of the feeling that the scientific approach does not meet his or her needs. Drawing these last few concepts together—folk medicine as a smaller version of culture and the differences between folk and scientific medicine—Alver completes her arguments with the following:

> In a modern folk belief system, health and quality of life are connected to concepts like harmony and balance. Sickness is linked with disharmony and disequilibrium: it is understood as a lack of balance within the body, as a disequilibrium between body and soul, and between human beings and the immediate environment. Also, it may be seen as a lack of balance between human beings and the "forces." Healing, then, involves help to dislodge the cause of the apparent disequilibrium and to re-instate harmony. (1995, 28–29)

Alver goes on to state that concepts such as these, when large enough, can be adapted to ideas present in scientific medicine, but the emphasis seems to be on the larger scale. Individual treatments are not often seen as part of this balancing act—a view that only serves to further distance the relativity of scientific medicine to the life of the average person.

Alver does recognize the importance of scientific medicine and acknowledges its marked ability to treat and cure many diseases. She says in response that scientific medicine "deals with sickness in terms of *how*, while alternative medicine asks *why*," and notes that while each of these questions are important, human beings are only satisfied when they have answers to both of them (1995, 31). And so the continued presence of folk medicine can once again be attributed to its meeting needs that are not adequately addressed by scientific medicine.

The last article in this section comes from Bonnie B. O'Connor and David J. Hufford. Published in Erika Brady's 2001 book *Healing Logics: Culture and Medicine in Modern Health Belief Systems*, "Understanding Folk Medicine" provides a succinct overview of the field and echoes many of the statements made by previous scholars in regard to the reasons folk medicine remains valid and present in modern society. O'Connor and Hufford state:

> However, it is precisely the health promoting capacities of any system or therapeutic modality that are of greatest importance to its proponents and users. People dealing with health problems are typically quite pragmatic in approaching and evaluating any form of treatment or remedy: if it seems not to work, or produces effects that are too unpleasant, it tends to be rejected; if it seems to work, it tends to be supported and retained in the repertoire of healing resources likely to be tried again (and recommended to others). This pragmatism operates at both individual and collective levels. Folk healing traditions' reputations for efficacy, based on aggregate observation and experience, are central to their persistence and continued vitality. (O'Connor and Hufford 2001, 15–16)

Folk medicine is thus not without logic or reason. Its treatments are chosen carefully and specifically, evaluated over long periods of time by hundreds, if not thousands, of practitioners and patients, and only absorbed into the category of useful treatments if such long-term observations conclude them worth their merit. Folk medicine is thus the ultimate patient-centered approach, especially considering the abandonment of treatments deemed too harsh. Not only is folk medicine interested in healing, it is interested in doing so in a manner comfortable to the patient.

In the closing paragraphs of their article, O'Connor and Hufford describe the links between folk and official medicines. They state that most people use folk medicine more frequently than official medicine, and that they continue to use folk medicine while undergoing treatment by doctors and other practitioners of official medicine for the same illness. Oftentimes, these doctors are not aware of such practices. This is made all the more complex by the fact that people are often recommended by their folk healers to seek treatment from hospitals, and these folk healers will sometimes enter hospitals to continue using their methods after or even while the patient is receiving treatment from hospital staff. "The conventional medical model," O'Connor and Hufford conclude, "can be incorporated rather easily along with folk models of illness, and in some instances may even serve to reinforce them." Folk medicine is thus more than willing to accept the presence and wisdom of scientific medicine, but such an attitude is hardly reciprocated. This, too, makes folk medicine the easier choice for the public: not only is it "comfortably consonant with their general worldviews," but it is more adaptable and willing to recognize the benefits—and sometimes superiorities—of other systems of healing (2001, 32).

The study of folk medicine is varied but generally points toward contextuality, especially within the field of folklore. The larger proportion of modern scholars have adopted a patient-oriented approach in their studies, focusing on the beliefs and attitudes of their interviewees regarding the treatments they use and the diseases for which they are selected. This approach appears across the field of folk medicine and has been applied to numerous health issues, including the psychological, the spiritual, and the corporeal. Applying such theories to SARS is at first blush no different than applying them to any other health issue, for the primary purpose of such investigations is simply to gain an understanding of the interviewee's culture, worldview, mind-set, etc. To an extent, many of the same questions could even be asked of a SARS interviewee: How do you treat this disease? Where did you learn of these treatments? Why are they important to you? What do they mean to you? Why do you use them?

From another perspective, the answers to these questions would largely be the same for SARS as they would be for any other disease. Alver's conclusions that folk medicine continues to present itself in modern culture because it fills niches and answers questions that scientific medicine does not are also applicable to SARS, even though this disease did not exist when Alver penned her texts. Interviewee answers to a question such as "Why do you use these treatments?" or even more basically, "What treatments do you use?" could therefore be expected to exhibit anti-medical establishment and/ or pro-nature sentiments. Take, for example, the following response from interviewees Angel and Rosita, who were asked what they did to prevent themselves from contracting SARS:

Angel: Preventing, like, avoid going to public places, like mall, like movie houses, restaurants specifically, restaurants, because they say that if you ate something and you, they didn't wash the dishes well, you know, you easily get SARS from eating [with], like, utensils they didn't wash well. So we try to avoid going to the mall or the fast foods or restaurant.

Rosita: Also, this fear, good thing we didn't have to go to, but this fear of going to funeral parlors. If somebody had died and you don't know why they died . . .

Angel: Yeah, yeah.

Rosita: . . . the SARS they said that if you were even in the funeral parlor you might get sick. [laughs] Or somehow transmit.

Angel: So one thing, you know, I'm afraid to go to the clinic, like if you are sick, like if you have colds, you would avoid going to see the doctors, because who knows, somebody before you has seen the doctors and left something, and then you go to see the doctors and you might have SARS. So that's one point, we are afraid to go to the doctors. Even [if] we, we are sick. (Angel and Rosita 2005)

The last paragraph clearly presents Angel's distrust of the medical community. Angel saw clinics not as places of healing but as places where people were likely to get sick, whether that illness came from medical professionals or from other patients. For Angel, the word hospital became synonymous with dirty, or perhaps diseased, and as such, hospitals became places to avoid. The medical profession's apparent lack of control over the virus caused and exacerbated such fears; even after the news broke worldwide about the coronavirus having spread from China, SARS continued over the next few weeks to spread elsewhere. The World Health Organization (WHO), the face most readily identified as responsible for containing such epidemics, seemed to be losing the battle. On a smaller level, hospitals and clinics also experienced great difficulties in containing the virus, as evidenced by the numerous instances of infected patients passing the disease to doctors, nurses, and other patients. Avoiding restaurants and funerals is a natural extension of such a negative perception, for if trained medical professionals have not proven themselves capable of preventing the spread of SARS, what assurances of safety could a waiter or funeral director possibly offer? In light of such failings, the only acceptable response for Angel was to take matters into his own hands.

The reasons why patients "take matters into their own hands"—a phrase used here in the larger, metaphorical sense of "removing some or all of the decision-making power from Western medicine in treating illness and disease"—are the crux of modern, contextual folk medicine studies. The reasons stated by those people interviewed for this chapter as to why they chose these approaches over, or at least in conjunction with, Western medicine are exactly those forwarded by Alver as well as O'Connor and Hufford: Western medicine, at least in some small part, was failing them, and folk medicine had the capability of offering more sound shoring.

Angel's avoidance of the medical clinic because of a perceived risk of contracting SARS is just one example of this failure. When interviewee Luis was questioned about his precautionary measures, he responded, "There is the . . . the most susceptible is if your resistance is low. So what we did during those times is we tried to boost our immune system by taking vitamin pills and extra milligrams or capsules or tablets of vitamin C. Those are the . . . and then don't overwork yourself, that way your resistance won't go down" (Luis 2005). Luis's response is subtler than Angel's, as Luis never openly admitted to discontent with Western medicine. He did express being afraid during the epidemic but seemed to believe in the power of local hospitals and global medical workers to combat the virus. Luis also watched the news and read local newspapers daily, following and apparently completely trusting any advice given to him from those "official" sources. But his inclusion of vitamins in his daily regime, and especially his notion of how overworking oneself leads to decreased resistance, still indicates that somehow his needs had not been fulfilled by those official sources.

What is interesting to note about SARS—what, in some small part sets it apart and may explain Luis's actions—is that almost all of the examples of folk medicine mentioned either by interviewees or through Internet and media sources were *preventatives*, not *curatives*. The thirteen interviewees specifically discussed having either used or having seen others use the following precautionary measures, in order of most to least noted:

1) masks or other coverings of the mouth and nose while breathing (ten mentions);
2) avoiding places (nine mentions);
3) washing hands/antibacterial or sanitizing hand gels (seven mentions);
4) tied at two mentions each were
   a) taking vitamins
   b) not shaking hands, and
   c) using herbs;
5) tied with only one mention each were
   a) using Windex as a surface disinfecting agent
   b) altered communion practices, and
   c) daily clothes washing

The reasons for such a proliferation of preventative medicines and efforts—to the virtual exclusion of curative medicines and efforts—are no doubt multiform. One of the largest reasons is also the most obvious: not many people contracted SARS, and far fewer died of it. Under such circumstances, cures make far less sense than preventatives, as there is little need for a cure to a disease that has not yet affected a large number of people. Preventing it from being contracted is sufficient.

If, for example, the lists of cures and preventatives for AIDS and SARS are compared, the natures of these differences are more apparent. AIDS has dozens of preventative measures that could be taken. Whatley and Henken give several examples, including "A shower after sex reduces the risk of getting AIDS"; "Withdrawal by a man before orgasm prevents transmission of HIV"; that only anal sex transmits AIDS, and therefore vaginal sex is safe (this contrasted with the opposing belief that only gay men get the disease through anal intercourse, so it is safe for heterosexual couples to practice anal sex to prevent contracting it vaginally); and that a 1:10 dilution of bleach will kill the virus—which is true for surfaces on which bodily fluids have spilled but is misinterpreted by women who use this dilution as a douche (Whatley and Henken 2000, 88).[1]

In terms of cures for the virus, Whatley and Henken again provide an example, noting the belief that a man can cure himself of AIDS by having sex with a virgin and "giving away" the disease to her—a belief that surfaced in rape trials of HIV-positive men in Zimbabwe and South Africa in the 1990s (Whatley and Henken 2000). Additional cures come from a wide range of sources and locales. A news report from MSNBC.com, dated February 20, 2007, covered the story of Gambia President Yahya Jammeh's claim of a cure for the virus, which consisted of a green herbal paste that he rubbed on the ribcages of victims, followed by the ingestion of a bitter yellow liquid and two bananas ("Gambia's President Claims He Has Cure for AIDS" 2007). Jonathan Campbell, who calls himself a "health consultant" in Boston, Massachusetts, writes of Ian Brighthope, whose book (written with Peter Fitzgerald) *The AIDS Fighters* details his successful use of zinc and massive oral and intravenous doses of vitamin C to cure patients (Campbell n.d.). Pam Rotella's website, devoted, in roughly equal parts, to vegetarian cooking, conspiracy theories, travelogues, and stories about rescued animals, contains an extensive section on Hulda Clark's ability to cure both cancer and AIDS through the use of radio frequencies (Rotella n.d.). And FOXNews.com reported in February 2007 that Iran, on the anniversary of the Islamic Revolution, was poised to reveal an herbal, nontoxic cure for AIDS called IMOD ("Report: Iran Set to Unveil Herbal AIDS Cure" 2007). There are dozens of further "cures" available for discussion, and this paragraph closes here only for reasons of brevity. Suffice

to say that AIDS does have numerous folk medical treatments, both curative and preventative.

The list of treatments for SARS, on the other hand, is almost exclusively dominated by preventative measures. Not a single interviewee discussed a method of getting rid of the virus once it had infected a person.
Instead, their examples focused on ways of staving off such an infection,
whether by boosting the immune system, killing the virus outside the body,
or physically preventing it from entering the body. Internet and media
searches reveal a similar skew: mothers buying vitamins to strengthen their
children's immune systems (Harmon 2003); people in China's Guangdong
province stripping store shelves of Western antibiotics, vinegar, and herbal
teas (Hoenig 2003); villagers in central China's Hunan province seeking
"help from sorcerers in incense-infused rites . . . Some [of whom] burn
fake money as an offering to the gods" (Ang 2003); a widespread rumor in
China that smoking prevented SARS (Mackay 2003); that drinking mung
bean juice made people impervious to the disease ("China vs SARS: A Good
Dog Is a Dead Dog" 2003); drinking teas made from (1) Banglangen (Isatis
root), (2) Hu Zhang (Polygonum cuspidatum), (3) ginseng, (4) Tremella
fuciformis (white fungus or silver ear mushroom), (5) chrysanthemum, and
(6) Andrographis (Dresser 2004); drinking a concoction for seven to ten
days that required boiling ten grams of dead silkworms and ten grams of
cicada skins in water with five herbs for twenty minutes (Dresser 2004); that
having the Ace of Spades with Saddam Hussein's face on it would keep away
SARS ("Bouncin' Around: SARS" 2005); etc. etc. etc., including the ever-
present surgical mask. Pessimistically, one might wonder if there is anything
that *doesn't* keep away SARS.

Conversely, cures for SARS are few and far between. The television show
South Park did claim satirically that SARS could be cured with a combination of chicken noodle soup, DayQuil, and Sprite. But real-life cures are
more difficult to find. Scouring the Internet revealed a Hong Kong religious
group claiming that drinking hydrogen peroxide would rid the body of the
virus (Cline 2004) and a website touting hydrogen peroxide as a cure for
SARS and several other ailments (McCabe 2003). Further surfing turned up
a claim that intravenous vitamin C would cure SARS (similar to the above
claim about an AIDS cure) (Cathcart n.d.) and a man named Clive Harris,
who claimed to be able to cure SARS (as well as Ebola, cancer, malaria,
AIDS, heart problems, and other diseases) because he had learned how to
"download the Mother lode of energy fields, then [separate] them, then
further [tailor] each individual's need to the specific energy form needed,"
which apparently resolves "energy field" problems in patients and allows the

body to naturally kill off the virus/bacteria/etc. ("Clinic Clive Harris" n.d.). One doctor contended that "ultraviolet blood irradiation therapy" cured viral pneumonias (Gupta 2003). Finally, a website claimed that a process called "Schlenzbath" effectively treated almost any disease, including SARS. The process involved sitting in water heated to 41 °C, or 105.8 °F (adding "Lindenblueten or Lime blossom" herbs to the water improved effectiveness) until the body's internal temperature—as measured by a fever thermometer—reached between 39 and 40 °C, or 102.2 to 104 °F. At this point the patient was instructed to lie down, wrapped heavily in towels, for the better part of an hour, or until their body temperature returned to normal ("There's an Ancient Cure to an Old Disease" n.d.).

Several notes should be made concerning these "cures." First, they were all collected from Internet sources on Google's search engine using the search term "SARS cure." Second, by far the larger number of websites returned by Google in response to this query were legitimate websites from legitimate sources detailing legitimate scientific advancements in the search for a vaccine or cure. Many of these websites included published reports by the WHO, the Food and Drug Administration (FDA), or the Federal Trade Commission (FTC) on the status of scientific progress in laboratories around the world. Third, mixed in with these legitimate reports of potential cures were dozens of websites warning the public of spam e-mails containing claimed SARS preventions and treatments, and noting the 2003 FDA and FTC crackdown on such bogus e-mails. Given these three points, it seems unlikely that any member of the public in search of a SARS cure on the Internet would be able to locate one without first coming across several dozen webpages noting that a) there is no cure for SARS, b) vaccines take years to develop, and c) many people have been scammed by bogus claims of cures that turned out to be little more than sinkholes for naïve consumers' funds.

A fourth note does not involve the websites themselves but an examination of the discovered cures. A close look at the remedies mentioned in the previous paragraphs will reveal that only the first of these—the Hong Kong religious group's suggestion of ingesting hydrogen peroxide—involves the claim of curing only a single disease. The rest of the entries all revolve around treatments claimed to be panaceas, cure-alls for virtually any malady.[2] SARS is related to them only in the sense that it is a disease, and these treatments cure all diseases. The status of these treatments as SARS cures only marginally relates to SARS itself, as the treatments were not specifically formulated to deal with the coronavirus but were created long beforehand in an effort to rid the body of any illness. Any emerging disease is simply added to the treatment's list of "treatable ailments," since the cure-all nature of the treatment entails its ability to cure anything, including (apparently) diseases that have not yet surfaced.

It is possible that somewhere someone created a folk cure specifically to treat SARS. But given the difficulties evident in locating such a cure, it seems safe to say that legitimate examples are rare—possibly a result of the coronavirus's limited presence in public consciousness, combined with its comparatively low mortality rate. More significant than an academic analysis of the types and numbers of cures and preventatives for SARS, however, are the opinions of the people who would have been surrounded by them. Interviewee Jennifer was quite opinionated about these remedies. When asked for her thoughts about people attempting self-treatment to avoid contracting SARS, she responded by using an example from her own culture:

> Again, it's sort of part of that human need for self-preservation. But it's entirely possible that you would, I mean in the Chinese culture, you would . . . animals and their body parts are sort of linked to human attributes of strength, and so I could see how people would think up, "Oh, if the bull is immune, or if the monkey was immune, that if we took"—and I think that's like what they base vaccines on, that you take a part . . . of the animal where it's the animal that is not affected or impacted and apply it to yourself, and that somehow you obtain their qualities of immunity. (Jennifer 2005)

Jennifer's proclivities toward empathy are strongly apparent here, as she takes care to not judge the practitioners of these remedies. Interestingly, Jennifer claimed to have been mostly unaffected by the epidemic and changed few of her habits. She never wore a mask, did not see the need to take extra vitamins or herbs, and did not change her daily routines—which included walking through Chinatown to get to work.

But Jennifer's generally nonjudgmental attitude evinced some wear when asked if she knew anyone who had avoided public places during the epidemic:

> I think my dad. I don't know if I can say that up to that point we ate regularly at Chinese restaurants, because we don't really eat at Chinese restaurants anymore, but I can't say if that was the date or period. But my dad's sort of a clean freak, and so is my younger brother, Charles. And I think for sure my dad said, "Okay, let's not eat at Chinese restaurants." Because he does have the perception that Chinese restaurants are not as clean, just regularly anyway, as other restaurants.

When asked for her opinion of people who reacted in such fashion to the epidemic, Jennifer responded:

> I think it's whatever a person is comfortable with. I mean, I sort of did feel as though it was unfounded. I mean, it was discriminatory, it is discriminatory. I

don't know. I don't think I judged him on it, or I think my brother, Charles,
would not . . . you know, he's also kind of a neat freak, and I think he avoided
[Toronto's public transportation system] because of that.

Jennifer is clearly torn here between her open-mindedness and what she
sees as discriminatory behavior. This is made all the more confusing for her
because of her ethnicity and the fact that her father, who was born in the
Philippines and whose parents were born in China, had these discriminatory attitudes toward people from his own culture. In an epidemic such as
SARS, however, it is not surprising to see the renegotiation of such lines.
Anyone perceived to be of Asian ethnicity was treated poorly because of it,
but Jennifer's father's actions show that this discrimination was not limited
to outsiders fearing Asians. In fact, some Asians feared contact with other
Asians—evidence that epidemics such as SARS can at least temporarily dis-
turb the cohesiveness that exists within a community. When one's neighbor
might be carrying a potentially deadly virus, one tends to avoid that neighbor regardless of his age, sex, or race. Disease, it may be said, is the great
leveler: it makes everyone afraid of everyone else.

Not all of the interviewees evinced such positive attitudes toward the use
of folk medicine. While no one actually displayed a serious, negative response
to people using herbs and teas to treat themselves, some informants joked
about the methods they saw people using. Mike, the EMT, recalled several
times when people crossed the street after seeing him coming toward them in
his medical uniform and seeing others cover their faces with their elbows or
otherwise hold jacket sleeves and clothing over their mouths. Asked his opinion of the efficacy of such a preventative method, Mike jokingly dismissed it
as a "put garlic in your sock and tie it over your head kind of thing" (Mike
2005). Mike also recalled a rumor concerning a method of creating a better
face mask that involved stuffing the standard masks with garlic and talc—an
act that created what he referred to as a mask looking "like a big doily or a
Maxi-Pad stuffed with herbs." In general, Mike's reactions to the panic he
saw in 2003 followed this same sort of good-natured teasing, though he did
not ultimately see these methods as pointless. While the actual efficacies of
these methods is questionable, Mike did quickly point out, when asked what
he thought of people who avoided public places,

I mean, paranoia strikes deep. People avoided Toronto as a whole. The number
of out-of-province license plates you saw that summer was few and far between.
You can't blame one . . . people would like to blame China, and you can't do
that. You can't blame the Guangdong province or the physicians there, or the
representatives from that country. I guess people were responding out of their
own fears and concerns.

Mike's final comments here echo Jennifer's feelings about Chinese medicine, and in general, most interviewees held this viewpoint: that scared individuals should not be judged for trying whatever they felt might help.

There were differing opinions, such as one gathered from interviewee Seny. Asked if she remembered hearing of any teas or vitamins that people took to prevent themselves from contracting SARS, she responded, "I don't think we had any of those. No, I don't think we had any of those. Because it was an unknown disease, right? It was [a] very new disease. So it wasn't something that you can strengthen your body to fight against, because it was still unknown" (Seny 2005). The media may have heavily influenced Seny's unique take on these matters, as she admitted to watching televised SARS updates "all the time . . . even at work," and most of the information she remembered came from these sources. Seny's opinions—that folk medicines cannot be used to treat diseases until those diseases are understood—stands in sharp distinction to the opinions of the rest of the interviewees, and moreover, parallels the operations of official medicine. That is, while the response of folk medicine to the SARS crisis was to offer a large list of potential preventatives, the response of official medicine was to try and stop the disease from spreading until the coronavirus's genome could be sequenced, allowing for the search for drugs that could halt or eradicate it altogether. Put more simply, the policy of official medicine in regard to SARS was to stop the epidemic from getting worse until better medical knowledge presented superior strategies. Seny's remarks thus more resemble the action sequences of official medicine than folk medicine—though they are an interesting hybridization of the two, as she still apparently believed in the importance and validity of folk treatments.

At the same time, it is hardly possible to say in the modern era that any response by folk medicine is not in some way a hybridization of folk and official practices. Many practitioners of folk medicine exist in comfortable cooperation with official medicine, offering their services at hospitals, recommending X-rays and vaccinations to their patients, and otherwise incorporating Westernized practices and knowledge into their own methods. However, as Alver, as well as O'Connor and Hufford, have pointed out, the reverse of this situation is far more rare. Doctors often look down upon practitioners of folk medicine, and patients receiving treatment from those practitioners are often advised by doctors to cease using any medicine that has not been scientifically tested and approved. Altogether this points to an interesting dilemma that official medicine presents to its patients, for it demands a great deal of patience from the public while scientists and other highly trained and educated people search for cures—a process that may take years. On the other hand, folk medicine is able to immediately deliver answers in the form of a multiplicity of remedies, some of which may have been around for decades. And this is in addition to all of the perceived benefits of folk medicine discussed elsewhere in this book, including its noninvasiveness, natural roots, and tendency to treat patients as people rather than statistics. For someone suffering from a disease that has barely been named, much less investigated, the choice is clear.

NOTES

1 Readers should note that Whatley and Henken's examples vary in accuracy and efficacy and should not be undertaken without first consulting a doctor.

2 But even the ingestion of hydrogen peroxide has been historically claimed as a cure-all—see not only the aforementioned McCabe 2003 but Douglass 1992; LeBeau 2001; McCabe 2004; and Trudeau 2007. The Cline article simply did not mention this connection.

7

This Little Virus Went to Market

A Comparison of H1N1 Narratives

In 2009, FOR A FRANTIC FEW MONTHS, a virus assaulted humanity with a fury that seemed apocalyptic, slipping the boundaries of cities, states, and countries to bound halfway around the world in a matter of hours. Its speed left doctors and researchers gasping in the wake, struggling to erect walls both physical and intellectual against the onslaught. But their reactions were nothing compared to the fear that gripped the nations of the world as they suddenly confronted a strange, invisible, and unexplained foe that killed thousands.

The virus was everywhere. Even when not physically present, its name was every day writ large on television screens and the covers of newspapers: H1N1. Headlines screamed the death tolls. The 9 o'clock news mapped out the new geographical areas where the virus had spread overnight. Radio announcers urged the public to receive vaccinations. The messages were impossible to avoid. H1N1 equaled fear. H1N1 equaled the unknown. H1N1 equaled the uncontrollable. H1N1 equaled death.

And then, almost as suddenly as it had arrived, the virus disappeared. There are those who predict that it will return. Only time will tell.

The rise and fall of the H1N1 virus in many ways parallels that of SARS, despite the six-year gap between outbreaks. Even a brief timeline such as the one that follows demonstrates many of these similarities. First announced by the World Health Organization (WHO) on April 24, 2009, the H1N1 virus roamed across the planet and disrupted lives for months. At its peak in North America, the pandemic was considered serious enough that President Barack Obama declared it a "national emergency" in a public announcement on October 24, 2009 ("Obama Declares H1N1 Emergency" 2009). By the end of the year, the WHO would note, "As of 27 December 2009, worldwide more than 208 countries and overseas territories or communities have reported laboratory confirmed cases

DOI: 10.7330/9780874219296.c007

of pandemic influenza H1N1 2009, including at least 12220 deaths" ("Pandemic (H1N1) 2009—Update 81" 2009).

Despite such numbers, that report noted that overall cases were declining in most parts of the world, including Asia; North, Central and South America; and the Caribbean. Only in Central and Eastern Europe was the virus still considered highly active, though the WHO acceded that the limited data available from Northern Africa suggested that it, too, might prove to be a hot zone.

Some sources claimed that the H1N1 flu yet had the capacity to infect millions. While cases declined in most of the United States in early 2010, the Centers for Disease Control and Prevention (CDC) reported widespread activity, as of January 7, in Delaware, New Jersey, Maine, and Virginia (S. Young 2010).[1] Across the Pacific, the Chinese health ministry warned on January 2, 2010, "The H1N1 strain of flu is rapidly spreading into China's vast countryside and there could be a spike in cases around the Lunar New Year period when millions head back to their home towns" ("China Says H1N1 Flu Spreading into the Countryside" 2010). This news report was seen as particularly unsettling, as the similarities between it and almost identical ones released during the 2003 SARS epidemic seemed to point to China having made inadequate progress in securing the safety of their people in the face of epidemics. Given this, it came as almost no surprise that Zhong Nanshan, a doctor based in China's Guangdong province who was noted for his efforts in fighting SARS in 2003, stated in November 2009 that he suspected China of withholding data concerning H1N1 flu deaths. At that time, the country had only reported 53 deaths, and Zhong found such a low number unlikely, asserting that many doctors were incorrectly treating and recording the deaths as the result of "ordinary pneumonia"—actions that Zhong deemed "irresponsible" ("China's Official H1N1 Death Count Suspect" 2009).

It is possible to find more similarities in the timelines of H1N1 and SARS, but such an investigation is not the focus of this chapter. Instead, we turn to the narratives themselves: the jokes and rumors, conspiracy theories and racist statements, cures and preventatives. As noted with SARS, the intent is not to prove that every narrative in H1N1 has its correlate elsewhere but to show that the same basic themes and types of narratives discussed so far in this book are also present in H1N1.

CURES, PREVENTATIVES, AND CONSPIRACIES

The H1N1 pandemic is unique among diseases referenced in this book in that a vaccine was made available a relatively short time after the offending virus entered public consciousness, before the disease was declared a pandemic. In part because of this, H1N1 is relatively devoid of the discussions of cures and preventatives that circulated so widely with other diseases. That is, the pandemic is relatively devoid of *unofficial* cures and preventatives. None of the people interviewed for this chapter recalled hearing of any such informal treatments, and even the Internet seems relatively free of them. One of the only examples gathered was an announcement from the Malaysian National News Agency that at Beijing Ditan Hospital in China, 88 out of 117 H1N1-infected patients recovered fully using only a specific mixture of four herbs, taken either as a tea or used as a mouthwash (Low 2009).

The pandemic was not, however, lacking in discussions of *official* cures and preventatives—namely, the H1N1 vaccine. In fact, many of the conspiracy theories generated during the H1N1 pandemic concerned vaccines. SARS, in comparison, featured few such rumors. The only salient example came from blogger "Izakovic," who, as discussed in chapter 2, claimed that SARS was man-made and targeted specific sections of the population; a vaccine could therefore be manufactured to keep safe those peoples who were not the intended targets of the coronavirus. H1N1 vaccine narratives, however, are multiform and widespread and exhibit a far bleaker outlook.

Among the many possible reasons for this exaggerated emphasis is the rapidity with which a vaccine became available to the public. The world's first introduction to the 2009 H1N1 flu came in April, and by October a vaccine was already in production. Such a brief turnaround aroused suspicions in some sectors, as concerned citizens wondered at the efficacy of a vaccine that had been produced in such a short time and the seemingly superhuman speed with which medical professionals, as well as the government, responded. After all, at the same time as the H1N1 vaccine was being mass-produced, one of the most prominent viral diseases in the world—AIDS—still lacked a vaccine some three decades after it had first appeared on the global radar. How is it possible that one could be manufactured for the H1N1 virus in only six months?

The answer lies in the cyclical, seasonal nature of the flu virus. Influenza outbreaks are common during winter months, and seasonal influenza vaccines have been available since the late 1940s. Modern influenza vaccine production is a streamlined process, and it is typical for vaccines to be produced in a matter of months:

> Every year, the World Health Organization and the Centers for Disease Control and Prevention collect data from 94 nations on the flu viruses that circulated the previous year, and then make an educated guess about which viruses are likely to circulate in the coming fall. Based on that information, the U.S. Food and Drug

Administration issues orders to manufacturers in February for a vaccine that
includes the three most likely strains. (Brownlee and Lenzer 2009)

While it is true that the 2009 H1N1 virus is novel, it is not lacking in
precursors. Variations of avian and swine flu outbreaks have occurred at
several points in recent history, including the 2005 avian influenza epidemic and the 1976 swine flu outbreak. Medicine is thus well acquainted
with the realities of these viruses and has developed measures to help counter their spread. The 2009 H1N1 vaccine can trace its origins to 2005,
when "worries of a bird flu epidemic prompted the Bush administration to
increase flu vaccine production capacity," thus setting the stage for a world
better prepared to deal with an outbreak of influenza ("Swine Flu (H1N1)
Vaccine" 2010).

Such explanations, however, do not seem satisfactory to those who claim
the vaccine to be suspicious for many reasons, including the rapidity with
which it hit the market. Echoing concerns that SARS was a virus created to
assist the New World Order (NWO) in their attempts to rid the world of
a large percentage of its population, H1N1 has also been called a purposeful pandemic: a "weaponized [virus] released on us in order to combat the
overpopulation of the world" ("H1N1 Conspiracy Voiced by the People"
2009).[2] At least one source has also claimed that the vaccines are little more
than a vehicle for the injection of microchips, or RFID chips, intended to
track and help control the population—a strategy also put in place by the
NWO ("H1N1 Conspiracy Update December 2009" 2009).

Far more common than conspiracy theories involving shady organizations such as the NWO, however, are narratives claiming that varying agencies have forced the vaccine on the population for monetary purposes. The
best and most extensive example of this was e-mailed by interviewee Kristian
and exists as an eighteen-slide PowerPoint presentation attached to an e-mail.[3]

It is not normally the charge of the folklorist to provide such an extended
debunking as the one that follows. As should be evident from the majority
of the narratives discussed in this book, the folklorist is normally concerned
not with the veracity of the narrative—that is, whether the events in the
story actually occurred, or at least could have occurred—but the "truth" of
the narrative as viewed by the teller and listener. If an interviewee considers
a story to be accurate and truthful, regardless of whether or not the facts in
that story are indeed correct, the folklorist treats the story with the same
level of care and respect as does the interviewee. As well, folklorists are usually interested in the *context* of the story: why it is told; what it says about
personal, local, or even regional worldviews; and what factors play a part in

the determination of the importance of a narrative. The paragraphs below break temporarily from this role. As one of the more commonly encountered conspiracy narratives, given the seriousness and specificity of the claims that it makes, it was also one of the more believable conspiracies of the H1N1 pandemic. Kristian's disbelief in the conspiracy makes the debunking efforts here morally easier by removing the guilt associated with proving an interviewee wrong in print. Nevertheless, three reasons highlight why this task was not undertaken lightly: (1) as noted, the conspiracy was widespread and believed by many; (2) few attempts have been made to disprove the narrative, and the following analysis will remedy this; and (3) the efforts will illuminate many problems inherent to conspiracy theories.

The conspiracy begins with a slide that declares, "News is just 'news' . . . / Not the absolute truth./Let's put swine flu (H1N1) into perspective."[4] A second slide provides viewers with a list of common H1N1 symptoms (fever, cough, sore throat, etc.), followed by a third slide which notes that the symptoms are so general that "Just about anyone could have Swine Flu." A strong conspiratorial tone already exists by this point in the slide show, the text hinting that even a cursory glimpse reveals that the symptoms for an H1N1 infection are suspiciously broad enough that virtually anyone who is sick could be included in the category of the diseased and treated as such.

Having set up the basic requirements for a conspiracy, the slide show moves into a series of panels that present basic H1N1 facts. Beginning with slide 4, under the headline "Deaths," the conspiracy notes the "816 deaths worldwide in 160 countries" and provides the following quote: "Given that countries are no longer required to test and report individual cases, the number of cases reported actually understates the real number of cases." The quote is not cited, but is a version of a caveat attached to many of the WHO's weekly updates on the H1N1 pandemic, this one appearing specifically on updates 59 through 76, dated July 27–November 2009 (available on the WHO's website, www.who.int). Appearing as it does in the presentation so proximate to the "816 deaths" listed on the same slide, the quote seems to be a warning about more deaths than facts dictate. Given the conspiratorial nature of the presentation, this commentary is likely the perception of scaremongering by official organizations. The quote and the 816 stated deaths also reveal the presentation's source (perhaps second- or third-hand) as update 59, which does provide that number for worldwide deaths as of July 27, 2009.

Following the establishment of these basic facts, slides 5–7 attempt to place the seriousness of the H1N1 pandemic into perspective by comparing the odds of dying from the disease to the odds of dying from various other causes. Slide 5 lists fourteen such factors, including the odds of "death by falling" (250:1), "death by drowning" (9,000:1), "death by lightning" (71,000:1), "death by dog attack" (137,000:1), and "death in the bathtub" (807,000:1). No sources are given for these odds, but a comparison to the list provided in the National Safety Council's (NSC) 2010 edition of *Injury Facts* demonstrates some discrepancies. Here the official statistics state that the odds of death by "Falls" are "1 in 184," death by "Accidental Drowning & Submersion" are "1 in 1,073," death by "Lightning" are "1 in 81,701," death by being "Bitten or Struck by Dog" are "1 in 119,998," and death by dying in a bathtub are "1 in 807,349" (National Safety Council 2010, 34–37).

Comparing the slide show to an official source in this manner evinces two problems. First, considerable variation sometimes exists between the numbers presented in the slide show and those given by the NSC. In some cases the numbers are quite close—the odds of dying in a bathtub are given as 807,000:1 in the slide show and 807,349:1 by the NSC—but in other cases are off by a large factor, as in the odds of dying from a dog attack (137,000:1 versus 119,998:1) or drowning (9,000:1 versus 1,073:1). Such discrepancies could have resulted from using older versions of the NSC's material, perhaps gleaned through secondhand or thirdhand sources. The second problem is that the NSC states that these odds are "one-year odds," calculated by dividing the worldwide population by the number of people who died from a given cause in a given year. This is separate from "lifetime odds," which are calculated by dividing the one-year odds by 76.9, which is the life expectancy of a person born in the year 2000. The lifetime odds of dying in a bathtub are thus 1 in 10,499. Both sources use the one-year odds, but by failing to include the lifetime odds, the slide show distorts the data.

Further problems are created when the slide show calculates the odds of dying from the H1N1 virus. Contrary to the earlier slide stating that 816 people died during the pandemic, slide 6 reports that "1154 people died (worldwide)," placing the odds of dying from H1N1 at "8,000,000[:]1," which slide 7 comments on with the note, "Yup, that's right / You at a greater risk from drowning in a bathtub." But using the one-year odds formula, this 8,000,000:1 figure can only be possible if the worldwide population is entered as 9,232,000,000, or some 2.5 billion people more than were alive as of mid-2010. The actual number, using a population of 6.8 billion (rounded), should be 5,892,547:1. This still places the odds higher than those of dying in a bathtub, but a second figure also needs altering: the number of worldwide deaths from H1N1. According to the WHO, the

1,154 stated deaths were only current as of July 31, 2009. The *total* number of deaths for 2009, as reported on December 27, was 12,220, placing the one-year odds at 556,465:1.[5] This makes dying from the H1N1 virus *more* likely than dying in a bathtub, at least in 2009.[6]

Having attempted to calculate the odds of dying during the pandemic, the slide show moves to comparing H1N1 to five of the more infamous diseases of the last fifty years. It begins by looking at influenza, which killed "more than 35,000 Americans every year"—a fact that can be verified using averages for the 1990s (see Thompson et al. 2003). Second on the list is "Bird flu," which includes the commentary "WHO reports (1 June 09) 436 cases and 262 deaths (was supposed to wipe us out)." The actual numbers are 432 cases and 262 deaths (see World Health Organization 2009a), but more significant is the subjective inclusion of the phrase "was supposed to wipe us out," which interrupts the factual nature of the slide with a contemptuous antiauthoritarianism, highlighting the conspiratorial nature of the overall presentation. The third noted disease is AIDS, which killed "More than 25m people . . . (up to July 07)"—a fact readily accessible on the Internet. Fourth is tuberculosis, which killed "1.6m . . . in 2005"—a plausible number, since official WHO estimates place the number of deaths in 2007 at roughly 1.8 million (World Health Organization 2009b). The slide ends with SARS. After erroneously calling it "Severe Adult Respiratory Distress Syndrome," it states, "167 deaths up to 2003 (was also supposed to kill millions)." As noted in chapter 1, SARS was responsible for 774 deaths. More significant, however, is the inclusion of a second antiauthoritarian comment on the same slide, reinforcing the message that official agencies are either incapable of accurately predicting the effects of a pandemic or are purposely overestimating (and perhaps lying about) them.

Evidence of a conspiracy thus firmly "established," the slide show shifts direction to investigate the source of the scheme. It begins by asking an obvious question: Who would benefit? Five groups are singled out in the answer: (1) "Drug companies—more medications sold"; (2) "Doctors— patients with mild cold will not 'take any chances'"; (3) "Medical institutions"; (4) "Media—more interest = more sales"; and (5) "Some politicians." With the possible exception of (2), this list centers on the idea that the groups in question somehow receive monetary compensation for overstating the dangers of H1N1. The second point is less clear but most likely also involves monetary compensation, the argument assuming that doctors receive kickbacks from drug companies for pushing H1N1 vaccinations, and that these doctors are somehow colluding with drug companies and media sources to increase public anxiety to the point where patients are demanding such vaccinations.

For slide 10, the presentation shifts focus again: "Only treatment/ Tamiflu/(also only treatment for bird flu)." The list of potentially responsible groups established in the previous slide is temporarily suspended, as if that list were so nebulous that any definite answers would be difficult to form. As such, a second approach is necessary to get at the heart of the conspiracy: if a list of groups is not immediately productive, a better approach involves looking at the "Only treatment," as that may reveal a source. Slide 11 then confirms the accuracy of this approach, revealing that the "Only licence for [o]seltamivir (Tamiflu) is to:/ Gilead Sciences Inc/ Roche— manufacturers it under licence/ Patent protection till 2016," implying that Gilead Sciences is at the heart of the matter. A fact check confirms Roche as the only US-licensed producer of Tamiflu (oseltamivir phosphate) during the H1N1 pandemic; the 2016 patent expiration date is also accurate—a patent that made headlines in 2005 when Roche warned foreign drug companies against producing generic versions of Tamiflu during the height of the avian flu epidemic (see "Tamiflu-Maker Roche Warns against Generic Versions" 2005).

But the presentation makes a critical error in these two slides because Tamiflu was not the only available treatment for H1N1. As detailed on the website of the CDC, Tamiflu was one of two FDA-approved "neuraminidase inhibitors," the other being Relenza (zanamivir), with a third neuraminidase inhibitor—peramivir—seeking FDA approval as early as October 2009 and "available through the CDC upon request of a licensed physician" ("Updated Interim Recommendations" 2009). GlaxoSmithKline and BioCryst held the patents for Relenza and peramivir, respectively. Furthermore, Relenza was discovered before Tamiflu, and its mid-2013 patent expiration creates further holes in the slide show's conspiracy theory by pointing out a second company that also benefited financially from the pandemic because of a drug monopoly. Further hurting the conspiratorial claims are news articles detailing two companies—one in Vietnam, one in India—which had been legally producing generic Tamiflu since 2005 and 2009, respectively; Roche granted the Vietnamese company a license to do so and the company in India won the right to do so in a court battle (see Minh 2005; "Cipla's Anti-Flu Drug Gets Nod" 2009).

Either ignoring or unaware of these contradictions, slide 12 continues to discuss Tamiflu, providing viewers a brief overview of the costs and numbers associated with the drug. Five statistics are given, including (1) "USA ordered 25m doses"; (2) "Total cost $2bn ($80 per course)"; (3) "65 governments have ordered"; (4) "Orders to 2008—200m doses"; and (5) "Price $70." These figures correspond to those found in various news sources, and even the conflicting costs of a course of drugs—$80 in (2) and $70 in (5)—still fall within the average cost for a ten-dose regimen. And the point of these numbers is clear: a lot of money is exchanging hands, and if we are to believe the previous few slides, it all goes to Roche.

But who is behind Roche? Slides 13 and 14 answer this question, bringing viewers to the heart of the conspiracy: the "Chairman of Gilead / Since 1997–2001 / Held major stocks" is none other than "Donald Rumsfeld / Former USA Secretary of defence." Rumsfeld's monetary gains from the pandemic are listed in detail on slide 15:

- Bush authorized $1.7Bn to fight bird flu—14% went to Gilead inc
- Gilead shares rose 700% since 2005 (when stock markets fell 40%)
- Total revenue for 2nd quarter 09 up 29% over 2008
- Net income for 2nd quarter 09 = $571.4m ($434m 2008)
- Royalties from Roche ($78.8m)
- 10% of every vaccine to Rumsfeld

Rumsfeld's status as former CEO of Gilead is accurate, as are the dates provided for his tenure there, and President George W. Bush did authorize $1.7 billion to fight bird flu, royalties from that figure having been estimated at 14–20 percent (Koh 2009). But stock charts for Gilead (NASDAQ: GILD) do not reveal a 700 percent rise in shares, as the cost of a single share on January 3, 2005, closed at $34.73, and the stock peaked on April 25, 2007, when it closed at $84.22—a rise of roughly 143 percent. A 2:1 stock split on June 25, 2007, cut the price in half—to $38.72 per share—making subsequent calculations more difficult. But the highest adjusted price for the stock between the time of the 2:1 split and the end of the H1N1 pandemic in mid-2010 came on August 13, 2008, when it closed at $56.81. Assuming a doubling of this price to account for the stock split, the non-adjusted price for this August 13 closing would be equivalent to a pre-split $113.62 closing cost, but that is still only a 227 percent rise—or slightly less than a third of what the slide show claims. Accurate revenue and net income reports for Gilead as of October 20, 2009, also reveal discrepancies, stating that the company "posted net income of $673 million, or 72 cents a share, compared with $496 million, or 52 cents a share, for the same period in 2008 . . . Revenue for the quarter rose 31% to $1.8 billion" (Kennedy 2009)—differences that may have arisen from reports filed earlier or later in the year. A report from Contract Pharma verifies that during the second quarter of 2009, Roche gained $78.8 million from royalties, of which $51.9 million came from Tamiflu ("Financial Report:

Gilead Sciences 2Q" 2009, which also confirms the second-quarter income of $571.4 million).

The accuracy of the claim that 10 percent of the sales of every vaccine went to Rumsfeld is dubious at best. Federal financial disclosures filed by Rumsfeld revealed that in 2005 he still held "a Gilead stake valued at between $5 million and $25 million," and that while "[t]he forms don't reveal the exact number of shares Rumsfeld owns . . . in the past six months fears of a pandemic and the ensuing scramble for Tamiflu have sent Gilead's stock from $35 to $47. That's made the Pentagon chief, already one of the wealthiest members of the Bush cabinet, at least $1 million richer." While it is thus clear that the former secretary of defense had considerable personal financial gain during the pandemic, the exact figures are not knowable due to the vagueness of the financial disclosures. Furthermore, an article by Nelson D. Schwartz details the distance Rumsfeld placed between himself and Roche when he assumed the cabinet position in 2001, recusing himself "from any decisions involving Gilead" at that time; and in September 2005, having "the Pentagon's general counsel issue additional instructions outlining what he could and could not be involved in if there were an avian flu epidemic and the Pentagon had to respond." In addition, during the early months of the avian flu epidemic, Rumsfeld considered selling off his shares of Gilead altogether, apparently to create further distance between himself and his former company, and sought counsel from the "Department of Justice, the SEC [Securities and Exchange Commission] and the federal Office of Government Ethics" on the matter, but as "Those agencies didn't offer an opinion . . . Rumsfeld consulted a private securities lawyer, who advised him that it was safer to hold on to the stock and be quite public about his recusal rather than sell and run the risk of being accused of trading on insider information" (Schwartz 2005). Thus, official reports point to Rumsfeld having dealt with his position as former CEO of Gilead with tact and due consideration, making all of his decisions and financial ties a matter of public record. It would be difficult at best to convict him of entanglement in a conspiracy because of such openness.

The slide show's final three slides close the argument. Having "revealed" the figurehead behind the "conspiracy," the presentation ends on a moral note, beginning with a slide that summarizes fatalities from various causes:

So lets understand . .

- Every month 50,000 people die from AIDS in South Africa
- Every day nearly 1,600 people die from AIDS
- Every year 18,000 people die on our roads

- 25,000 people are murdered
- Every year 80,000 die of TB

Slide 17 notes, "But we are forced to focus on / Influenza A (H1N1) / Swine flu" and slide 18 concludes, "Because the Powers / Don't make money from treating AIDS, TB, measles, malnutrition." Deconstructing these arguments, we begin with raw data. According to UNAIDS.org, "In 2008, an estimated 1.4 million AIDS-related deaths occurred in sub-Saharan Africa" (UNAIDS 2009), or 116,666 deaths per month. But in the country of South Africa, which is referenced specifically in the slide show, yearly deaths in 2007 were around 350,000, or 29,166 per month ("South Africa: HIV & AIDS Statistics" 2010). This data suggests that, while the slide show exaggerated the numbers for South Africa, they are in fact well below the worldwide average for *daily* AIDS-related deaths. Almost 1,000 people per day died of AIDS in 2007 in South Africa, but estimates place the number of worldwide AIDS-related deaths in 2008 at 2 million, or 5,479 per day ("Worldwide HIV & AIDS Statistics" 2010).

The figures given for the number of yearly deaths on roads and by murders are problematic, since the presentation does not make clear which country is being referenced—that is, who is the "our" in the sentence. Information from the US National Highway Traffic Safety Administration, however, places the number of "Fatal Crashes" in 2008 at 34,017, or slightly less than double the figure provided in the slide show ("National Statistics" n.d.). Homicides in the United States did approach the presentation's stated number in the early 1990s—24,700 in 1991 and 24,530 in 1993—but have since declined, with only 16,272 in 2008 (Disaster Center 2009). And as has been noted in the investigation of slide 8, tuberculosis deaths in 2007 approached 1.8 million—another instance of the slide show contradicting itself.

As for the claim that the reason we are forced to focus on the H1N1 virus is because the "Powers"—presumably the government—do not make money off of "AIDS, TB, measles, malnutrition," we only need to look at the first of these diseases to find a contradiction. And we find it in a company that has already been discussed at length: Roche. According to the company website in late 2012, Roche manufactures two patented HIV/AIDS drugs—Fuzeon and Invirase—and four different analysis and testing systems for AIDS researchers (see http://www.roche.com/index.htm). Since Rumsfeld held between $5 and $25 million of Roche stock in 2005, he definitely made money "treating AIDS" during his tenure as secretary of defense.

As can be seen from the above analysis, the conspiracy theory pinning responsibility for creating the panic associated with the H1N1 pandemic on Donald Rumsfeld is dubious at best. Not only does the conspiracy contradict itself at several points, but its inaccurate data, and the assumptions made with that data, only work when significant countertrends and key facts are ignored. The conspiracy's continued existence despite these shortcomings serves as a demonstration of public perceptions of governments and politicians—namely, that they are looking out for themselves more than they are for the common person and have little compunction when it comes to creating widespread panic if doing so results in an influx of cash.

Government conspiracies such as this one are common, as noted in previous chapters, where various diseases have been linked to Saddam Hussein, the CIA, and other governmental organizations and personnel. Whether detailing attempts to eradicate large portions of the worldwide population or plans to make the rich even richer, they all play off the notion that we are not in control of our own lives. But the Rumsfeld conspiracy takes additional advantage of a powerful tool: statistics. Kathleen Woodward, in "Statistical Panic," examines the role statistics play in creating fear and anxiety. Statistics are pointed out as being equitable to risk, especially when it comes to health. In our modern society we are surrounded by figures and facts that tell us, for example, the likelihood that we will contract breast cancer, or fall down a flight of stairs, or be eaten by sharks. Statistics is, in fact, "a discourse of risk. We are at risk, it seems, of anything and everything" (Woodward 1999, 179).

One of the many problems Woodward points out concerning statistics is that they are too easily read in a negative sense and often promote "a sense of foreboding and insecurity" (1999, 180). If someone is told that they only have a 1 in 10 million chance of being eaten by a shark, they do not necessarily receive the message that it is extraordinarily unlikely for such an event to occur but simply that such an event *can possibly* occur. Given this fact, and the statistic-rich nature of the modern world, Woodward claims that, in some ways, our lives are essentially a series of statistical panics, one occupying our minds for a fleeting moment until another shoves out the first one, and so on. Statistics can cause an especially acute panic, largely because of the uncertainty intrinsic to the statement: "What in fact panics us, however, is that we cannot be certain of our own future, however much [it has been] quantified . . . for us" (187). In the end, Woodward claims that, following the work of Ulrich Beck, industrial society has been replaced by the risk society, where "What we fear is risk itself" (180).

Besides using statistics as a persuasive device, the slide show also plays on our natural fear of diseases, especially those originating somewhere else.

Margaret Humphreys's "No Safe Place: Disease and Panic in American History" examines several instances of fear and anxiety that arose during modern epidemics and health scares such as cholera, malaria, heart disease, and the anthrax-laden letters mailed in 2001, among others. Humphreys contends that modern Americans have largely forgotten what it means to "feel that our place is contaminated, diseased, and unsafe" (Humphreys 2002, 845), and so scares such as the anthrax letters often result in panics disproportionate to their actual morbidity. Such reactions are not solely limited to North America or novel anxiety-inducing health situations. In fact, Humphreys states that, in general, "diseases do not cause panic in direct proportion to their morbidity and mortality, a fact that seems counterintuitive," and illustrates this by noting that women are more afraid of breast cancer than heart disease, despite the latter's far more prevalent and deadly presence (846).

Humphreys also notes that central to panic is the "crossing of boundaries" both real and artificial (2002, 847). She comments, "The scariest diseases are traveling diseases. Strange plagues that threaten the place of sanctuary arouse the most fear. This is particularly true when the disease can be tracked" (850). She adds that there is a direct correlation between the speed of mortality and the escalation of panic. The spread of panic, however, depends directly upon the spread of information (or disinformation) surrounding the disease; the media plays a role in this circulation. Humphreys even goes so far as to claim that "disease panic and the news media form their own generative circle," where the panicked public demands more information from the media, and upon its presentation, such information begets more panic, which creates a call for more information, etc. (846).

In the H1N1 pandemic, this fear made possible the creation of government conspiracy narratives such as the one detailed above, which play off of our apprehensions about our own mortality. But these are not the only narrative forms that arose from this fear; H1N1 also resulted in the creation of a fresh round of anti-vaccination narratives. Such narratives, which argued that the H1N1 vaccine was not effective at best, and at worst was more harmful than helpful, were arguably the most common type of conspiracy theory. Shannon Brownlee and Jeanne Lenzer's article "Does the Vaccine Matter?" provides a well-researched, investigative look into influenza vaccinations in general, detailing many of the problems that are voiced in anti-vaccination narratives. One of their more troubling revelations is that vaccination concerns are held by some doctors and medical researchers besides being endemic to the lay population. More than 100 million Americans every year—or roughly one-third of the population—receive the flu vaccine, state Brownlee and Lenzer, and the vaccine has been a centerpiece in the US government's public health policy ever since the 1957 avian flu epidemic, which resulted in the deaths of some 70,000 Americans. But the flu vaccine has rarely been without some controversy. Proponents of the vaccine often defend it by pointing out the effectiveness of other vaccines, including those for polio and whooping cough, both of which have dramatically reduced the occurrences of those diseases. The flu vaccine, proponents claim, serves a parallel purpose for influenza, and several studies have determined that "people who get a flu shot in the fall are about half as likely to die that winter—from any cause—as people who do not" (Brownlee and Lenzer 2009).

Opponents of the flu vaccine are not as easily persuaded by such studies. Influenza, they note, causes only a small percentage of deaths in the United States, and even after adding in deaths to which the flu could have contributed—via lung disease, heart failure, etc.—the National Institute of Allergy and Infectious Diseases has concluded that the flu accounts for no more than 10 percent of winter deaths among the elderly. Any claims that the vaccine reduces overall mortality rates by half are therefore suspect. Tom Jefferson, a doctor and head of the Cochrane Vaccines Field at The Cochrane Collaboration, summarizes these problems succinctly: "For a vaccine to reduce mortality by 50 percent and up to 90 percent in some studies means it has to prevent deaths not just from influenza, but also from falls, fires, heart disease, strokes, and car accidents. That's not a vaccine, that's a miracle" (Brownlee and Lenzer 2009).

Another problem noted by medical opponents to the influenza vaccine involves the few times in recent history when vaccines were either available only in limited supply or did not match up with the viruses against which they were supposed to provide protection. For example, in 2004 medical facilities were unable to produce the amount of vaccine required, resulting in a 40 percent decrease in immunization rates. And in both 1968 and 1997, the "educated guess" that the WHO and the CDC made concerning which viruses would be circulating in the upcoming flu season proved incorrect: "the vaccine that had been produced in the summer protected against one set of viruses, but come winter, a different set was circulating. In effect, nobody was vaccinated" (Brownlee and Lenzer 2009). Despite these problems, mortality rates did not rise during any of these years, causing some researchers to question whether influenza vaccines had been useful during the years when it was correctly matched and had been produced in sufficient quantities.

A final problem is the "healthy-user effect." Detailed in the work of Lisa Jackson, a physician and senior investigator with the Group Health

Research Institute in Seattle, Washington, the healthy-user effect hypothesizes that lower mortality rates among vaccinated patients may actually be the result of the overall health of those patients, not the vaccine itself. Jackson's work, which involved combing through eight years of medical data on some 72,000 senior citizens, "showed that *outside of flu season*, the baseline risk of death among people who did not get vaccinated was approximately 60 percent higher than among those who did, lending support to the hypothesis that on average, healthy people chose to get the vaccine, while the 'frail elderly' didn't or couldn't" (Brownlee and Lenzer 2009, emphasis in original). In other words, the lowered mortality rates noted by vaccine proponents may result from the fact that healthy people, who are less likely to die over the short term, are simply more likely to get vaccinated than people who are ill.

Problems such as these have caused some researchers to call for a reexamination of the effectiveness of the influenza vaccine using placebo-controlled, double-blind studies. Among many questions to be answered is whether the vaccine is actually useful for those who need it the most (i.e., the elderly, who account for most flu deaths but who have weakened immune systems that are less capable of responding positively to vaccines) and whether the vaccine is actually needed by those for whom it is the most useful (i.e., healthy people, whose immune systems do respond well to vaccines but who are better capable of fighting off an illness). Such controlled studies, however, are unlikely to happen anytime soon. As explained by Lone Simonsen, research professor and research director in the Department of Global Health at the George Washington University School of Public Health and Health Services, "It is considered unethical to do trials in populations that are recommended to have vaccine" (Brownlee and Lenzer 2009). Although Simonsen is a proponent of such trials, her statements concerning the backward logic of influenza vaccines will, for the conspiracy theorist, only provide further evidence of the suspicious nature of all vaccines.

Portions of the population thus consider all influenza vaccinations suspect, and the H1N1 vaccination has not escaped this treatment. Some of the more radical conspiracy theorists claimed the inoculations part of a New World Order conspiracy. By far the more commonly circulated vaccine-related narratives, however, revolved around the vaccine's ingredients and method of production. Specifically, many of the narratives expressed concern over the vaccine's adjuvants—agents added to the vaccine cocktail for several purposes, including enhancing the inoculated person's immune response, preserving the vaccine, and providing for the sterility over time and repeated usage of the glass vials in which the vaccine was packaged.

Numerous anti-adjuvant websites sprung up during the H1N1 pandemic, all proclaiming the dangers of these "untested" chemicals. An example of such a website—chosen because of its high placement in Google's search engine in response to the query "H1N1 vaccine adjuvants"—may be found at PreventDisease.com, a not-for-profit organization based in Toronto, Canada. This website promotes prevention as the key to health, and its January 2010 front page contained article titles ranging from "Mango Effective in Preventing Colon and Breast Cancer" to "Exercise Improves Cognitive Function," to "Almost Half of All Fast Food Soda Contains Bacteria that Grew in Feces," to "Drug Firms Cashed In On Swine Flu Scam." The website as a whole is neatly organized and geared toward an intelligent audience, but more significantly, each featured article provides references, many of which come from scientific studies published in peer-reviewed journals. For example, the article on soda containing fecal bacteria references a study published in volume 137, number 1 (January 2010) of the *International Journal of Food Microbiology*, and the abstract provided by that journal does confirm that coliform bacteria was found in 48 percent of the ninety beverages the authors procured from thirty different locations (White et al. 2010). In other words, PreventDisease.com is not an ordinary, run-of-the-mill conspiracy website but a highly intelligent site with contents likely to be perceived by readers as truthful and accurate.

When a website of this nature publishes the following statement, it can be assumed that readers take it seriously:

> It appears that both the U.S. and Canada are prepared to skip all of the normally required safety and efficacy procedures and allow for the massive testing of [a] novel adjuvant on thousands of paid clinical trial participants in tests of the new H1N1 vaccine. This is despite documented government warnings that adjuvanted vaccines can induce more pronounced side effects than ordinary vaccines, a definite downside because vaccines, unlike most other pharmaceuticals, are given to healthy people.
>
> There has been no confirmation, but many vaccine experts have speculated that the H1N1 flu vaccine ingredients will be very similar, if not identical to the H5N1 flu vaccine which was also developed by GlaxoSmithKline. The biological index of that vaccine includes chicken embryos, formaldehyde, squalene adjuvant, thiomersal (mercury derivative), polysorbate 80 (preservative) and aluminum adjuvant among others. ("The H1N1 Vaccine Is a Much Greater Risk to Your Health Than the Flu Itself" 2009)

From this point the article moves into a detailed discussion of the dangers present in some of the referenced adjuvants. It begins with squalene and notes that a study published in *The American Journal of Pathology* in

2000 "demonstrated that a single injection of the adjuvant squalene into rats triggered a chronic, immune-mediated joint-specific inflammation, also known as rheumatoid arthritis." Among further dangers claimed to be associated with squalene include that: "The Polish Academy of Sciences has shown that in animals, squalene alone can produce catastrophic injury to the nervous system and the brain. The University of Florida Medical School has shown that in animals, squalene alone can induce production of antibodies specifically associated with systemic lupus erythematosus." The second adjuvant warning involves thimerosal, a mercury derivative—mercury being "a toxin linked with autism and neurological disorders." The section concludes with a note, laden with conspiratorial overtones: "Epidemiologist Tom Verstraeten and Dr. Richard Johnston, an immunologist and pediatrician from the University of Colorado, both concluded that thimerosal was responsible for the dramatic rise in cases of autism but their findings were dismissed by the CDC."

The information available on PreventDisease.com makes for interesting analysis. The website smartly corroborates many of its statements by citing legitimate scientific research. Its facts, therefore, come across as well investigated and accurate. Any reader wishing to disprove any of these articles faces numerous obstacles, including negating, or at least arguing, the conclusions of peer-reviewed papers. With such data behind them, the articles available on this website thus carry a compelling note of veracity. It is true that not every website that discusses H1N1 conspiracy theories and adjuvant problems is similarly as intelligent, but many of them make similar claims. PreventDisease.com has the additional advantage of serving as one of the more popular health-oriented websites, with an average of 30,000 unique visitors per month—a number that spiked to roughly 80,000 during the height of the H1N1 pandemic in November 2009, according to web analytics company Compete. It can be assumed that readers of PreventDisease.com take seriously the information they gather there. And as has been noted, many of the H1N1 articles available on the website do not paint a flattering picture of the pandemic, nor of the available vaccines.

The presence of refutations of H1N1 "myths" in national newspapers is a better indicator of the popularity of anti-vaccination narratives.[7] For example, *The New York Times* has published extensive overviews of the pandemic, including one article with a "Frequently Asked Questions" section that answers twenty of the most common H1N1 queries, many of which involve rumors and conspiracies. Two of these questions address the issues raised by PreventDisease.com:

Q: Do adjuvants added to flu vaccine increase risk of an autoimmune reaction?
A: This is a myth perpetuated on some health Web sites. Although substances called
   adjuvants are sometimes added to vaccines to make them more effective,
   no flu vaccine sold in the United States, including the H1N1 2009 vaccine, contains any adjuvants.

Q: Does the new vaccine contain the mercury compound thimerosal?
A: Flu vaccine packaged in a multidose vial contains thimerosal, a preservative
   that prevents contamination of the vial during repeated use. One dose
   from a multiuse vial contains about 25 micrograms of mercury. By
   comparison, a tuna fish sandwich contains about 28 micrograms of
   mercury. Repeated studies have shown thimerosal to be safe. However,
   people who want to minimize mercury exposure can ask for a vaccine
   in a single-dose package, which has only trace amounts. Thimerosal is
   not used in the production of FluMist. ("Swine Flu (H1N1) Vaccine"
   2010)

The New York Times does effectively counter anti-adjuvant narratives, and
with roughly 15 million unique visitors per month (statistics again provided by Compete), its website reaches a far larger audience than does
PreventDisease.com. One may argue that the *Times*, in restating the rumors,
has effectively assisted in their dispersal, but such arguments are not the
focus of this chapter. What is important is the appearance in a major newspaper of an article devoted primarily to rumor control, which is a clear
indicator of the popularity of those rumors. Such popularity can only result
from those rumors speaking to common beliefs, uncertainties, and fears,
such as the concern that our fates are being affected by variables outside of
our control and influence.

HUMOR AND JOKES

In North America, three different names, or titles, circulated simultaneously
among the public for the entirety of the pandemic: Mexican flu, swine flu,
and H1N1. This situation is unique among major diseases in recent history, for it is the normal trend that new names simply replace older names.
For example, AIDS was initially referred to as GRID (Gay-related immune
deficiency), but use of the GRID acronym ceased after the introduction
of the AIDS acronym. A second unique quality of the H1N1 pandemic is
the naming of more than one offending party—Mexicans and pigs—in the
title, resulting in the fragmentation of the types of narratives in circulation.
In fact, the jokes included in this chapter are divided fairly equally among
the three "official" names—that is, one-third of the jokes concern Mexicans,
one-third concern pigs or swine, and one-third concern the H1N1 acronym

itself. These ratios seemed to stay constant throughout the majority of the pandemic, meaning that when it came to humor, at no point in time was one group—whether human, animal, or viral—singled out by the public as the sole culprit.

The tripartite nature of these jokes stands in defiance of official efforts to avoid naming a specific group of people or animals as the cause of the pandemic. As early as April 2009, governments around the world were debating what to name the new disease, as detailed in *The Guardian*:

> Trouble began yesterday when a health minister in Israel raised an objection to "swine flu" on the grounds of Jewish and Muslim sensitivities over pork. Yakov Litzman, a member of an ultra-Orthodox Jewish community, came up with his own alternative: "Mexican flu."
>
> That had the advantage of sparing Jews and Muslims discomfort. It had the disadvantage, however, of causing Mexicans even greater discomfort. (Pilkington 2009)

The debate over these terms would rage for weeks, and even the introduction of the non-blameful H1N1 acronym in early May would not completely stymie the discussions. Instead, it moved them into the public realm, where they became joke fodder.

Indeed, some jokes acknowledged this discussion, highlighting the problems created by naming a disease after a specific group or animal, as exemplified in a joke e-mailed by interviewee Lynne: "So, the press was trying to figure out what to call this flu, and they realized they couldn't call it the Mexican flu, because that wouldn't be PC, and when they tried calling it swine flu, the pig farmers got mad, so they decided to call it the 'Other White Flu'" (Lynne 2010). Although the initial facts in the joke have been largely distorted to create the humorous ending—the media was not solely involved in onomastics—the joke itself saliently describes the "othering" that occurs when one group is labeled as responsible for an unwanted or negative occurrence. The punch line, featuring a play on words referring to a campaign by pork manufacturers to publicize the healthiness of their product by referring to it as "The Other White Meat," diffuses the tension that exists between blaming either pigs or people from Mexico, neither of which presents an ideal level of political correctness. The punch line also serves to move the blame away from those groups altogether, focusing it instead on white people. Given that the pandemic quickly spread beyond Mexico's borders and became a global problem, this shift is appropriate, though it should be noted that substituting *white* for *Mexican* creates the same othering problem that existed initially. At the same time, the word *white*, connoting Caucasians, demands a reciprocity and self-examination that few disease narratives exhibit, pointing out that those who participate in othering are not themselves so free of fault.

The above example constitutes what might be termed a formal joke. It has a set-up and a punch line and any retellings should closely approximate the original. The mechanism that triggers laughter at the punch line's revelation is incongruity, defined by Patricia Keith-Spiegel as "disjointed, ill-suited pairings of ideas or situations or presentations of ideas or situations that are divergent from habitual customs" (Keith-Spiegel 1972, 7). Incongruity is, however, found in almost every type of humor, and Elliott Oring has gone so far as to say that an "appropriate incongruity"—meaning one relevant and fitting to the joke—is one of the more pervasive structures in humor (Oring 1992). Thus, while a formal joke such as the one above relies on an appropriate incongruity, it could be said that most, if not all, situations that create laughter—whether formal or informal, planned or spontaneous, pre-written or improvised—also rely on incongruities. An example of a spontaneous, improvised piece of humor that exhibits these characteristics comes from interviewee Cara Nina, who e-mailed the following: "My best friend called a few days after the swine flu hit the news. He said he felt sick and was worried about the swine flu. I told him to chill out, [because] he probably just had a cold. Then he added, 'But the other night I rimmed a Mexican!'" (Cara Nina 2010). Many things could be said of such humor, beginning with the recognition of its racist, inappropriate nature, which Cara Nina acknowledged in her e-mail by concluding the story with the coda "Maybe not the best for an academic text." The joke itself, though, is an excellent example of a spontaneously administered appropriate incongruity, relying for its effect on the listener's comprehension that some diseases can be transmitted through sexual activities, though in this case juxtaposed with an anal-oral form of sexual activity that is particularly offensive to polite sensibilities.[8] It is also a second illustration of the joking that arose from the nomenclature Mexican flu, demonstrating the pervasiveness of such humor, and by extension, evincing that only a few days after the flu had entered the public consciousness, it had fast become associated with a single group of people.

Cara Nina's second contribution also played on the Mexican flu title. As she stated in an e-mail: "whenever I was inconvenienced by school closures or had to stay home from work because of sick kids, I told my 1/4 Mexican housemate that she was 1/4 responsible for swine flu." Such a comment was obviously intended to be a jest, and when asked how frequently she made these comments, as well as how they were received by her roommate, Cara Nina answered, "I would say she was 1/4th as amused as I was and I said it about 400 times." Critical to an analysis of this joke, at least for the purposes of this chapter, is the strong correlation made between ethnicity and pandemic, such that a person who was only "1/4 Mexican" could still be definitively associated with the H1N1 virus. This incident echoes the stories in chapter 3 of Jennifer and "Rita," who were so stigmatized during the SARS epidemic because of their Asian ethnicity that people refused to sit near them on buses. Also notable in Cara Nina's joke is the ease with which it switches between the implied title of Mexican flu and the openly stated swine flu, evidence that both titles existed comfortably and simultaneously in the teller's mind. A narrative such as this exposes the difficulties inherent in attempting to remove the stigmatization of an ethnic group by changing the name of the pandemic, as the introduction of the newer title does not necessarily erase the existence of the older one. In fact, both names come to rest easily in the public consciousness, and the newer one may even serve to reinforce the existence of the older one because the latter is now seen as taboo, and joking about its existence frees the teller from the task of keeping the forbidden thing under repression (see Gagnier 1991; Gray 1994; and Grotjahn 1957). It would thus seem apparent that to lessen stigmatization, any new outbreak must carry from the beginning a name that does not connect it with any race, ethnicity, or society.

The second name proposed during the H1N1 pandemic—swine flu— at least removed any reference to a group of humans, and many jokes circulating during the pandemic featured pigs and porcine-related material. From one perspective, this could be seen as a welcome departure from the Mexican jokes, as it would seem that the new name would provide fewer chances for outright racism. The first piece of collected humor that used *swine* as part of the punch line was, in fact, quite a "clean" joke, compared to those featured so far. The story comes again from Cara Nina, who noted simply, "a few friends and I always reply to Facebook posts about being sick with a solitary 'OINK.'" Like her earlier contributions, this narrative follows no formal joke outline. It is also the shortest piece of humor in this chapter, since in its natural form the entirety of the joke is the single word *OINK*. The set-up, likely something along the lines of "I feel sick," does provide introductory phrasing and is thus part of the joke. But the poster did not originally intend it as such, instead merely wanting to inform friends of an illness. Only after the inclusion of the onomatopoeic word does the nature of the initial posting change to become part of a piece of humor. Because of the brevity of such an exchange, the joke-maker must be confident that the initial poster (as well as other viewers) will understand the reference; made too far beyond the boundaries of an outbreak, a reply such as "oink" would not make sense, the referenced outbreak too far out of easy recall to understand the nature of the remark. That only a single unexplained word is needed in Cara Nina's exchange demonstrates that the joke-maker thinks it fairly safe to conclude that anyone coming across a discussion wherein one party notes an illness and the other replies with an oink will understand the reference, thus providing evidence for the firmness with which the phrase "swine flu" had entered the public consciousness.

The second piece of collected humor that referenced pigs in the punch line comes from interviewee Christine, who e-mailed, "People used to say that the day there was a black President of the United States would be the day that pigs fly. Swine Flu" (Christine 2010). This piece returns to both a more formalized joke structure and racism, as exhibited in the idea that a black man (i.e., Barack Obama) becoming president is as likely as a flying pig. The punch line relies on the homophonic pun created by the similar pronunciations of *flew* and *flu*, without which the joke would be nonsensical. From an analytical perspective, this pun is interesting because it provides one of the few ways that a joke about swine flu could be made to be racist. Further research turned up few other mechanisms for this, and the only approximate humor involved the word *pig* functioning as derogatory slang for *police*, as in the following, gathered off of a website: "Anyone else awaiting the first Policeman to be diagnosed with Swine Flu?" (Domaticus 2009).

The larger number of collected swine flu jokes relied on puns or hyperbole (or, occasionally, both) for the transmission of humor. Puns, contrary to the above example, were rarely used to express racist sentiments, and instead presented a markedly forced and less serious nature. Examples (all of which appeared on the website FunnyandJokes.com) included "My friend thought she had swine flu so she oinked a appointment with her docter"; "What's the difference between bird flu and swine flu? With bird flu the doctor gives you tweetments. With swine flu he'll just give you some oinkment"; "I think iv got swine flu, im feeling pigheaded. I need the hambulense to come"; and "I have swine flu and I feel Offal . . . but I have been told I will be bacon my feet real soon." Like the other humorous pieces in this chapter, these puns seem designed to downplay the seriousness of the pandemic, or at least serve as mediators to help deal with stress and worry. The same could be said of swine flu jokes that relied on hyperbole. In this case, however, the jokes exist to specifically point out the exaggerated responses of the public, the media, and the government, as in the following:

A bear, a lion and a pig meet.
The bear says, "If I roar in the forest, the entire forest is shivering with fear."
The lion says, "If I roar in the jungle, the entire jungle is afraid of me."

[The] pig says, "Big deal . . . I only have to cough, and the entire planet shits itself." (Raghav 2009)

The escalating fearful reactions in this joke are indirectly proportionate to the danger of the animals, the domesticated pig being less frightening on the whole than a bear or lion. In this way, the joke serves as metacommentary on the reactions exhibited by the public during the pandemic, where a small virus was given a larger place of importance than, for example, an international political scandal. By lampooning such reactions, the joke points out the backward nature of such structures and causes the listener or reader to question their own ideas about pandemics.

The final joke in the swine flu category, taken again from FunnyandJokes.com, serves the same metacommentary function on the H1N1 pandemic as the previous entry, but on an even larger scale, displays a keen perception of the correlations between narratives extant in separate pandemics:

This little piggy went to market.
This little piggy stayed at home.
This little piggy had roast beef.
This little piggy had none.
And this little piggy went "cough, sneeze" and the whole world's media went mad over the imminent destruction of the human race, and every journalist found out that they didn't have to do too much work if they just did "Find 'bird,' replace with 'swine'" on all their saved articles from a year ago, er, all the way home. (Domaticus 2009)

The children's rhyme referenced in this joke provides an ideal substructure, as it already features pigs as central characters. Building on this, the joke moves into a discussion of the exaggerated reactions present in the media during the H1N1 pandemic and in this way closely resembles the earlier joke about the bear, lion, and pig. The narrative then takes a second turn, noting that many of the articles published during the H1N1 pandemic closely resemble those of the avian flu epidemic, and then sarcastically comments that the current articles appear to be little more than quick rewrites of the older ones via a word processing program's find and replace tool. Such commentary makes several implications regarding media sources: (1) that they are quick to recognize a news opportunity; (2) that they are equally quick to recognize a chance to sell newspapers; (3) that they are willing to exaggerate the nature of the news opportunity to sell newspapers (as evinced by the phrase "imminent destruction of the human race"); (4) that the individuals working for the media are inherently lazy; (5) that because they are lazy, but want to sell newspapers, these individuals are prone to bad journalism (i.e., using a computer's find and replace tool, which could be seen as representative of a host of bad practices such as poor fact-checking, lack of proofreading, etc.); and (6) that because of such bad journalism, the media cannot be trusted to accurately report events. In order for a series of commentaries such as this to exist—in joke form or otherwise—the public must first perceive a media that, if it does not closely approximate that presented in the joke, is at least ambivalent enough to allow for such a possibility. The media, the joke says, is made of people, and people are fallible.

Having covered examples of humor related to the terms *Mexican flu* and *swine flu*, this examination now turns to the final, and ultimately official, name: H1N1. Two of the diseases discussed elsewhere in this work also bore acronyms as titles—SARS and AIDS—and in both of those cases a proportion of the collected narratives appropriated those acronyms, rewording them for specific purposes. Following such appropriation, SARS stood not for "Severe Acute Respiratory Syndrome" but "Saddam's Awesome Retaliation Strategy," and various redefinitions for AIDS have included "Abstinence Is Definitely Smart," "Another Idiot Dies Standing," and "After Intercourse Die Standing." By itself, the process of appropriating an acronym in this fashion is not remarkable, and humorous examples of this process can be found for many common acronyms. But the process of appropriating an acronym is not confined to the invention of new meanings for that acronym; it can include any effort made in the process of altering the acronym for other purposes.

The H1N1 flu provided an easy target in this sense, the letter-number format of the name visually approximating the word *heinie*, a slang term for the buttocks. An example of the humor made possible by this pronunciation comes in an e-mail from Kristian, who worked as a security officer at a Toronto-area hospital during the pandemic: that "everyone at the hospital calls it the [heinie] flu [because] first they thought it was a crock of shit" (Kristian 2010). The reasons for such a reaction among hospital staff were in part created by the safety protocols established during the pandemic, including, as explained by Kristian, "having security posted at every door screening for the virus in full PPE" (Personal Protective Equipment), including "a yellow isolation gown, a n95 respirator mask, gloves and in some cases a hair net." As noted by Mike, the EMT in chapter 3, such gear is not only uncomfortable but inhibits the wearer's ability to interact normally with the public, who perceive the equipment as threatening, frightening, or worrisome, and so the benefits of the equipment's protective nature become entangled with the inhibited abilities of hospital staff to do their jobs.

Protective equipment was, however, not the only cause of staff complaints during the pandemic. As described by Kristian, other newly established protocols, including those governing patient-doctor interactions and patient admittance procedures, also hindered the normal working environment. When asked how these protocols affected her job, Kristian responded:

> We had a security guard stationed at the front door of the ER wearing [PPE] and asking everyone who entered if they had specific symptoms. The guard would also pump hand [sanitizer] into the hand of everyone who entered. Anyone with symptoms was given a mask, a red number and directed to their own waiting area/red triage . . . they also changed the ER voice recording to tell patients to proceed inside, wash their hands and speak to the security guard . . . talk about scary walking into a hospital!!!

Clearly evident in this description is the quandary created by the juxtaposition of strict security protocols and the empathy felt by security staff, who recognized the frightening nature of such protocols for patients. But the above example comes from the middle of the pandemic. At the beginning, as described by Kristian, the situation was potentially worse: "In the first few days when they didn't know much about the virus all patients had to wear facemasks [whether] they had symptoms or not and anyone who was ill was not allowed to even have their [spouse] accompany them to see the Dr. Only children under 16 were allowed to have one parent with them." Under conditions such as these, where family members are denied entry and patients are treated as if they were sick, regardless of circumstances—a guilty-until-proven-innocent mind-set—it is extraordinarily difficult at best to produce a healthy, calm, productive working environment. And when combined with the frightened reactions of some members of the public, the situation quickly spiraled down, as Kristian described it, "People actually came into the ER crying and panicking because their child had a cough or a [runny] nose. It was chaos for the first little while."

The second piece of H1N1-specific humor was e-mailed by interviewee Philip and also features the *heinie* pronunciation of the acronym. In this case, however, the pronunciation refers not to anatomy but to a popular alcoholic beverage: "I arrived at my wife's sister's house for supper in December [2009] with a box of Heineken beer and my 20-something nephew said, 'Oh, Heineys! the official beer of the H1N1 epidemic!'" (Philip 2010). Adding a critical layer to the story, Philip noted, "He said 'H-one-N-one' but he was obviously referring to the pronunciation 'Hi, knee' and it raised a quick laugh." That the nephew made such a joke was possible because of the audience's knowledge of the *heinie* pronunciation—something that the nephew took for granted, evincing at least a local diffusion of the pronunciation. The joke itself provides at least two levels of commentary. The first plays off of the ubiquitous claims by beer makers that their beverages are "the official beer of" a given time, event, place, etc. Many of these claims are legitimate, as in Coors Light serving as the "Official Beer Sponsor of Super Bowl XLIII," which it was in 2009. But many of the claims seem spurious or laughable, as in Chico, California's Butte Creek Brewing claiming to have "The Official Beer of Planet Earth." Claiming a beer to be "the official beer of the H1N1 epidemic" falls under the same category as this latter example. The joke also provides further evidence of widespread recognition of the H1N1 epidemic, as well as the acronym, for without such recognition any joke about the event needing an official beer would fall flat.

The final joke in this section comes from interviewee Gillian, who e-mailed, "This one was written on the chalk board at work in December [2009] and involves a local mall (Bonnie Doon mall [in Edmonton, Alberta]) that had been housing a makeshift flu clinic in the same spot that they would later house Santa[:]—Bonnie Doon mall recently stopped vaccinating against H1N1 in exchange for HOHO—" (Gillian 2010). Many— perhaps most famously Sigmund Freud (1990) in *Jokes and their Relation to the Unconscious*—have argued how laughter and humor provide a "release." The nature of this release varies by joke and could result from, for example, fear, pleasure, or hostility. In the narrative provided by Gillian, at least two of these—fear and pleasure—play crucial roles. The H1N1 pandemic created widespread fear. But by replacing the numeral 1 in the acronym with a capital *O*, the joke turns the acronym into an utterance widely associated with Santa Claus—*Ho ho ho*—transforming the word from fearful into pleasurable. Removal of this fear provides a release. At the same time, the introduction of an element associated with Christmas, a time of joy and celebration, reminds the audience of more pleasant times. Thus, while the removal of the fearful aspects of the acronym by itself produces a more pleasant situation, the addition of the holiday element reinforces this, and the resultant symbiosis creates a stronger release.

Notable in these last three examples is the lack of an appropriation of the H1N1 acronym in the same fashion as those displayed with SARS and AIDS, where new words are substituted in acrostic fashion. An obvious explanation for this has to do with the nature of the original acronyms. Whereas SARS and AIDS are acronyms for terms that have, if not familiar, at least pronounceable words, the H1N1 acronym provides no such firm ground. The *H* and *N* stand for *hemagglutinin* and *neuraminidase*, respectively, which are viral proteins, and the numeral 1 after each letter refers to the subtype of that protein, hemagglutinin having sixteen subtypes and neuraminadase having nine (Picard 2009). Such terms hardly roll off the tongue, and while easily located online, they could hardly be considered common knowledge. By itself, this makes the process of appropriation more difficult. But the H1N1 acronym also consists of numbers as well as letters, and numbers do not make for easy acrostics. Perhaps this explains the proliferation of the other forms of appropriation described above.

Other differences could be noted regarding H1N1 jokes and those that relate to other diseases, many of which involve surface-level constructs such as different places, times, events, and punch lines. But when examined for deeper constructs, far more similarities than differences emerge. To begin with, all of these outbreaks *have* jokes, and whether these jokes were created to challenge conventions, deal with taboo topics, or provide a release from the stress of the outbreak (or, as is more likely, some combination of all three), the impetus of those jokes was the outbreak itself, evincing humor as a common reaction to disease. Moving deeper, these jokes have a finite set of constructs, or building blocks. Racism constitutes one of these blocks and is featured widely in jokes and many forms of disease narratives. Paranoia is another block and often appears hand-in-hand with racism. Where there is racism and paranoia, there is often othering, which leads to the stigmatization of a different race, group, or person as culpable. Closing the circle, othering often leads to questions of etiology: Where did this come from, and how did it get here?

When it comes to disease-related humor, only a few building blocks can construct thousands of narratives. Such a multiplicity of narratives can be explained in several ways, beginning with the realization that each individual has the opportunity to use those basic building blocks in new ways. A wider explanation is that, despite the laughter that many of these jokes are intended to elicit, they are all ultimately quite serious and express real human concerns about sickness and mortality.

THE CURTAIN FALLS?

On April 26, 2009, the US Department of Health and Human Services (HHS), noting the emergence of a new strain of the H1N1 influenza virus that had the capacity to become a pandemic, declared a Public Health Emergency (PHE). On June 23, 2010, that PHE expired without challenge for renewal, marking a significant shift in the government's attitudes about the seriousness of the pandemic. Official reports from the HHS list the reasons for this shift as follows:

> Many factors have changed since H1N1 flu first arrived in the United States. More than 80 million Americans have now been vaccinated against H1N1 influenza. And, today, a little over a year after declaring our initial public health

emergency, the Centers for Disease Control and Prevention . . . reports that there is little 2009 H1N1 virus currently circulating in the United States. Hospitalizations from influenza-like illnesses have fallen to their usual low levels for this time of year, and there is no longer a significant demand for the medical countermeasures that required a public health emergency determination and emergency use authorizations. It is likely that other countries will be taking similar actions in the coming weeks and months based on their own assessments. ("H1N1 Influenza Public Health Emergency Determination Expired on June 23" 2010)

Although the report recognized the absence of the H1N1 virus in the United States, it still cautioned the public to take "seasonal flu seriously" and advocated hand washing, coughing and sneezing into sleeves or tissues, and staying at home when ill as the best preventative measures.

This report was not the final word on the pandemic. Not even the WHO's August 10, 2010, declaration of the end of the H1N1 pandemic (see "2009 H1N1 Flu" 2010) brought the discussions to a close. The HHS acknowledged that the virus was still circulating and could potentially return during the 2010–2011 flu season. There were also ongoing criticisms of how the government was handling the situation, the most serious of which called into question the WHO's strategies and objectives as well as their ties to pharmaceutical companies. The most prominent and serious of these objections came from the *British Medical Journal* (*BMJ*), wherein a June 3, 2010, article titled "WHO and the Pandemic Flu 'Conspiracies'" began with this abstract:

> Key scientists advising the World Health Organization on planning for an influenza pandemic had done paid work for pharmaceutical firms that stood to gain from the guidance they were preparing. These conflicts of interest have never been publicly disclosed by WHO, and WHO has dismissed inquiries into its handling of the A/H1N1 pandemic as "conspiracy theories." (Cohen and Carter 2010)

The six-page article then enumerates a laundry list of complaints and concerns, including that the WHO exaggerated the severity of the virus, claiming 2 billion possible cases; that they took advice from several experts with strong ties to Roche and other pharmaceutical companies; and that the WHO changed how a pandemic could be defined by removing the phrase "enormous numbers of deaths and illness" from the definition, thus making it easier to define the H1N1 outbreak as a pandemic.

In reply, the WHO published two separate statements, one on June 8, 2010, addressed to the editors of *BMJ*, and a more general version two days later. Both responses attempted to clear up the concerns specified by the *BMJ*. Dr. Margaret Chan, Director-General of the WHO, personally wrote the June 8 statement, stating at one point, "let me be perfectly clear on one point. At no time, not for one second, did commercial interests enter my decision-making" (Chan 2010). She further reminded the *BMJ* editors of comments she made on June 11, 2009, when she "drew attention to the fact that the worldwide number of deaths was small, and clearly stated that we did not expect to see a sudden and dramatic jump in the number of severe or fatal infections," and called for the formation of an independent review committee to evaluate the WHO's performance during the pandemic (Chan 2010).

The WHO's second statement more strongly addressed the remainder of the *BMJ*'s claims. In it, the WHO admitted changing the definition of a pandemic but noted that such changes are common, and they created the current definition before the outbreak's inception:

> Definitions changed over time in line with . . . evolving knowledge and the need to increase the precision and practical applicability of phase definitions. The 2009 guidelines, including definitions of a pandemic and the phases leading to its declaration, were finalized in February 2009. The new H1N1 virus was neither on the horizon at that time nor mentioned in the document.

Claims that the WHO employed experts with ties to pharmaceutical industries were also admitted, though explained by noting that the small population of experts present in the United States, as well as the WHO's need to communicate with pharmaceutical industries, makes such ties unavoidable. Furthermore, all expert advisers are required "to declare their professional and financial interests when they participate in advisory groups and consultations," and these declarations are examined to determine the existence of any conflicts ("The International Response to the Influenza Pandemic: WHO Responds to the Critics" 2010).

A preliminary examination of these responses seems to absolve the WHO of wrongdoing, and as Chan stated in one of the closing paragraphs in her statement:

> Without question, the BMJ feature and editorial will leave many readers with the impression that WHO's decision to declare a pandemic was at least partially influenced by a desire to boost the profits of the pharmaceutical industry. The bottom line, however, is that decisions to raise the level of pandemic alert were based on clearly defined virological and epidemiological criteria. It is hard to bend these criteria, no matter what the motive. (Chan 2010)

Only time will tell whether these accusations will continue to harangue the WHO or whether that organization has responded with enough sufficiency to quell conspiracy theorists. If the past is any indicator, the world will be hearing of these matters for a long time to come.

NOTES

1 In direct conflict, a Boston-area news report filed twenty-nine days later, on February 5, stated, "Federal health officials report that for the fourth week in a row, no states have widespread flu activity" (Germano 2010). Such conflicting information may have contributed to public uncertainty.

2 Worth noting here is that the H5N1 "bird flu" virus has also been claimed by conspiracy theorists as a vehicle for the purposeful depopulation of the world—see ProTo Fire Fox 2008.

3 The version examined here is only one of many, as the conspiracy exists in various forms on dozens of websites, not all of which use the PowerPoint slide show format or need to be circulated by e-mail.

4 The transcriptions presented here of these PowerPoint slides use a single forward slash—/—to indicate where hard returns and forced line breaks appeared in the original material.

5 The European Centre for Disease Prevention and Control lists total deaths for the H1N1 pandemic, including 2010 fatalities, as 14,286 (European Centre for Disease Prevention and Control 2010).

6 The 807,349:1 odds provided by the NSC mean that some 8,423 people died in a bathtub in 2009.

7 The field of folklore usually defines myths as sacred narratives, consisting of traditional, often religious, stories dealing with supernatural beings, heroes, or ancestors that are often used to pass down important cultural mores and values. A folklorist would therefore not refer to the examples in this section as myths—misunderstandings, confusions, or inaccurate statements would be more appropriate.

8 Again, the word *appropriate* here means that the incongruity is relevant and necessary for the joke to be perceived as humorous, and not that the type of humor is proper or politically correct.

8

Full Circle
The Recycling of Disease Narratives

THE DISEASE-RELATED NARRATIVES THAT FILL THIS BOOK were collected from hundreds of oral and written sources, in some cases have existed for scores of years, and have circulated in dozens of countries. In addition, these narratives have been told at varying times about a significant number of diseases. The SARS narratives alone constitute an adequate cross-section of the rumors, gossip, legends, jokes, and other oral forms that circulated during the 2003 epidemic. But when these are placed against narratives pertaining to AIDS, Hansen's disease, influenza, syphilis, H1N1, etc., patterns begin to emerge. Like photo mosaics, where thousands of individual photos are grouped by tone, pattern, and coloring to form a single larger picture, the individual disease narratives in this book construct a larger representation of reality. Underlying the multiple ways this new, larger picture can be interpreted is how the picture is representational of the health beliefs of millions, if not billions, of people.

This is not to say that everyone has the same beliefs—any statement to that effect ignores decades of scholarship. It means that, at least concerning novel diseases, people use certain sets of narratives to discuss the presence of illness, mediate their fears of it, come to terms with it, and otherwise incorporate its presence into their daily routines. Past experience with disease does influence future perception of newer diseases (see Duffin and Sweetman 2006). Some of these narratives express a harsher, more paranoid view of reality than others, some are openly racist and xenophobic, and some are more concerned with issues of treatment and prevention than blame—but all revolve around a single emotion in all its many forms: fear.

If all of the individual narratives that comprise this larger picture are borne of fear, if all these narratives can be separated into a finite subset of mediating reactions, and if the narratives in these subsets can be organized

DOI: 10.7330/9780874219296.c008

by common themes and elements, it is thus possible to establish at least a basic typology of disease narratives. This does seem to be the case, and though this volume is one of the first to examine SARS narratives at length in relation to this organizational method, it is not the first volume to recognize the existence of such a method. As Diane Goldstein says in the introduction to *Once Upon A Virus*:

> As I write this introduction, another deadly disease, SARS (Severe Acute Respiratory Syndrome) has hit the world stage. In these initial weeks of the outbreak of the disease, one cannot help but notice that epidemiologists and the general public alike have become obsessed with story making. While members of the public engage in rumors about who has the disease, places and people to avoid, mandatory quarantines, and government health conspiracies, epidemiologists create and recreate plots that they hope will establish links of transmission. Both sets of stories mirror the narratives discussed in this volume. They explore notions of animal origins, superinfectors, hidden carriers, and numerous other themes entrenched in our stories about AIDS but also seen in reaction to virtually any devastating disease we have experienced historically. Already, only a few weeks into the SARS outbreak, we can see how story comes to define risk. (Goldstein 2004, xiv)

In fact, the nature of the disease itself is almost of secondary consideration when it comes to narrative: regardless of which outbreak is making headlines—whether it's AIDS or SARS or H1N1—the basic stories are the same. Narratives are recirculated from one outbreak to the next, modified not in their themes but in the specific details necessary to link the narratives to current situations.

An example of a single narrative that exemplifies this process of modification is the blood libel legend. This legend is at least two thousand years old, and in its earliest forms was either anti-Semitic (describing the murder of Catholics by Jews) or anti-Catholic (describing the murder of Roman children by recent converts to Catholicism). In both cases the murders were done ritually, as part of religious ceremonies. In the several centuries that have passed since this legend's inception, many different groups have been accused of ritual murder, and the narrative has been altered to fit. Communists, Chinese people, neo-pagans, Satanists, and gang members have all been fingered as guilty of such crimes. While the main theme of ritual murder has remained in each case, the specifics of the story—names, dates, places, and other details—have been updated to increase the story's relevance, believability, and impact (Alexander 1987; Bennett 2005b; Dundes 1991; Rives 1996).

It is true that not every disease narrative has a history as long as the blood libel legend, or with as many permutations. But a significant enough number of these narratives do contain sufficient examples to allow for the construction of a typology (see Appendix). The importance of such a typology will allow scholars to cross-reference and examine previous narratives as well as present to those scholars a list of common themes and elements that can be expected to appear in future outbreaks. Since xenophobia is a common element in the collected narratives, it is logical to assume that it will also be a common element in future narratives. And since most major outbreaks have resulted in conspiracy theories detailing governmental deception, secrecy, and misconduct, it can be assumed that future outbreaks will contain similar theories. Recognizing that these patterns exist, and are relatively easy to isolate, is a boon for health care workers everywhere who are forced to deal with the negative effects of such narratives. Understanding that any new disease outbreak is going to result in conspiracy theories, xenophobic gossip, etiological arguments, and so forth, and that these will appear in a finite number of permutations, allows health workers the opportunity to better prepare themselves for the onslaught.

An initial examination of this idea also points to the possibility of using this information to counter such narratives even before they are born. But narrative forms such as legends—especially contemporary legends—and conspiracy theories are notoriously difficult to eradicate post-creation, and while knowledge of impending racist narratives is beneficial, predicting the exact narrative forms that such racism will take in future narratives is an extraordinarily complex task, perhaps even an impossible one.

What *can* be addressed here is the possibility of eradicating or countering narratives that do exist. This is not a new idea, having been discussed in academic circles for the last few decades. The problem is that narratives have a troubling tendency to exist: little seems to affect them. Allan J. Kimmel and Robert Keefer discovered that the transmission of an AIDS rumor was strongly linked to the anxiety caused by the rumor—that is, the more anxious someone felt about the information contained in the rumor, the more likely they were to pass it on. In addition, rumors seen as personally consequential and relevant were more likely to be believed and cause anxiety (Kimmel and Keefer 1991). Spreading rumors is thus a purposive action for both narrator and listener (Bordia and DiFonzo 2005). This information alone points out the difficulties inherent in eliminating a narrative: any rumor—and presumably any narrative form, such as legend or gossip—that is deemed important or pertinent enough to provoke a fearful reaction is likely to be retold. Such is the nature of people. We naturally want to warn those close to us of danger.

But spreading rumors is not an action that merely involves attempting to protect those close to us. It is also a social act, shaped by the communities we have been raised in. We think in patterns taught to us by friends and family (Fine and Khawaja 2005). Rumors are in this sense understood within the context of "local meanings and recent histories" and "are drawn from a store of historical and contemporary allusions that have been kept alive and given new and renewed meanings by the fractious arguments of diverse social groups" (White 2005, 241, 244). Rumors are often grounded in prejudices and misunderstandings so old that they are not recognized as inaccurate, so any attempt to challenge the rumor inherently challenges deeply ingrained belief systems and ideas.

Making the issue of dealing with racist rumors more difficult is that, as Gary Alan Fine has noted, the modern world has proven their model breeding ground:

> The transformation of the global economy and the expansion of transnational migration patterns have proven to be a rich source of rumor and fears for national identity. Moreover, even in the most remote corners of the globe people are increasingly aware of diversity. With expanding migration between developing and developed nations, the character and actions of migrants have become more salient. As the homogeneous cultures of industrialized nation-states mutate, becoming more multicultural, rumors that target recent immigrants (legal or illegal, temporary or permanent) frequently appear. These workers bring their own cultural patterns, including such diverse matters as food preferences, standards of cleanliness, public decorum, sexuality, family dynamics, and religious beliefs. These patterns of behavior and display may contrast with those of the receiving nation, leading to misunderstanding, suspicion, and mistrust. Observations of cultural diversity are transformed into rumor alleging that these cultural choices are immoral or dangerous. The majority transforms events, some real and some imagined, into patterns of depravity through truth claims reported in rumor. (Fine 2005, 3–4)

Dealing with rumors in this light is a truly Herculean task, for not only can racist sentiments be deep-seated, but they can also be continually aggravated by the influx of foreign peoples into "our" territory. It is not even necessary that a narrator *believe* a rumor to have some impetus for passing it on—only a belief that the events in the narrative *could have* happened (Fine and Khawaja 2005).

Moving beyond rumor, Véronique Campion-Vincent has noted the popularity of conspiracy theories—how they are used "to provide meaningful and accurate explanations of the world's condition" and are "part of an everyday struggle to make sense of a rapidly changing world" (Campion-Vincent 2005, 103). These narratives are used—wittingly or not—to increase group cohesion through the naming of enemies, whether those enemies are from other races or ethnicities or are members of different classes within the ethnicity of the conspiracy theorist. Fine has remarked that the telling of antigovernment conspiracy theories reveals "uncertainty about procedural democracy . . . [the narratives] frequently reflect the inchoate disaffection of citizens, diverting allegiance, but lacking any positive program of change" (2005, 5). Conspiracy theories constitute important and critical avenues for the discussion of unknown situations, providing form and shape to, and release from, stress. Like rumors, conspiracy theories exist because they serve a purpose and because the need for informational vacuums to be filled is strong enough to support the existence of the narrative.

Not surprisingly, those articles that deal with the issue of eradicating rumors and conspiracy theories are mixed in their judgments of the effectiveness of any given method. Bill Ellis discusses several methods in his essay "Legend/AntiLegend: Humor as an Integral Part of the Contemporary Legend Process," beginning with the idea that most scholars have focused their efforts on the birth and spread of such narratives rather than on their demise. He then states,

> Only three factors, according to Fine and Turner, combine to make a rumor (or legend) disappear: boredom, saturation of the community, and intervention of social interest groups . . . That is, legends are news, and when everyone has heard them, they cease to have the attraction of novelty, and so when more credible information is available, they have no reason for being. (Ellis 2005, 123)

So one possible response to the question of eradicating a narrative is to simply wait it out—it will eventually get rid of itself. Proof of this is found in the SARS epidemic. As soon as the virus disappeared and ceased to make headlines, the stories died. This tactic, however, is problematic in an outbreak, where the narrative can cause massive psychological and even real-world damage before it ceases to circulate. In such instances, it would be better to contain the narrative to the largest extent possible. Waiting for the legend to take care of itself is also problematic because, as with the blood libel legend, some narratives—even those two thousand years after their creation—are arguably more popular than ever. Narratives are additionally continually reshaped and are almost infinitely flexible in their ability to adapt to new situations. Quoting Fine and Turner again, Ellis notes that "some legends may not die so much as they *dive*, that is, remain latent in the communities in which they circulate, ready to be verbalized later as a social need arises" (123–24, emphasis in original).

If waiting for the legend to die out is not an option, the logical conclusion is to attempt to force its early demise. Many efforts have been made in this direction, but as Ellis notes, the results have been inconsistent:

Fine and Turner concede that formal rumor control has had "mixed success," and in any case there are no control data available to determine what might have happened in the absence of such efforts. Official denials do no harm, they conclude, but whether they in fact do shorten the duration of rumors by providing "authoritative information" is unclear . . . Some research by Jean-Noël Kapferer . . . on the Mickey Mouse LSD legend, in fact, suggests that formal efforts to debunk legends are not especially convincing and may in fact communicate the rumor to those who have not yet heard it. If the authority challenging the legend is seen as a low-credibility source, then taking time to deny a claim suggests that it may be doing so to cover up its own culpability. (124)

In addition, as Jean-Bruno Renard points out, Western postwar generations have been found to be more likely to question and distrust governments and are thus more receptive to conspiracy theories and other such negative narratives (Renard 2005). Patricia A. Turner (1993) points out further problems with official denials by noting that African Americans often dismiss such denials—such as the CIA creating AIDS or the KKK owning Church's Chicken—because of a deep-seated distrust of a primarily white government and economy. Because of this, any attempts to deal with rumors and gossip must take into account the tenacity of such narratives, along with race and ethnic relations that may prohibit or lessen the effectiveness of communications.

One potential avenue for dealing with unwanted narratives is the antilegend, a parody narrative designed to counter a legend by presenting its information in a humorous, satiric, or scornful light. By "creatively distorting" the narrative structure of a legend, the antilegend can prove more effective in demonstrating the logical flaws and absurdities present in legends (Ellis 2005, 124). Ellis note that antilegends have at times proven effective, citing the antilegends of the Good Times computer virus legend, which have not only fairly effectively halted the circulation of the original legend but have proven more popular in the long run than the original legend. The problems with antilegends, however, are (1) that they can exist comfortably beside the original legends, commenting on them rather than negating them, and (2) "the dynamics of the antilegend require a conduit that supports both belief in and skepticism about some of the elements of the legend on which it is based" (Ellis 135). In other words, in order for an antilegend to succeed, there must be some extant skepticism about the original legend, or at least an environment in which a skeptical attitude can be fostered. Given the right circumstances, an antilegend might prove effective. In the case of Turner's African American dismissals of official denials, however, an antilegend would stand far less of a chance of succeeding in negating the original legend, as that legend exists because of deep-seated distrust and strong emotions. There are few chinks in such armor into which an anti-legend could be thrust. Similarly, it is questionable whether an antilegend would prove effective in dealing with narratives that espouse racism and xenophobia. Such sentiments are also entrenched and may have been present in an individual's psychological matrix since early childhood, having been learned from parents and peers.

The methods discussed thus far in dealing with problematic narratives have all come from folklore and related fields. There are, however, approaches from other disciplines and organizations that will prove useful in combating the dissemination of these rumors. One comes from the US Department of Justice (DOJ), which, between January 25 and 27, 2009, tested the security awareness of its own workers by sending them hoax e-mails that attempted to phish for sensitive "supply account information related to the federal retirement savings program" (Mills 2009). Those workers who responded to the e-mails and provided the sensitive information were contacted shortly thereafter by superior officers and retrained in their security awareness. According to a DOJ spokesperson, such training programs have been conducted for at least three years.

Although this approach was only intended to combat problems within the DOJ, its implications and possible applications did not go unnoticed outside that agency. At least one source has claimed that an altered use of such a program could spell the "end of spam" and could function as follows:

A number of government security organisations around the world—think national spam centres—would routinely send out what looked like spam to all email users.

In appearance, these would be identical to the real thing: they would offer all the improbable improvements to parts of your anatomy, or access to multi-million pound bank accounts for very little effort. All the usual—and highly-effective—tricks of social engineering would be deployed in order to persuade users to respond.

Most people would simply ignore these fake spams, as they do other junk that they find in their inboxes. But a few—as always—would respond. That's good: for these are precisely the people who make spam viable, providing enough incentive for spammers to send out billions of mails to the rest of us.

These are also the people who click on infected Word documents, or visit dodgy Web sites and infect the rest of the ecosystem. So it is precisely these people that need to be educated.

The fake spam would allow that to happen. For instead of receiving information about wondrous pills, or large sums of money, those who succumb to the siren-like call of the spam would, instead, receive a gentle warning—by email or from special Web sites the fake spam respondents would be directed to—from the national spam centres explaining that had this been a real spam email, they would have suffered various negative consequences, and that maybe it would be best to ignore such offers in the future. (Moody 2009)

Although Glyn Moody's suggestions do not address narratives that crop up during disease outbreaks, it is not difficult to imagine a slight revision of these fake spam e-mails that could incorporate such rumors. The efficacy of such a system is debatable—not to mention the problems associated with setting up such a program in the first place—but it does seem to offer a promising new approach.

One of the most useful sources of suggestions on the problem of rumors is the field of psychology. The psychological study of rumor transmission is usually credited as beginning in 1945 with the work of Floyd H. Allport and Milton Lepkin, who found that the more false war-time rumors were heard, the more likely people believed them. In addition, Allport and Lepkin concluded that subjects were more likely—33.9 percent more likely, to be exact—to believe a rumor they had heard before, compared to a novel rumor. They did, however, find an inverse correlation between rumor belief and the number of times a subject had read the "Rumor Clinic" column in a local newspaper, leading them to conclude that official rumor debunking does have some measurable effect (Allport and Lepkin 1945).

Allport and Lepkin's study may have been revolutionary, but it was not the last of its kind. It was also not the definitive study, as other researchers have come to contradictory conclusions. In 2007, for example, Schwarz et al. conducted a study wherein participants were given an official CDC flier containing "myths" about the flu vaccine. The flyer followed a simple format, presenting in sentence form various commonly held beliefs, labeling them clearly as either true or false. Immediately after reading the flyer, participants were questioned on its contents, and initially they demonstrated high levels of comprehension, misidentifying only 4 percent of the incorrect statements as true and 3 percent of the correct statements as false. Only thirty minutes later, the test was re-administered, and this time the participants misidentified 15 percent of the incorrect statements as true while the percentage of correct statements wrongly identified as false remained stable. These findings were not unexpected, the authors explaining that the human brain has a tendency to assume that familiar statements are true, which explains why the number of false positives increased, as well as why the number of false negatives did not (Schwarz et al. 2007).

A second study—reported in the same article—exposed groups of "younger adult" and "older adult" participants either once or three times to statements that were clearly marked as true and false. The subjects were then tested immediately on the contents and again three days later. In almost all cases, the number of true statements misidentified as false was low and rose only marginally over the three-day wait—by roughly 6 percent across the board. But the results for the number of false statements misidentified as true varied widely, and not only over time but also according to age. The young adults given the information only once increased their incorrect answers from 10 percent to 24 percent over the three-day period while the young adults given the information three times increased their errors from 7 percent to 14 percent, showing that, for younger adults, increased repetition improved accurate recall. For the older adults, however, the number of errors for those who heard the information once remained steady at 28 percent, between days one and three, while the older participants who heard the information three times actually *increased* their number of incorrect responses over time, from 17 percent on day one to 40 percent on day three, demonstrating that, for older adults, increased repetition *lessened* accurate recall. Schwarz et al. state that this results from the decreased memory function of older adults, which forces them to rely more on "familiarity" as evidence of truth than recollection of accurate facts (Schwarz et al. 2007).

Additional psychological studies add to the complexities of rumor perception. Weaver et al. determined that repetition increases the likelihood of a statement being determined as prevalent among a group and that the statement does not have to be made by all members of that group. In fact, an outsider who only hears a statement repeated by one member of a group is likely to assume that statement holds true for every member of the group. And within that group, participants were more likely to agree with that frequently repeated statement, even though they knew it came from only one member (Weaver, et al. 2007).

The last piece of the puzzle comes from Ruth Mayo, Yaacov Schul, and Eugene Burnstein, who examined the effects of time on the memory of certain statements. The researchers gave participants a series of descriptions, then examined recollection over time based on the presence of "bi-polar" and "uni-polar" negations. Briefly, "a bi-polar description has a well-defined opposite construct which is easily accessible, whereas a uni-polar description does not" (Mayo, Schul, and Burnstein 2004, 440). An example of a bi-polar description is "warm," which has the easily understandable opposite of "cold," whereas a uni-polar description would be "responsible." The word *responsible* does not have an easily accessible opposite; the most immediate antonym is "not responsible" or "irresponsible," which is linguistically far closer to the parent word than "hot" is to "cold"—and in fact "not responsible" and "irresponsible" both contain the parent word in the negation.

The results of the study found that, while 83 percent of respondents accurately remembered the bi-polar description "not warm" as meaning "not warm," only 62 percent accurately remembered the uni-polar description "not responsible"—the other 38 percent misremembered it as "responsible" (444). In real-world terms, this study gives reasons for why people cleared of criminal charges are still stigmatized afterwards: someone who is declared "not guilty of harassment" is more likely to be remembered as "guilty of harassment" due to the uni-polar nature of the word *harassment*. The study concludes in part that at times one is better off not denying a false claim. Instead, a more effective approach is to create a new, positive claim that makes no reference to the false claim (i.e., declaring, "I am innocent" instead of "I am not guilty").

The implications of these studies in terms of rumor negotiation are vast. Many rumor control methods have been historically ineffective and often result in the dispersal of incorrect information rather than its correction. The above studies help provide reasons for such results and point toward a course of action that, at least theoretically, should provide rumor debunkers with a better outcome. Not all rumors are harmful, and thus not all merit such attention as might result in their demise. But for dangerous or harmful rumors, a few strategies can be employed to help counter their effects. Summarizing the information presented in the previous paragraphs, we come up with the following series of statements: (1) if we naturally assume that familiar statements are true and (2) we tend to misremember false statements as true and (3) if bi-polar descriptions are better remembered than their uni-polar counterparts, then (4) accurate, oft-repeated, positive descriptions are superior to efforts made in rehashing narratives only to deny their veracity. Studies would be needed to confirm these conclusions, but the logic behind them suggests that in a selection of disease narratives, the following courses of action would find better results:

1) Instead of denying the presence of SARS in an Asian neighborhood, city officials could comment that the disease has equally affected all parts of the city—or alternately, that SARS has only been discovered to exist in other cities (if there is no evidence that the virus has broached city limits).

2) Instead of denying that AIDS can be transmitted by having sex with a virgin (or any other harmful, unofficial course of action), health officials could comment that the only proven treatments are FDA-recognized drugs.

3) Instead of denying that smoking prevents people from contracting SARS, health officials could comment that the best courses of action are to wear a mask, avoid crowded places, and stay away from people who are infected.

4)   Instead of denying conspiracy theories about the origins of H1N1, health officials could comment that current evidence points toward an animal virus that has adapted to humans as the source of the infections.

In each of these cases, the negative rumor has been bypassed entirely, and the answers instead rely on repeating accurate, positive information. Inaccurate information is neither repeated nor summarized to avoid its further spread. For best results, the accurate, positive information should be repeated frequently to help solidify its public recognition and familiarity. Any phrase that begins with "X is not true" should be avoided altogether, as should, in general, the word *not*, as it too often leads to confusion, especially when used in conjunction with uni-polar descriptions. Response to rumors should be rapid, for best results, and wherever possible, presented by people who have some recognized authority, either on a local or national level.

Who should these authorities be? Church leaders, mayors, police, and doctors are all fine candidates. But individually, these people have only limited exposure to a small section of a city. In order to get the messages across, a dispersal system is needed—one that is nearly ubiquitous, highly visible, and frequently used. Such a system already exists: the media. Consider this excerpt from interviewee Luis (2005), who was asked how the public reacted to the epidemic:

> Based on what I see . . . you couldn't go on the bus. People tried to avoid sneezing and coughing. [laughs] That was very, very obvious sight you can see in the public. Even in churches or public places, people sneezing, people try to turn their head away, you know? [laughs] It's really very scary during that time. Because especially newspapers say that it can be transmitted by, when you sneeze, saliva or something from your nasal excretion. Those are the things I remember quite well . . . It's just human nature to be cautious. It's normal. You try to avoid, you know? Especially newspapers, how this can be contracted, then they tell you what to do, what to avoid. We just follow most of this from what we heard in the news . . . You open the TV, you hear SARS stories. You see the, you read the newspaper, you have SARS stories front page. (Luis 2005)

Another example, this one from Angel and Rosita (2005), who, when asked if they had heard any rumors about the origin of SARS said:

> Rosita: Well for us, there's always it's coming from civet rats or something from China, so that's in our mind that that's where it came from. And then it moved to Hong Kong, and one person from Hong Kong brought it over. That was very clear in my mind, that was what everybody kept saying. I didn't hear any other sources, did you?
> Angel: That's the only one, yes.
> Rosita: Because it was very clear, they kept saying, "This is exactly where it came from."

In fact, of the thirteen people interviewed for this chapter, twelve mentioned that media sources provided them with at least part of the information they had gathered during the epidemic, and several informants stated that media sources provided them with the greater part of their critical information. It is true that some of this information wasn't correctly recalled—the SARS virus came from civet cats, not civet "rats," as Rosita stated—but even here the wrong answer is still close to the right one. More importantly, Rosita's answer demonstrates the power of media sources in dispersing information.

These findings agree with at least two studies of the SARS crisis. The first was conducted in Qatar and examined the knowledge, attitudes, and practices of the people of the region in response to the epidemic. The researchers handed out questionnaires at airports and health centers and ultimately received 1,386 responses. The results showed that 73 percent of respondents were aware of the highly infectious nature of SARS, 69.9 percent recognized that close contact with an infected person was a primary transmission vector, and 67.4 percent knew that a high fever was the first symptom of infection. Roughly half of the subjects reported having gained most of their knowledge of SARS from media sources—primarily television and radio programs (Bener and Al-Khal 2004). The second article detailed the results of a study of community responses in Hong Kong to the SARS epidemic. The study consisted of a number of telephone surveys conducted during the crisis, examining the measures people thought effective in preventing the spread of the virus. Of the 1,397 participants, 82 percent rated wearing masks as effective in preventing infection, 93 percent said the same for washing hands, and 75 percent said the same for disinfecting the home—and these numbers remained constant throughout the epidemic. The researchers concluded that government- and media-based dissemination of accurate information in a timely manner was responsible for the high numbers of people who provided knowledgeable answers and who so quickly adopted the appropriate SARS prevention measures (Lau et al. 2003).

The media thus *does* work, at least in the sense of serving as an effective vehicle for the distribution of information. The problem lies in the type of information that is disseminated. Following the steps laid out in this chapter would greatly increase the dispersal of accurate information and inhibit the spread of negative and harmful rumors. Using local spokespersons recognized for their honesty and authority on the matter would also increase the chances that this accurate information would be trusted and believed. Knowing that certain narratives are more likely to appear in epidemics, health officials could better prepare themselves for the kinds of rumors and gossip that they are likely to encounter, and even prepare a short list of accepted responses. Again, real-world tests need to be conducted to prove or disprove these theories, but the simplicity and cleanliness of the logic that underlies them is compelling. With any luck, the next outbreak—whatever it may bring—will be better managed in light of these conclusions.

Epilogue
. . . And the World Moved On?

IN 2003, FOR A FRANTIC FEW MONTHS, SARS brought the world to its knees. But it vanished just as suddenly as it had appeared. Life quickly returned to normal, and for the better part of a decade the disease was all but forgotten.

Then on September 23, 2012, the World Health Organization (WHO) detailed the case of a forty-nine-year-old male Qatari national who had been admitted into an ICU in Qatar on September 7, 2012, presenting acute respiratory syndrome and renal failure. Due to the nature of his symptoms, this man was transferred to a hospital in the United Kingdom on September 11. Subsequent testing by the Health Protection Agency of the United Kingdom revealed that the man had been infected by a coronavirus. The virus itself was novel, having only been encountered once before—earlier that same year, when a sixty-year-old Saudi Arabian national perished after contracting it (World Health Organization 2012b). Over the next three months, the WHO would report seven more cases of infected individuals. By December 21, the WHO had established nine laboratory-confirmed cases of individuals infected with the new strain of coronavirus. Somewhat troublingly, five of those nine victims perished, indicating that, while the virus was not particularly contagious, it was highly dangerous when contracted. Possibly recognizing the potential for public concern, given these statistics and the SARS-like nature of the coronavirus, the update also contained this note: "WHO recognizes that the emergence of a new coronavirus capable of causing severe disease raises concerns because of experience with SARS. Although this novel coronavirus is distantly related to the SARS [coronavirus], they are different. Based on current information, it does not appear to transmit easily or sustainably between people, unlike the SARS virus" (World Health Organization 2012a).

As of this writing, the last published update on this novel coronavirus, now officially called MERS-CoV (for "Middle East respiratory syndrome coronavirus"), dated October 31, 2013, reported a total of 149 laboratory-confirmed infections, including 63 deaths, for a mortality rate of roughly

182

DOI: 10.7330/9780874219296.c009

42 percent. Almost all of the victims contracted the virus in the Middle East, and those few infected outside that region contracted the virus from someone recently returning from there. Because of the continued low transmission rate, the WHO noted that they do "not advice special screening at points of entry with regard to this event," nor do they "recommend the application of any travel or trade restrictions." Instead, they recommend that countries and health care providers "maintain vigilance" and that anyone returning from the Middle East who develops a respiratory infection should be tested for MERS-CoV (World Health Organization 2013).

Given so few confirmed cases of almost any other type of virus, it is difficult to imagine media sources conceiving of the topic as worthy of attention. But the fact that this was a coronavirus resulted in the immediate publication of several news articles. One of the main differences between those articles and the updates released by the WHO was that while the WHO only stated that this novel coronavirus was in the same family of viruses that cause SARS, media sources quickly made a more firm connection. On September 24, only a day after the WHO's first update on the coronavirus, websites for both *TIME* and CNN carried articles with titles containing the phrase "new SARS-like virus," and both articles briefly rehashed the 2003 SARS epidemic, making obvious the connections they thought were present.

The tones of the two articles, however, were markedly different. The article in *TIME* noted that the virus had proven lethal in one case and had badly sickened the second victim, but it also stated that "experts believe it is not very contagious" and featured a quote from Dr. Peter Openshaw, director of the Centre for Respiratory Infection at Imperial College London, who said, "For now, I would be watchful but not immediately concerned" (Park 2012). In contrast, the CNN article struck a darker tone, and while it did recognize that the virus did not seem to be overly contagious, it noted first that the two victims "not only suffered from severe respiratory illness, they also had kidney failure, something that wasn't seen in SARS patients." It followed with a quote from Dr. William Schaffner, chairman of the Department of Preventive Medicine at Vanderbilt University Medical Center, who said, "There is reason to be interested and even concerned" about the new coronavirus, then moved into openly questioning whether there have "been other serious cases that haven't been reported yet" (Falco 2012).

The differences between these two articles is astonishing, especially since both used the WHO's release as one of their main sources, and points again to the problematic nature of the media as a reliable source of unbiased, objective information. Readers interested enough in this new virus to surf through several media sources for information would likely be left unsure as to whether or not they should be concerned, and anyone who only read the CNN article would walk away with an entirely different set of information than anyone who only read the article on *TIME*'s website.

A second point of interest that emerges from this novel coronavirus comes from the public reactions expressed as comments to these news articles. Only eighteen hours after the CNN article appeared online, it had gained 103 comments, 18 of which bore an eerie resemblance to those expressed during the 2003 SARS epidemic. The first comment, posted by someone taking the name "Mary Jane," drew on the identities of the two victims of the coronavirus to conclude that the disease was "More proof that Muslims are dirty people ruining the planet." Some small comfort can be gained from the fact that, of the 31 comments posted in direct response to Mary Jane, the vast majority took offense, many calling her comment racist. But other comments agreed with Mary Jane, such as one by "Lixi," who noted, "Mary's right. Islam is filth and we let them into our countries with their intestinal diseases, with their developmental delays born from an inbreeding program. Just throw in some Ebola, Influenza, Meningitis and Aids and you have yourself a muslim buffet." As with the 2003 SARS epidemic and the 2009 H1N1 pandemic, the process of othering is immediately present: this disease came from somewhere else, and the people responsible for it are lesser humans.

Another set of comments to the CNN article evoked the same aura of conspiracy theory present in 2003. One poster, "Dondi Cook," said, "Relax and breath deeply the tainted air . . . This must be the super virus I've been heareing so much about in the alternative Media . . . It iis man made by the United States government to decimate a large portion of the WORLD Population and is Obama's Brain-Child." Another, posted by "Jay Hobe Sound," stated, "One might reasonably wonder if this SARS-like virus is a man-made virus that was released into the population by accident or was it released into the population for a sinister reason. It is very realistic to realize that the potential for a soft-weapon like a virus is both possible and plausible." A third respondent, "doubt it," openly called the two cases "Biological warfare," seemed to wonder if the existence of the new virus was someone "just seein' if it would work," and closed by positing "maybe we could put in those planes that make chem trails then we could completely destroy humanity. Looks like that's where we are going."

The existence of such comments reveals again the cyclical nature of disease narratives and demonstrates that, even in this new millennium, humans continue to react to novel disease outbreaks the same way we have for the greater part of recorded history. While SARS may be forever wiped from the Earth, the fears and attitudes that underscored the narratives that sprang up around the disease are as present now as they have ever been. The recent H1N1 and novel coronavirus outbreaks further reveal that racism and xenophobia still seethe just under the surface of humanity and establishes that humans will continue to create legends, rumors, jokes, and bits of gossip to mediate the fears and stresses that result from the introductions of novel diseases.

Furthermore, those news articles that covered the 2012 coronavirus attacks reveal that the media is as guilty now of scaremongering as ever.[1] American novelist and polemicist Upton Sinclair reportedly once said, "It is difficult to get a man to understand something when his salary depends upon his not understanding it." In the current climate, it seems more appropriate to modify this statement: "It is difficult to get a journalist not to make a big deal out of a little situation when his salary depends upon it." It is imperative that media sources begin to recognize their roles in spreading rumor and legend and the damage that they can cause. By repeating racist narratives—even if only as examples—newspaper and television journalists, as well as their editors and managers, are complicit in the hate crimes and xenophobia that follows.

But such blame cannot be solely placed upon journalists and media sources. They are indeed selling a problematic product, but they can only keep selling it because someone is buying. We the people are creating the information vacuums that these xenophobic narratives fill, and if fingers should be pointed anywhere, they should point toward the public. Why then place such emphasis on having media sources alter their practices when the problem lies with those who demand the narratives? Because it is far easier to ask a score of businesses to change than it is to demand the same from millions of individuals. For if the former task is daunting, the latter is truly Sisyphean.

***

The purpose of this book has been threefold: demonstrate the links between disease narratives, study the various vectors through which those narratives have been transferred, and examine the effects that these narratives have had on the world. Panic and racism are to disease narratives as the chicken is to the egg: each exists because of the other, whirling together in a generative dance that began long before living memory and will persist long after the child born today dies of old age. But it is not enough to say that these narratives define us. They *are* us: body and soul, flesh and idea, moral and ethic—a connection that goes beyond mere metaphor. And just as these narratives are our friends and homes, they are also our enemies and the things we hate and fear. When in story we crucify and ridicule other people for their differences, we reveal to the world our true faces—the ones we only loosely hold back by our concerns over political correctness and to maintain social niceties.

Looked at properly, disease narratives tell us much about humanity. Not only do they reveal widely held beliefs about a specific disease, but studying them on a larger scale reveals overarching beliefs that pass among diseases, highlighting areas of concern and cultural importance that do not always coincide with those espoused by doctors and scientists. Understanding these differences will lead to improved communications between laypersons and medical personnel and may point to preventive measures that could be undertaken by entities such as the World Health Organization to preemptively combat the racist and xenophobic narratives that come out of epidemics.

The problem, however, lies less in understanding what the narratives say about people than it does in persuading the appropriate entities to begin to take responsibility for their actions and convincing the appropriate people to guard their words more carefully. What we think and say and do constitutes our reality, and a reality that is beset by xenophobia, distrust in authority, fear, and scaremongering is the poorer because of it. Unfortunately, no herbal remedies can fix the media; no vaccines can cure racism. Only concerted, intelligent efforts to educate people in the delicate intricacies of cause-and-effect relationships stand any chance of succeeding. Even so, the changes will not come easy, nor will they come quickly. But we must still attempt them. If we do not, the next world will look a lot like this one.

NOTE

1 A fact that did not go unnoticed in the comments to CNN's September 24, 2012, article. One respondent wrote, "CNN seems to be more overdramatic than a school full of teenagers," while another commented, "I'm surprised they didn't say 'New AIDS type SARS virus from Saudi Arabia sweeping through London starting with 2 people.'"

Appendix

A Contribution toward a Typology of Disease Narratives

APPROPRIATED ACRONYMS

AIDS, 64
H1N1, 162–64
SARS, 64, 111–12

CURES AND PREVENTATIVES

Ace of Spades Showing Saddam Hussein's Face
  SARS, 133
Adjuvants
  H1N1, 153–56
Alcohol, Consumption of (General/Unspecified)
  SARS, 28
Altered Sexual Practices
  AIDS, 132
Antibiotics
  SARS, 133
Bathing and Showering
  AIDS, 132
Bleach
  AIDS, 132
  SARS, 25
Blockading of Villages
  SARS, 84, 96
Campbell's Chicken Noodle Soup
  SARS, 113
Communion Bread/Wafers
  SARS, 19, 116, 131

Covering the Face
  SARS, 85, 112, 136
DayQuil
  SARS, 113
Disinfectants, Antibacterials, and Antiseptics (General/Unspecified)
  SARS, 28
Energy Fields, Manipulation of
  AIDS, 133
  Cancer, 133
  Ebola, 133
  Heart problems, 133
  Malaria 133
  SARS, 133
Face/N-95/Surgical Masks and Shields
  H1N1, 162–63
  SARS, 13, 23, 35, 39, 41, 52, 80, 82, 85, 94–96, 102, 110, 112, 131, 135–36, 180
Firecrackers
  SARS, 28
Fresh Air
  SARS, 37
Gloves
  SARS, 41, 82, 85, 112, 162
Green Bean Soup
  SARS, 29
Hand Sanitizer
  H1N1, 163

DOI: 10.7330/9780874219296.c010

References

Due to the unpredictable archiving practices of online news sources, many of the referenced Internet-based sources are no longer available at the URLs at which they originally appeared. Keeping track of these sources is made the more difficult because of the practice of rewording titles, and even adding to or deleting content from the body of news articles when they are reprinted by secondary news sources. Where possible, alternate sources for these news articles have been located. If no alternate sources were found, the citation will state that the article is "No longer available online."

Aglionby, John. 2003. "Electronic Chip to Detect SARS." *TheGuardian.com*. October 5. http://www.theguardian.com/world/2003/oct/06/sars.johnaglionby (accessed February 22, 2013).

Alexander, Tamar. 1987. "A Legend of the Blood Libel in Jerusalem: A Study of a Process of Folk-Tale Adaptation." *International Folklore Review: Folklore Studies from Overseas* 5: 60–74.

Allen, Ron. 2003. "Hong Kong Fights Stigma of SARS." MSNBC.com. June 23. http://www.nbcnews.com/id/3076734#.USgbh-iRrNM (accessed February 22, 2013).

Allport, Floyd H., and Milton Lepkin. 1945. "Wartime Rumors of Waste and Special Privilege: Why Some People Believe Them." *Journal of Abnormal and Social Psychology* 40 (1): 3–36. http://dx.doi.org/10.1037/h0058110.

Alver, Bente Gullveig. 1982. "Folk Medicine as an Open Medical System." In *Folk Medicine and Health Culture: Role of Folk Medicine in Modern Health Care*, edited by Tuula Vaskilampi and Carol P. MacCormack, 124–39. Kuopio, Finland: University of Kuopio.

Alver, Bente Gullveig. 1995. "The Bearing of Folk Belief on Cure and Healing." *Journal of Folklore Research* 32 (1): 21–33.

Ang, Audra. 2003. "Chinese Turning to Occult to Fight SARS." *Yahoo! News*. May 14. http://pekingdork.blogspot.com/2003/05/chinese-turning-to-occult-to-fight.html (accessed April 2, 2008).

Angel and Rosita. 2005. Interview by author. 12 July. Toronto. Tape recording.

"Another SARS Death in Toronto." 2003. *CNN.com*. June 2. http://www.cnn.com/2003/HEALTH/06/02/sars/index.html (accessed June 2, 2003).

Ansfield, Jonathan. 2004. "SARS Strain May Be Shadow of Its Former Self." *Yahoo! News*. January 14. http://rense.com/general47/SARSstrainmay.htm (accessed April 2, 2008).

Ansfield, Jonathan, and James Peng. 2003. "WHO Says China Doctors Still Under-Reporting SARS." *Yahoo! News*. May 17. http://www.timesofmalta.com/articles/view/20030518/local/who-says-china-doctors-still-under-reporting-sars.149919 (accessed February 22, 2013).

Anthony, Ted. 2004. "U.N. Team Returns to China in SARS Probe." *Yahoo! News*. January 14. http://www.redorbit.com/news/general/42646/un_team_returns_to_china_in_sars_probe/ (no longer available online, accessed April 2, 2008).

DOI: 10.7330/9780874219296.c011

"Are Some Better SARS Transmitters?" 2003. MSNBC.com. April 21. http://www.msnbc .com/news/903175.asp (no longer available online, accessed April 23, 2003).

"Australia Probes Two Suspect SARS Cases." 2004. *Yahoo! News*. January 14. http://www .mywire.com/pubs/AFP/2004/01/14/351328?extID=10051 (no longer available online, accessed April 2, 2008).

"Bats Passed SARS to Civet Cats: Expert." 2005. *Chinadaily.com*. October 4. http://www .chinadaily.com.cn/english/doc/2005-10/04/content_482632.htm (accessed February 22, 2008).

Becker, Howard S. 2002. "Outsiders." In *Deviance: The Interactionist Perspective*, edited by Earl Rubington and Martin S. Weinberg, 7–10. Boston: Allyn & Bacon.

Beech, Hannah. 2003. "How Bad Is It?" *TIME Asia*. May 5. http://content.time.com/time /world/article/0,8599,2047288,00.html (accessed January 24, 2004).

"Beijing Hopeful of SARS Decline." 2003. *CNN.com*. May 9. http://www.cnn.com/2003 /WORLD/asiapcf/east/05/09/sars/index.html (accessed May 14, 2003).

"Beijing Shuts Anti-SARS Headquarters." 2004. *Yahoo! News*. June 2. http://findarticles .com/p/articles/mi_kmafp/is_200406/ai_kepm479235 (accessed April 2, 2008).

Bener, Abdulbari, and Abdullatif Al-Khal. 2004. "Knowledge, Attitude and Practice Towards SARS." *Journal of the Royal Society for the Promotion of Health* 124 (4): 167–70. http://dx.doi.org/10.1177/146642400412400408. Medline:15301314

Benjamin. 2005. Telephone interview by author. 17 August. St. John's, Newfoundland. Tape recording.

Bennett, Gillian. 2005a. *Bodies: Sex, Violence, Disease, and Death in Contemporary Legend*. Jackson: University Press of Mississippi.

Bennett, Gillian. 2005b. "Towards a Revaluation of the Legend of 'Saint' William of Norwich and Its Place in the Blood Libel Legend." *Folklore* 116 (2): 119–39. http:// dx.doi.org/10.1080/00155870500140156.

Berger, Michele Tracy. 2004. *Workable Sisterhood: The Political Journey of Stigmatized Women with HIV/AIDS*. Princeton, NJ: Princeton University Press.

Berger, Peter L., and Thomas Luckmann. 1967. *The Social Construction of Reality: A Treatise in the Sociology of Knowledge*. New York: Anchor.

"Berkeley Eases SARS Restrictions." 2003. MSNBC.com. May 10. http://www.sfgate.com /health/article/UC-Berkeley-relaxes-ban-tied-to-SARS-Campus-now-2649136.php (accessed February 22, 2013).

"Berkeley Turns Away Students from SARS-Hit Regions." 2003. *CNN.com*. May 6. http:// www.cnn.com/2003/EDUCATION/05/05/berkeley.sars.ban/ (accessed May 14, 2003).

Bird, S. Elizabeth. 1996. "CJ's Revenge: Media, Folklore, and the Cultural Construction of AIDS." *Critical Studies in Mass Communication* 13 (1): 44–58. http://dx.doi.org /10.1080/15295039609366959.

Black, William George. (1883) 1967. *Folk-Medicine: A Chapter in the History of Culture*. Nendeln, Liechtenstein: Kraus Reprint.

"Bloody Animal Trade Thrives in Post-SARS China." 2003. *Yahoo! News*. October 26. http://rense.com/general43/asasr.htm (accessed April 1, 2008).

Bodeen, Christopher. 2003a. "China Threatens to Execute SARS Spreaders." *Yahoo! News*. May 15. http://www.emsworld.com/news/10341914/china-threatens-to-execute -sars-spreaders (accessed April 2, 2008).

Bodeen, Christopher. 2003b. "China Bans Wildlife Cuisine on SARS Fears." *Yahoo! News*. May 31. http://www.redorbit.com/news/science/1121/china_bans_wildlife_cuisine _on_sars_fears/ (accessed April 2, 2008).

Bondy, Filip. 2003. "SARS May Wreak Havoc with Games." *MSNBC.com*. April 27. http://www.msnbc.com/news/905923.asp (no longer available online, accessed May 14, 2003).

Bordia, Prashant, and Nicholas DiFonzo. 2005. "Psychological Motivations in Rumor Spread." In *Rumor Mills: The Social Impact of Rumor and Legend*, edited by Gary Alan Fine, Véronique Campion-Vincent, and Chip Heath, 87–101. New Brunswick, NJ: Aldine Transaction.

Bosk, C. L. 1980. "Occupational Rituals in Patient Management." *New England Journal of Medicine* 303 (2): 71–76. http://dx.doi.org/10.1056/NEJM198007103030203. Medline:6104293

"Bouncin' Around: SARS." 2005. *Bouncin' Around* (blog). October 27. http://bouncaround .blogspot.com/2005/10/sars.html (accessed April 27, 2008).

Boyle, Alan. 2003. "Cosmic Log: Quantum Fluctuations in Space, Science and Explora-tion." MSNBC.com. April 23. http://www.msnbc.com/news/750150.asp?0bl=-0 (no longer available online, accessed April 24, 2003).

Brandon, Elizabeth. 1976. "Folk Medicine in French Louisiana." In *American Folk Medi-cine: A Symposium*, edited by Wayland D. Hand, 215–34. Berkeley: University of California Press.

Bray, Marianne. 2003. "'Shortcomings' in HK SARS Outbreak." *CNN.com*. October 2. http://www.cnn.com/2003/WORLD/asiapcf/east/10/02/hk.sars.report/ (accessed October 2, 2003).

Briggs, Charles L. 2005. "Communicability, Racial Discourse, and Disease." *Annual Review of Anthropology* 34 (1): 269–91. http://dx.doi.org/10.1146/annurev. anthro.34.081804.120618.

Brown, DeNeen L. 2003. "SARS Fears Grow in Canada." MSNBC.com. April 18. http://www .msnbc.com/news/902431.asp (no longer available online, accessed April 23, 2003).

Brown, Phil. 1992. "Popular Epidemiology and Toxic Waste Contamination: Lay and Pro-fessional Ways of Knowing." *Journal of Health and Social Behavior* 33 (3): 267–81. http://dx.doi.org/10.2307/2137356. Medline:1401851

Brownlee, Shannon, and Jeanne Lenzer. 2009. "Does the Vaccine Matter?" *Atlantic*. November. http://www.theatlantic.com/magazine/archive/2009/11/does-the-vaccine-matter/307723/ (accessed January 4, 2010).

Brundtland, Gro Harlem, Julio Frenk, and Christopher J. L. Murray. 2003. "WHO Assess-ment of Health Systems Performance." *Lancet* 361 (9375): 2155. http://dx.doi.org /10.1016/S0140-6736(03)13702-6. Medline:12826452

Brunvand, Jan Harold. 1986. *The Mexican Pet: More "New" Urban Legends and Some Old Favorites*. New York: W. W. Norton.

Brunvand, Jan Harold. 2004. *Be Afraid, Be Very Afraid: The Book of Scary Urban Legends*. New York: W. W. Norton.

Buckler, Grant. 2003. "PC Grids Take Aim at SARS in Battle against Disease." *Globe and Mail*. June 19. http://www.theglobeandmail.com/technology/pc-grids-take-aim-at -sars-in-battle-against-disease/article1162899 (accessed April 1, 2008).

Calnan, Michael. 1987. *Health and Illness: The Lay Perspective*. London: Tavistock.

Campbell, Jonathan. "A Cure for AIDS?" http://www.cqs.com/aidscure.htm (accessed October 3, 2007).

Campion-Vincent, Véronique. 2005. "From Evil Others to Evil Elites: A Dominant Pat-tern in Conspiracy Theories Today." In *Rumor Mills: The Social Impact of Rumor and Legend*, edited by Gary Alan Fine, Véronique Campion-Vincent, and Chip Heath, 103–22. New Brunswick, NJ: Aldine Transaction.

"Canada Fears New SARS Outbreak." 2003. *Yahoo! News*. May 31. http://www.accessmy library.com/coms2/summary_0286-23419.407_ITM (accessed April 2, 2008).

"Canada's Active SARS Caseload Falls by Five to 16." 2003. *Yahoo! News*. May 13. http:// www.accessmylibrary.com/coms2/summary_0286-23273415_ITM (no longer avail-able online, accessed April 2, 2008).

"Canada Waits for SARS News as Asia under Control." 2003. *Yahoo! News*, June 2. http://www.smh.com.au/articles/2003/06/01/1054406076596.html (accessed April 3, 2008).

"Canadian Tourist Industry Nervous as SARS Stigma Lingers." 2003. *Yahoo! News*. June 11. http://www.accessmylibrary.com/coms2/summary_0286-23530526_ITM (accessed April 1, 2008).

Cara Nina. 2010. "H1N1." January 8. E-mail to author.

"Carlo Urbani." 2003. *BMJ* 326 (7393): 825.

"Cat Delicacy Could Be SARS Key." 2003. *CNN.com*. May 28. http://articles.chicago tribune.com/2003-05-24/news/0305240137_1_civet-cat-sars-virus-sars-like-virus (accessed February 22, 2013).

Cathcart, Robert. "SARS." http://vitamincfoundation.org/www.orthomed.com/index2 .htm (accessed October 5, 2007).

"CDC Team Arrives in Toronto." 2003. MSNBC.com. April 22. http://www.msnbc.com /news/893950.asp (no longer available online, accessed April 23, 2003).

Centers for Disease Control and Prevention. 2006. "CDC Health Information for International Travel, 2005–2006." http://www.mediscon.com/contissue/inflightdisease transmission/index.html (accessed October 22, 2006).

Centers for Disease Control and Prevention. 2009. "Updated Interim Recommendations for the Use of Antiviral Medications in the Treatment and Prevention of Influenza for the 2009–2010 Season." 2009. H1N1 Flu. December 7. http://www.cdc.gov /h1n1flu/recommendations.htm (accessed June 28, 2010).

Centers for Disease Control and Prevention. 2010. 2009 H1N1 Flu. August 11. http://www.cdc.gov/h1n1flu/ (accessed September 5, 2010).

"Chances of Containing SARS Much Improved—Expert." 2003. *Yahoo! News*. October 30. http://news.yahoo.com/news?tmpl=story2&cid=571&u=/nm/20031030/hl_nm /health_sars_dc&printer=1 (no longer available online, accessed October 30, 2003).

Chan, Margaret. 2010. "WHO Director-General's Letter to BMJ Editors." World Health Organization. June 8. http://www.who.int/mediacentre/news/statements/2010 /letter_bmj_20100608/en/index.html (accessed July 1, 2010).

Chan-Yeung, Moira, and W. C. Yu. 2003. "Outbreak of Severe Acute Respiratory Syndrome in Hong Kong Special Administrative Region: Case Report." *BMJ* 326 (7394): 850–52. http://dx.doi.org/10.1136/bmj.326.7394.850. Medline:12702616

Chen, Melody. 2003. "SARS Epidemic: DOH Denies Rumor of Disease Fatalities." *Taipei Times*. April 27. http://www.taipeitimes.com/News/taiwan/archives/2003/04/27 /203669 (accessed January 24, 2004).

"China Admits First 2004 SARS Death." 2004. *CNN.com*. April 30. http://www.cnn. com/2004/WORLD/asiapcf/04/30/china.sars/index.html (accessed April 30, 2004).

"China Checks SARS Rumor Messages." 2003. MSNBC.com. May 13. http://en.minghui .org/html/articles/2003/5/14/35665p.html (accessed May 14, 2003).

"China Plans SARS Vaccine Trial." 2003. *CNN.com*. November 23. http://www.cnn.com /2003/HEALTH/11/23/sars.vaccine.ap/ (no longer available online, accessed November 23, 2003).

"China Quarantined Too Many in SARS Outbreak—Study." 2003. *Yahoo! News*. October 30. http://www.nytimes.com/2003/10/31/world/world-briefing-asia-china-too-many -quarantined-in-sars-outbreak.html (accessed February 22, 2013).

"China: SARS Battle Remains 'Grave.'" 2003. *CNN.com*. May 6. http://www.cnn.com /2003/HEALTH/05/06/sars/ (accessed May 14, 2003).

"China SARS Numbers Pass 5,000." 2003. *CNN.com*. May 12. http://www.cnn.com/2003 /HEALTH/05/12/sars/index.html (accessed May 14, 2003).

"China Says H1N1 Flu Spreading into the Countryside." 2010. *Yahoo! News.* January 2. http://www.rferl.org/content/China_Says_H1N1_Flu_Spreading_Into_The _Countryside/1919856.html (accessed January 6, 2010).

"China's Official H1N1 Death Count Suspect." 2009. *China Digital Times.* November 18. http://chinadigitaltimes.net/2009/11/chinas-official-h1n1-death-count-suspect/ (accessed January 4, 2010).

"China to Stop Daily SARS Report." 2004. *Yahoo! News.* June 1. http://www.apnews archive.com/2004/China-s-Health-Ministry-Stops-SARS-Report/id-ea57808f285e2e 2c66d9b81c2b1d7928 (accessed February 22, 2013).

"Chinatown Businesses Hurt by SARS Hoax." 2003. *The Boston Channel.* April 3. http:// www.thebostonchannel.com/news/2089377/detail.html (no longer available online, accessed January 24, 2004).

"China vs SARS: A Good Dog Is a Dead Dog." 2003. *Asia Times.* May 31. http://www .atimes.com/atimes/China/EE31Ad04.html (accessed April 27, 2008).

Chinoy, Mike. 2003. "Experts Issue SARS Warning." *CNN.com.* June 19. http://edition. cnn.com/2003/HEALTH/06/19/sars.wrap/index.html (accessed June 20, 2003).

Christine. 2010. "H1N1." January 12. E-mail to author.

Chuang, Angus. 2003. "Taiwan Sees Record SARS Rise; China to Cooperate." *Yahoo! News.* May 18. http://www.timesofmalta.com/articles/view/20030519/local/taiwan -sees-record-sars-rise.149833 (accessed February 22, 2013).

Cindy. 2003. "SARS Paranoia." *Elephant Soap Archives.* May 9. http://www.elephantsoap .com/archives/000016.html (accessed January 24, 2004).

"Cipla's Anti-Flu Drug Gets Nod." 2009. *Times of India.* May 14. http://timesofindia. indiatimes.com/Business/India-Business/Ciplas-anti-flu-drug-gets-nod/articleshow /4526891.cms (accessed June 29, 2010).

"City of Toronto Disputes World Health Organization Travel Advisory." 2003. *Toronto.* April 23. http://wx.toronto.ca/inter/it/newsrel.nsf/9da959222128b9e885256618006 646d3/38b0d2f7c9fea7a385256df60045c817 (accessed April 25, 2003).

Cline, Austin. 2004. "Bleach as Cure for SARS?" *About.com.* January 17. http://atheism .about.com/b/2004/01/17/bleach-as-cure-for-sars.htm (accessed October 5, 2007).

"Clinic Clive Harris." N.d. http://clinic.cliveharris.org/index.php (no longer available online, accessed October 5, 2007).

Cohen, Deborah, and Philip Carter. 2010. "WHO and the Pandemic Flu 'Conspiracies.' " *BMJ* 340 (2912): 1274–79.

Cohen, Jon. 2003. "Travel Bug." MSNBC.com. April 3. http://www.slate.com/articles /health_and_science/medical_examiner/2003/04/travel_bug.html (accessed February 22, 2013).

Cohen, Margot, Gautam Naik, and Matt Pottinger. 2003. "Inside the WHO as It Mobi- lized To Fight Battle to Control SARS." *Wall Street Journal.* May 2. http://online.wsj .com/article/SB10518264649952700.html (accessed May 10, 2007).

Cohen, Stanley. 2002. *Folk Devils and Moral Panics: The Creation of Mods and Rockers.* 3rd ed. New York: Routledge.

Compton, Lauren. 2003. "Is SARS from Outer Space?" *CNN.com.* May 23. http://www.cnn .com/2003/TECH/space/05/23/sars.fromspace/index.html (accessed May 26, 2003).

Department of Health and Human Services. 2010. "H1N1 Influenza Public Health Emer- gency Determination Expired on June 23." June 25. http://www.flu.gov/news /h1n1pheexpiration.html (no longer available online, accessed June 25, 2010).

de Vos, Gail. 1996. *Tales, Rumors, and Gossip: Exploring Contemporary Folk Literature in Grades 7–12.* Westport, CT: Libraries Unlimited.

Disaster Center. 2009. "United States Crime Rates 1960–2008." http://www.disastercenter .com/crime/uscrime.htm (accessed June 30, 2010).

Doheny, Kathleen. 2004. "SARS Review Shows Toronto Fought a Good Fight." *Yahoo! News*. June 2. http://consumer.healthday.com/infections-disease-information-21 /misc-infections-news-411/sars-review-shows-toronto-fought-a-good-fight-519301. html (accessed April 2, 2008).

Domaticus. 2009. "Swine Flu Jokes." June 19. http://www.funnyandjokes.com/swine-flu -jokes.html (accessed October 30, 2013).

Douglas, Mary. 1988. "Purity and Danger." *An Analysis of the Concepts of Pollution and Taboo*. London: Ark Paperbacks.

Douglass, William Campbell. 1992. *Hydrogen Peroxide: Medical Miracle*. Atlanta, GA: Second Opinion.

Dresser, Norine. 2004. "SARS—No Laughing Matter?" http://www.norinedresser.com /sars.html (accessed April 20, 2008).

Duffin, Jacalyn, and Arthur Sweetman, eds. 2006. *SARS in Context: Memory, History, Policy*. Montreal: McGill-Queen's University Press.

Dundes, Alan, ed. 1991. *The Blood Libel Legend: A Casebook in Anti-Semitic Folklore*. Madison: University of Wisconsin Press.

Eaton, Lynn. 2003. "SARS Could Still Affect the United Kingdom, Health Secretary Warns." *BMJ* 326 (7396): 948. http://dx.doi.org/10.1136/bmj.326.7396.948/b. Medline:12727743

Edelstein, Michael. 2007. "Hanford: The Closed City and Its Downwind Victims." In *Cultures of Contamination*, Volume 14: *Legacies of Pollution in Russia and the US (Research in Social Problems and Public Policy)*, edited by Michael R. Edelstein, Maria Tysiachniouk, and Lyudmila V. Smirnova, 253–306. Greenwich, CT: JAI Press. http://dx.doi.org/10.1016/S0196-1152(06)14012-0.

"Editorial: Eves Needs to Call SARS Review Soon." 2003. *Toronto Star*. June 10. http:// www.torontostar.com/NASApp/cs/ContentServer?GXHC_gx_session_id_=d0ffa 9fc6fac0dff (no longer available online, accessed June 18, 2003).

Ellis, Bill. 2005. "Legend/AntiLegend: Humor as an Integral Part of the Contemporary Legend Process." In *Rumor Mills: The Social Impact of Rumor and Legend*, edited by Gary Alan Fine, Véronique Campion-Vincent, and Chip Heath, 123–40. New Brunswick, NJ: Aldine Transaction.

Emboden, William A., Jr. 1976. "Plant Hypnotics among the North American Indians." In *American Folk Medicine: A Symposium*, edited by Wayland D. Hand, 159–67. Berkeley: University of California Press.

Emery, David. 2003. "SARS Infects Restaurant Workers in Asian Neighborhoods." *About. com*. April 11. http://urbanlegends.about.com/library/bl-sars-restaurants.htm (accessed January 24, 2004).

Emery, Theo. 2003. "SARS Fear Roils Chinatown Neighborhoods, from Frisco to Boston." *ABC News*. April 8. http://yellowworld.org/health/87.html (accessed April 27, 2008).

Epstein, Steven. 1996. *Impure Science: AIDS, Activism, and the Politics of Knowledge*. Berkeley: University of California Press.

European Centre for Disease Prevention and Control. 2010. "ECDC Daily Update: 2009 Influenza A (H1N1) Pandemic." January 18. http://ecdc.europa.eu/en/healthtopics /Documents/100118_Influenza_AH1N1_Situation_Report_0900hrs.pdf (accessed October 30, 2013).

"Evidence SARS 'Jumped from Animals.'" 2003. *CNN.com*. May 28. http://edition.cnn .com/2003/WORLD/asiapcf/east/05/28/sars.source/ (accessed June 2, 2003).

Fairchild, Amy L. 2003. *Science at the Borders: Immigrant Medical Inspection and the Shaping of the Modern Industrial Labor Force*. Baltimore, MD: Johns Hopkins University Press.

Falco, Miriam. 2012. "New SARS-like Virus Poses Medical Mystery." *CNN.com*. September 24. http://thechart.blogs.cnn.com/2012/09/24/new-sars-like-virus-poses -medical-mystery/ (accessed September 25, 2012).

Falk, Gerhard. 2001. *Stigma: How We Treat Outsiders*. Amherst, NY: Prometheus Books.

Feagin, Joe R., and Pinar Batur. 2004. "Racism in Comparative Perspective." In *Handbook of Social Problems: A Comparative International Perspective*, edited by George Ritzer, 121–38. Thousand Oaks, CA: SAGE Publications. http://dx.doi.org/10.4135 /9781412973526.n8.

"Federal Agents Trained to Spot SARS." 2003. *MSNBC.com*. May 7. http://www.nbcnews .com/id/3076747/ns/health-infections_diseases/ (accessed April 2, 2008).

"Financial Report: Gilead Sciences 2Q." 2009. *Contract Pharma*. July 22. http://www .contractpharma.com/contents/view_breaking-news/2009-07-22/financial-report -gilead-sciences-2q-2009-07-22-10-20-00/ (accessed June 29, 2010).

Fine, Gary Alan. 2005. "Rumor Matters: An Introductory Essay." In *Rumor Mills: The Social Impact of Rumor and Legend*, edited by Gary Alan Fine, Véronique Campion- Vincent, and Chip Heath, 1–7. New Brunswick, NJ: Aldine Transaction.

Fine, Gary Alan, and Irfan Khawaja. 2005. "Celebrating Arabs and Grateful Terrorists: Rumor and the Politics of Plausibility." In *Rumor Mills: The Social Impact of Rumor and Legend*, ed. Gary Alan Fine, Véronique Campion-Vincent, and Chip Heath, 189–205. New Brunswick, NJ: Aldine Transaction.

Fleck, Fiona. 2003. "WHO Says SARS Outbreak Is Over, But Fight Should Go On." *BMJ* 327 (7406): 70. http://dx.doi.org/10.1136/bmj.327.7406.70-c. Med- line:12855506

FlorCruz, Jaime. 2003. "China Censors CNN SARS Report." *CNN.com*. May 15. http:// www.cnn.com/2003/WORLD/asiapcf/east/05/14/sars.censor/ (accessed May 25, 2003).

Foreman, William. 2003a. "SARS Virus Keeps Schools Shut in Beijing." *Yahoo! News*. May 4. http://www.apnewsarchive.com/2003/SARS-Virus-Keeps-Schools-Shut-in-Beijing /id-3ea7c96b94e7dbe9e5825d359fba2448 (accessed April 2, 2008).

Foreman, William. 2003b. "Villagers Attack China Offices over SARS." *Yahoo! News*. May 5. http://www.apnewsarchive.com/2003/Villagers-Attack-China-Offices-Over-SARS /id-5d3af6676f3a80bb55aaa10594c359c0 (accessed April 2, 2008).

Fox, Maggie. 2003a. "West Nile Seen Scarier than SARS for U.S., Canada." *Yahoo! News*. May 15. http://www.planetark.org/dailynewsstory.cfm/newsid/20804/newsDate /15-May-2003/story.htm (accessed April 2, 2008).

Fox, Maggie. 2003b. "'Cattle Car Syndrome' Offers SARS Insights." *Yahoo! News*. May 20. http://www.planetark.org/dailynewsstory.cfm/newsid/20859/story.html/ (accessed April 3, 2008).

Fox-Baker, Jack. 1981. "Mexico: Folk Medicine, Magic and Mind-Molding." In *Folk Medi- cine and Herbal Healing*, edited by George G. Meyer, Kenneth Blum, and John G. Cull, 121–38. Springfield, IL: Charles C. Thomas.

Freud, Sigmund. (1905) 1990. *Jokes and Their Relation to the Unconscious*. New York: W. W. Norton.

Gagnier, Regenia. 1988. "Between Women: A Cross-Class Analysis of Status and Anarchic Humor." *Women's Studies* 15 (1–3): 135–48.

"Gambia's President Claims He Has Cure for AIDS." 2007. *MSNBC.com*. February 20. http://www.nbcnews.com/id/17244005/ (accessed October 3, 2007).

Gamble, Vanessa Northington. 1997. "Under the Shadow of Tuskegee: African Americans and Health Care." *American Journal of Public Health* 87 (11): 1773–8. http://dx.doi .org/10.2105/AJPH.87.11.1773. Medline:9366634

Gardner, Amanda. 2003. "Life 'Surreal' for Nurse under SARS Quarantine." *Yahoo! News.* May 30. http://findarticles.com/p/articles/mi_kmhea/is_200305/ai_kepm413923 (accessed April 2, 2008).

Garro, Linda C. 1992. "Chronic Illness and the Construction of Narratives." In *Pain as Human Experience: An Anthropological Perspective,* edited by Mary Jo DelVecchio Good, Paul E. Brodwin, Byron J. Good, and Arthur Kleinman, 100–37. Berkeley: University of California Press.

Gaudet, Marcia. 2004. *Carville: Remembering Leprosy in America.* Jackson: University Press of Mississippi.

Gebhard, Bruno. 1976. "The Interrelationship of Scientific and Folk Medicine in the United States of America since 1850." In *American Folk Medicine: A Symposium,* edited by Wayland D. Hand, 87–98. Berkeley: University of California Press.

Germano, Beth. 2010. "Is the Swine Flu Epidemic Over?" *WBZTV.* February 5. http://wbztv.com/local/swine.flu.epidemic.2.1473031.html (no longer available online, accessed May 25, 2010).

Gillian. 2010. "H1N1." January 8. E-mail to author.

Glazer, Mark. 2003. "FW: SARS Jokes." May 2. E-mail to author.

"Global Tech Giants Take a Hit from SARS." 2003. *Yahoo! News.* June 11. http://news .yahoo.com/news?tmpl=story2&cid=1506&u=/afp/20030611/ts_alt_afp/heath _sars_companies.htm (no longer available online, accessed June 16, 2003).

Goffman, Erving. 1963. *Stigma: Notes on the Management of Spoiled Identity.* Englewood Cliffs, NJ: Prentice-Hall.

Goldberg, Marshall. 1987. "TV Has Done More to Contain AIDS than Any Other Single Factor." *TV Guide.* November 28.

Goldstein, Diane E. 2004. *Once Upon a Virus: AIDS Legends and Vernacular Risk Perception.* Logan: Utah State University Press.

Gottlieb, Scott. 2003. "Chinese Scientists Must Test Wild Animals to Find the Host of SARS." *BMJ* 326 (7399): 1109. http://dx.doi.org/10.1136/bmj.326.7399.1109. Medline:12763976

Goudsmit, Jaap. 2004. *Viral Fitness: The Next SARS and West Nile in the Making.* New York: Oxford University Press. http://dx.doi.org/10.1093/acprof:oso/9780195130348.001 .0001.

Grauwels, Stephan. 2003. "WHO: SARS Could Be Coming to an End." *Yahoo! News.* June 12. http://www.apnewsarchive.com/2003/WHO-SARS-Could-Be-Coming-to-an -End/id-39e1006a278681a753ac04c8cef40162 (accessed April 3, 2008).

Gray, Frances. 1994. *Women and Laughter.* Charlottesville: University of Virginia Press.

Griffith, Dorsey. 2003. "Worries Add to the Confusion of SARS." *sacbee.com.* April 9. http://www.sacbee.com/content/news/medical/story/6424157p%2D7376204c.html (no longer available online, accessed December 5, 2004).

Grotjahn, Martin. 1957. *Beyond Laughter.* New York: Blakiston.

Guerra, Francisco. 1976. "Medical Folklore in Spanish America." In *American Folk Medicine: A Symposium,* edited by Wayland D. Hand, 169–74. Berkeley: University of California Press.

Gupta, Chris. 2003. "SARS—Treatments Available and Cost-Effective." *MasterNewMedia.* April 23. http://www.masternewmedia.org/2003/04/23/sars_treatments_available _and.htm (accessed October 5, 2007).

"H1N1 Conspiracy Update December 2009." 2009. *News Independent.* December 3. http://www.news-independent.com/h1n1-conspiracy-update-december/ (accessed January 5, 2010).

"H1N1 Conspiracy Voiced by the People." 2009. *News Independent.* May 7. http://www.news -independent.com/h1n1-conspiracy-voiced-by-the-people/ (accessed January 5, 2010).

"The H1N1 Vaccine Is a Much Greater Risk to Your Health Than the Flu Itself." 2009. *PreventDisease.com.* August 7. http://preventdisease.com/news/09/080709_swine_flu_hype.shtml (accessed January 12, 2010).

Hand, Wayland D. 1980. *Magical Medicine: The Folkloric Component of Medicine in the Folk Belief, Custom, and Ritual of the Peoples of Europe and America.* Berkeley: University of California Press.

Harmon, Amy. 2003. "SARS Rumor Mill Working Overtime on the Internet." *Salt Lake Tribune.* April 6. http://www.sltrib.com/2003/Apr/04062003/nation_w/45469.asp (no longer available online, accessed January 24, 2004).

Havely, Joe. 2003. "Mystery Bug Sets Tongues Wagging." *CNN.com.* April 1. http://www.cnn.com/2003/WORLD/asiapcf/east/04/01/hk.bug/index.html (accessed January 24, 2004).

"Health Officials Concerned over New SARS Cluster, Exported Case to US." 2003. *Yahoo! News.* June 10. http://www.accessmylibrary.com/coms2/summary_0286-23519616_ITM (no longer available online, accessed June 10, 2003).

"Health Officials Ponder What Next after SARS." 2003. *Yahoo! News.* June 17. http://groups.yahoo.com/neo/groups/beritamalaysia/conversations/topics/60129 (accessed February 22, 2013).

Heather. 2005. Interview by author. 9 September. St. John's, Newfoundland. Tape recording.

Hesketh, Therese. 2003. "China in the Grip of SARS." *BMJ* 326 (7398): 1095. http://dx.doi.org/10.1136/bmj.326.7398.1095.

"HK, China Discuss SARS Warning System." 2003. *Yahoo! News.* June 20. http://muzi.com/cc/english/10006,19931.shtml?q=1266892&cc=&ccr=24205 (accessed April 3, 2008).

"HK Government Defends Points System to Evict Unruly Public Housing Tenants." 2003. *Yahoo! News.* May 31. http://www.accessmylibrary.com/coms2/summary_0286-23411895_ITM (accessed April 2, 2008).

"HK Health Chief Quits over SARS." 2004. *CNN.com.* July 7. http://asianfanatics.net/forum/topic/21571-hk-health-chief-quits-over-sars/ (accessed April 2, 2008).

Hobie. 2003. "SARS—a Poison, and Not a 'Bug' at All . . .?" *Rumor Mill News Reading Room.* December 29. http://www.rumormillnews.com/cgi-bin/archive.cgi?read=42079 (accessed January 24, 2004).

Hodgson, Jeffrey. 2003. "Canada Marks Another SARS Death, but Cases Decline." *Yahoo! News.* June 17. http://news.yahoo.com/news?tmpl=story2&cid=585&u=/nm/20030617/sc_nm/health_canada_sars_dc.htm (no longer available online, accessed June 18, 2003).

Hoenig, Henry. 2003. "Beijing Goes High-Tech to Block Sars Messages." *New Zealand Herald.* June 16. http://www.nzherald.co.nz/world/news/article.cfm?c_id=2&objectid=3507534 (accessed April 27, 2008).

"Hong Kongers Shun Karaoke Amid Virus Fears." 2003. *The Age.* April 3. http://www.theage.com.au/articles/2003/04/03/1048962867381.html (accessed December 5, 2004).

"Hong Kong Reports Three More SARS Cases, Three Deaths." 2003. *Yahoo! News.* June 1. http://www.accessmylibrary.com/coms2/summary_0286-23448889_ITM (accessed April 3, 2008).

"Hong Kong to Use HIV Drug to Treat SARS." 2003. *CNN.com.* September 25. http://www.aegis.org/news/re/2003/RE030948.html (accessed April 1, 2008).

"Hong Kong University to Finance Top-Level SARS Lab." 2003. *Yahoo! News.* September 12. http://www.advocate.com/health-news/2003/09/26/hong-kong-use-hiv-drug-treat-sars-9985 (accessed February 22, 2013).

Hoo, Stephanie. 2004. "China OKs Human Trials of SARS Vaccine." *Yahoo! News.* January 19. http://www.ustc8312.com/drugnews/messages/126.html (accessed April 2, 2008).

Hookway, James. 2008. "For Vietnamese, the Year of the Rat Starts with Lunch." The Wall Street Journal.com. February 6. http://online.wsj.com/news/articles/SB12022248893 8344263 (accessed November 1, 2013).

Hopkins, Jim. 2003. "SARS Scare Hurts Business in Chinatowns." *USA Today.* April 25. http://usatoday30.usatoday.com/news/nation/2003-04-24-chinatown-usat_x.htm (accessed February 22, 2013).

Horowitz, Leonard. 2004. "SARS—A Great Global Scam." *Conspiracy Planet: The Alternative News & History Network.* May 12. http://www.rense.com/general36/scam.htm (accessed December 5, 2004).

"Hospitals in China Battle SARS Burden." 2003. *CNN.com.* May 5. http://www.cnn.com /2003/HEALTH/05/05/sars/index.html (accessed May 14, 2003).

"How Vietnam Beat the Bug." 2003. *CNN.com.* April 28. http://www.cnn.com/2003 /WORLD/asiapcf/east/04/28/sars.vietnam/index.html (accessed May 14, 2003).

Huang, Annie. 2003a. "Toronto Reports 8 New SARS Infections." *Yahoo! News.* May 26. http://www.apnewsarchive.com/2003/Toronto-Reports-8-New-SARS-Infections /id-1667988e41a02af2d7767e418d85aef8 (accessed February 22, 2013).

Huang, Annie. 2003b. "Taiwan Rejects China's Help in SARS Fight." *Yahoo! News.* May 25. http://z1.invisionfree.com/triforce_news/ar/t2.htm (accessed April 2, 2008).

Hufford, David J. 1976. "A New Approach to the 'Old Hag': The Nightmare Tradition Reexamined." In *American Folk Medicine: A Symposium,* edited by Wayland D. Hand, 73–85. Berkeley: University of California Press.

Hufford, David J. 1982. *The Terror That Comes in the Night: An Experience-Centered Study of Supernatural Assault Traditions.* Philadelphia: University of Pennsylvania Press.

Humphreys, Margaret. 2002. "No Safe Place: Disease and Panic in American History." *American Literary History* 14 (4): 845–57. http://dx.doi.org/10.1093/alh/14.4.845.

"Italy to Check for SARS on Travellers." 2003. *CNN.com.* May 9. http://www.cnn. com/2003/TRAVEL/ADVISOR/05/09/sars.italy.reut/index.html (accessed May 14, 2003).

Izakovic. 2003. "SARS Kills 50% Patients over 65—A Perfect Age-Specific Weapon." *Rumor Mill News Reading Room.* December 30. http://www.indiadivine.org /showthread.php/918748-SARS-KILLS-50-PATIENTS-OVER-65-A-PERFECT -AGE-SPECIFIC-WEAPON (accessed January 24, 2004).

Jansen, William Hugh. 1959. "The Esoteric-Exoteric Factor in Folklore." *Fabula: Journal of Folktale Studies* 2 (2): 205–11. http://dx.doi.org/10.1515/fabl.1959.2.2.205.

"Japan Businesses Report SARS Impact." 2003. *Yahoo! News.* May 20. http://www .highbeam.com/doc/1P1-74039875.html (accessed April 3, 2008).

Jennifer. 2005. Interview by author. 11 July. Toronto. Tape recording.

Jonathan. 2005. Interview by author. 13 July. Toronto. Tape recording.

Jones, Alex S. 1989. "The Media Business; Publisher of TV Guide Joins New York Post." *New York Times.* April 6. http://www.nytimes.com/1989/04/06/business/the-media -business-publisher-of-tv-guide-joins-new-york-post.html (accessed January 2, 2007).

Kahn, Chris. 2003. "House Cats, Ferrets Can Get SARS." *Yahoo! News.* October 30. http:// www.blackherbals.com/house_cats.htm (accessed April 2, 2008).

Kataria, Sunil. 2003. "WHO Chief: More SARS-like Diseases Likely." *Yahoo! News.* September 12. http://ww1.aegis.org/news/re/2003/RE030917.html (accessed April 1, 2008).

"Keep up the Guard on SARS, Health Experts Say at Paris Conference." 2003. *Yahoo! News.* October 30. http://www.accessmylibrary.com/coms2/summary_0286 -24892430_ITM (accessed April 2, 2008).

Keith-Spiegel, Patricia. 1972. "Early Conceptions of Humor: Varieties and Issues." In *The Psychology of Humor: Theoretical Perspectives and Empirical Issues*, edited by Jeffrey H. Goldstein and Paul E. McGhee, 3–39. New York: Academic.

Kelly, Kevin. 1998. *New Rules for the New Economy: 10 Radical Strategies for a Connected World*. New York: Viking.

Kennedy, Val Brickates. 2009. "Gilead Reports Higher Profit, Revenue." *MarketWatch.com*. October 20. http://www.marketwatch.com/story/gilead-reports-higher-profit -revenue-2009-10-20 (accessed June 29, 2010).

"Key Developments with the SARS Virus." 2003. *Yahoo! News*. May 17. http://www .highbeam.com/doc/1P1-73979773.html (accessed April 2, 2008).

Kimball, Ann Marie. 2006. *Risky Trade: Infectious Disease in the Era of Global Trade*. Aldershot, UK: Ashgate.

Kimmel, Allan J., and Robert Keefer. 1991. "Psychological Correlates of the Transmission and Acceptance of Rumors about AIDS." *Journal of Applied Social Psychology* 21 (19): 1608–28. http://dx.doi.org/10.1111/j.1559-1816.1991.tb00490.x.

Kleinman, Arthur, and Sing Lee. 2005. "SARS and the Problem of Social Stigma." In *SARS in China: Prelude to Pandemic?*, edited by Arthur Kleinman and James L. Watson, 173–95. Stanford, CA: Stanford University Press.

Knopf, Terry Ann. 1975. *Rumors, Race, and Riots*. New Brunswick, NJ: Transaction.

Koh, Wilson. 2009. "Blockbuster Antivirals and Vaccines: Real Options in a Flu Pandemic." *Social Science Research Network*. July 12. http://papers.ssrn.com/sol3/papers. cfm?abstract_id=1433145 (accessed June 29, 2010). http://dx.doi.org/10.2139/ssrn .1433145.

Koven, Mikel J. 2001. "'Buzz Off!': The Killer Bee Movie as Modern Belief Narrative." *Contemporary Legend* 4: 1–19.

Kraut, Alan M. 1995. *Silent Travelers: Germs, Genes, and the "Immigrant Menace."* New York: Basic Books.

Krishnan, Barani. 2003. "SARS Mystery Lives on as Cases Dwindle." *Yahoo! News*. June 18. http://oldsite.nautilus.org/archives/napsnet/dr/0306/JUN18-03.html#item9 (no longer available online, accessed February 22, 2013).

Kristian. 2010. "H1N1." January 13. E-mail to author.

Kuhlman, T. L. 1988. "Gallows Humor for a Scaffold Setting: Managing Aggressive Patients on a Maximum-Security Forensic Unit." *Hospital & Community Psychiatry* 39 (10): 1085–90. Medline:3229742

Lacourcière, Luc. 1976. "A Survey of Folk Medicine in French Canada from Early Times to the Present." In *American Folk Medicine: A Symposium*, edited by Wayland D. Hand, 203–14. Berkeley: University of California Press.

Lakshmanan, Indira A. R. 2003. "Exploring China's Silence on SARS—New Details Surface on Initial Cover-up." *Boston Globe*. May 25. http://en.minghui.org/emh/ articles/2003/5/27/36215.html (accessed April 27, 2008).

Lau, J. T. F., X. Yang, H. Tsui, and J. H. Kim. 2003. "Monitoring Community Responses to the SARS Epidemic in Hong Kong: from Day 10 to Day 62." *Journal of Epidemiology & Community Health* 57 (11): 864–70. http://dx.doi.org/10.1136/jech.57.11 .864. Medline:14600111

LeBeau, Conrad. 2001. *Hydrogen Peroxide & Ozone*. West Allis, WI: Vital Health.

Lichtenstein, Bronwen. 2004. "AIDS as a Social Problem: The Creation of Social Pariahs in the Management of an Epidemic." In *Handbook of Social Problems: A Comparative International Perspective*, edited by George Ritzer, 316–34. Thousand Oaks, CA: SAGE Publications. http://dx.doi.org/10.4135/9781412973526.n19.

Lin, Paul. 2003. "China Has Cooked Up 'American SARS' Scam." *Association for Asian Research*. May 27. http://www.asianresearch.org/articles/1387.html (accessed January 24, 2004).

Lodge, David M. 2003. "Biological Hazards Ahead." *New York Times*. June 19. http://www
.nytimes.com/2003/06/19/opinion/biological-hazards-ahead.html (accessed June 20,
2003).

Loury, Glenn C. 2002. *The Anatomy of Racial Inequality*. Cambridge, MA: Harvard University Press.

Low, Vincent. 2009. "Chinese Herbs Prove Effective in the Cure of Influenza A (H1N1)."
Malaysian National News Agency. July 24. http://www.bernama.com.my/bernama/v5
/newsgeneral.php?id=427649 (accessed January 13, 2010).

Lui, John. 2003. "Cell Phone Firm Offers SARS Alerts." *MSNBC.com*. April 18. http://
www.news.cnet.com/Cell-phone-firm-offers-SARS-alerts/2100-1039-997457.html
(accessed April 4, 2008).

Luis. 2005. Interview by author. 12 July. Toronto. Tape recording.

Luk, Helen. 2003. "Hong Kong to Set up SARS Alert System." *Yahoo! News*. September
22. http://www.apnewsarchive.com/2003/Hong-Kong-to-Set-Up-SARS-Alert
-System/id-70a22d50b118630edbde98771e6e1a00 (accessed February 22, 2013).

Lyn, Tan Ee. 2003a. "Virus Spreads in Hong Kong, Cockroaches Eyed." *Yahoo! News*.
April 8. http://www.iol.co.za/news/world/cockroaches-eyed-as-sars-spreads-in-hong-
kong-1.104313#.USfebOiRrNM (no longer available online, accessed February 22,
2013).

Lyn, Tan Ee. 2003b. "Bone Disease Worry for Former SARS Patients." *Yahoo! News*. October 10. http://www.freerepublic.com/focus/f-news/998751/posts (accessed April 1,
2008).

Lyn, Tan Ee. 2003c. "Website Hoax on Killer Virus Triggers Hong Kong Panic." *Yahoo! News*.
April 1. http://www.inreview.com/archive/topic/1727.html (accessed April 27, 2008).

Lynch, David J. 2003. "Wild Animal Markets in China May Be Breeding SARS." *USA
Today*. October 29. http://usatoday30.usatoday.com/news/health/2003-10-28-sars
-wild-animals_x.htm (accessed February 22, 2013).

Lynne. 2010. "H1N1." January 9. E-mail to author.

MacCormack, Carol P. 1982. "Traditional Medicine, Folk Medicine and Alternative Medicine." In *Folk Medicine and Health Culture: Role of Folk Medicine in Modern Health
Care*, edited by Tuula Vaskilampi and Carol P. MacCormack, i–xxv. Kuopio, Finland:
University of Kuopio.

Mackay, Judith Longstaff. 2003. "SARS—An Agatha Christie novel." *Pulmonary Perspectives*. September. http://www.chestnet.org/downloads/education/physician/pp
/sept03.pdf (no longer available online, accessed January 24, 2004).

Markel, Howard. 1999. *Quarantine!: East European Jewish Immigrants and the New York
City Epidemics of 1892*. Baltimore, MD: Johns Hopkins University Press.

Marks, Lara, and Michael Worboys, eds. 1997. *Migrants, Minorities and Health: Historical
and Contemporary Studies*. New York: Routledge. http://dx.doi.org/10.4324/978020
3208175.

Martín-Barbero, Jesús. 1987. *De los medios a las mediaciones: Comunicación, cultura y hegemonía*. Barcelona: Editorial Gustavo Gili.

Maxwell, W. 2003. "The Use of Gallows Humor and Dark Humor during Crisis Situations." *International Journal of Emergency Mental Health* 5 (2): 93–98. Medline:12882095

Mayo, Ruth, Yaacov Schul, and Eugene Burnstein. 2004. "'I Am Not Guilty' vs 'I Am
Innocent': Successful Negation May Depend on the Schema Used for Its Encoding."
Journal of Experimental Social Psychology 40 (4): 433–49. http://dx.doi.org/10.1016
/j.jesp.2003.07.008.

McCabe, Ed. 2003. "SARS Anthrax West Nile Smallpox Flu AIDS the Common Cold."
http://curezone.com/art/read.asp?ID=4&db=14&C0=24 (accessed October 5, 2007).

McCabe, Ed. 2004. *Flood Your Body with Oxygen.* Miami Shores, FL: Energy Publications.

McDonald, Joe. 2004. "WHO Finds Evidence Animals Play SARS Role." *Yahoo! News.* January 16. http://www.firstcoastnews.com/news/local/story.aspx?storyid=13588 (accessed April 2, 2008).

McNeil, Donald G., Jr. 2003. "SARS Fight in Taiwan Is Impeded by Resistance to Segregation." *New York Times.* May 12. http://goldismoney.info/forums/archive/index.php/t-1082.html (no longer available online, accessed April 2, 2008).

McNeil, Donald G., Jr., and Lawrence K. Altman. 2003. "Is SARS Spread by a Modern-day Typhoid Mary?" *New York Times.* April 15. http://www.iht.com/articles/93282.html (no longer available online, accessed November 17, 2004).

Meyer, George G. 1981. "The Art of Healing: Folk Medicine, Religion and Science." In *Folk Medicine and Herbal Healing,* edited by George G. Meyer, Kenneth Blum, and John G. Cull, 1–12. Springfield, IL: Charles C. Thomas.

Mike. 2005. Interview by author. 12 July. Toronto. Tape recording.

Miles, Tom. 2003. "U.S. Health Chief Sees SARS Deaths in Europe, U.S." *Yahoo! News.* May 20. http://www.freerepublic.com/focus/f-news/914843/posts (accessed April 3, 2008).

Mills, Elinor. 2009. "Report: Justice Department Sends Hoax E-mail to Test Workers." *CNET News.* January 30. http://news.cnet.com/8301-1009_3-10153795-83.html?part=rss&subj=news&tag=2547-1_3-0-20 (accessed May 18, 2009).

Minh, Tran Van. 2005. "Vietnam to Produce Generic Bird-Flu Drug." *Washington Post.* November 9. http://www.washingtonpost.com/wp-dyn/content/article/2005/11/09/AR2005110900384.html (accessed June 29, 2010).

"MLB Issues Guidelines for Toronto." 2003. *MSNBC.com.* April 23. http://dailycollegian.com/2003/04/24/mlb-concerned-about-sars/ (accessed April 23, 2003).

Montalk. 2003. "Metaphysics of Immunity: SARS and Chemtrails." *Educate-Yourself.* April 28. http://educate-yourself.org/cn/metaphysicsofimmunity07may03.shtml (accessed March 23, 2006).

Moody, Glyn. 2009. "Is This the Solution to Spam?" *ComputerworldUK.* February 2. http://blogs.computerworlduk.com/open-enterprise/2009/02/is-this-the-solution-to-spam/index.htm (accessed May 18, 2009).

Morris, Meaghan. 1999. "Things to Do with Shopping Centres." In *The Cultural Studies Reader.* 2nd edition. Edited by Simon During, 391–409. London: Routledge.

Moss, Ralph W. 1992. *Cancer Therapy: The Independent Consumer's Guide to Non-Toxic Treatment & Prevention.* Brooklyn: Equinox.

Moss, Ralph W. 1998. *Herbs Against Cancer.* Brooklyn: Equinox.

Muzzatti, Stephen L. 2005. "Bits of Falling Sky and Global Pandemics: Moral Panic and Severe Acute Respiratory Syndrome." *Illness, Crisis & Loss* 13 (2): 117–28.

National Highway Traffic Safety Administration. N.d. "National Statistics." Fatality Analysis Reporting System Encyclopedia. http://www-fars.nhtsa.dot.gov/Main/index.aspx (accessed June 30, 2010).

National Safety Council. 2010. *Injury Facts,* 2010 edition. Itasca, IL: National Safety Council.

New Milford Visiting Nurse Association. 2003. "SARS—More Coming for Sure: The Sky Is Falling!" *NM VNA & Hospice.* June. http://www.newmilfordvna.org/newsletter.html (no longer available online, accessed January 24, 2004).

"New SARS Deaths a Blow for Taiwan." 2003. *CNN.com.* May 25. http://www.cnn.com/2003/HEALTH/05/25/sars.wrap.new/index.html (no longer available online, accessed February 22, 2013).

"New SARS Outbreaks Feared in Taiwan, Singapore." 2003. *MSNBC.com.* May 14. http://www.timesofmalta.com/articles/view/20030515/local/new-sars-outbreaks-feared-in-taiwan-singapore.150166 (accessed February 22, 2013).

"New SARS Travel Warning Issued." 2003. *MSNBC.com.* April 23. http://bbs.clutchfans. netarchive/index.php/t-56190.html (no longer available online, accessed April 4, 2008).

"No China Sars Deaths for First Day in Six Weeks." 2003. *Yahoo! News.* June 1. http:// www.timesofmalta.com/articles/view/20030602/local/no-china-sars-deaths-for-first -day-in-six-weeks.148813 (accessed February 22, 2013).

"Nokia Sinks on Latest Warning." 2003. *CNN.com.* July 18. http://www.cnn.com/2003 /BUSINESS/07/17/nokia/ (accessed April 3, 2008).

"Nurses Say Toronto Not Prepared If SARS Reappears." 2003. *Yahoo! News.* September 22. http://news.yahoo.com/news?tmpl=story2&cid=571&u=/nm/20030922/hl_nm /sars_canada_nurses_dc&printer=1 (no longer available online, accessed September 23, 2003).

"Obama Declares H1N1 Emergency." 2009. *CNN.com.* October 24. http://www.cnn. com/2009/HEALTH/10/24/h1n1.obama/index.html (accessed January 4, 2010).

Obrdlik, Antonin J. 1942. "'Gallows Humor'—A Sociological Phenomenon." *American Journal of Sociology* 47 (5): 709–16. http://dx.doi.org/10.1086/219002.

O'Connor, Bonnie Blair. 1995. *Healing Traditions: Alternative Medicine and the Health Professions.* Philadelphia: University of Pennsylvania Press.

O'Connor, Bonnie B., and David J. Hufford. 2001. "Understanding Folk Medicine." In *Healing Logics: Culture and Medicine in Modern Health Belief Systems,* edited by Erika Brady, 13–35. Logan: Utah State University Press.

Oliveira, Mike. 2003. "Local Businesses Punished by SARS Rumours." *Toronto Star.* March 29. http://www.thestar.com/NASApp/cs/ContentServer?pagename=thestar/Layout /Article_Type1&c=Article&cid=1035780135837&call_pageid=968332188492& col=968705899037 (no longer available online, accessed April 7, 2003).

Omi, Michael, and Howard Winant. 1986. *Racial Formation in the United States: From the 1960s to the 1990s.* New York: Routledge.

"One 'Probable' SARS Case in India: WHO." 2003. *Yahoo! News.* May 12. http://www. accessmylibrary.com/coms2/summary_0286-23253039_ITM (accessed February 22, 2013).

"Origin of New SARS Outbreak in China a Mystery, Raccoon Dogs Culled." 2004. *Yahoo! News.* January 14. http://www.terradaily.com/2004/040114092430.mdcambww. html (accessed April 2, 2008).

"Origin of SARS Virus Still a Puzzle." 2003. *MSNBC.com.* May 12. http://www.nbcnews. com/id/3076743/ns/health-infectious_diseases/#.USgleOiRrNM (accessed February 22, 2013).

Oring, Elliott. 1992. *Jokes and Their Relations.* Lexington: University Press of Kentucky.

Park, Alice. 2012. "New SARS-Like Virus Detected: Should We Be Worried?" *TIME.* September 24. http://healthland.time.com/2012/09/24/new-sars-like-virus-detected -should-we-be-worried/ (accessed September 25, 2012).

Parry, Jane. 2003a. "Hong Kong and US Scientists Believe Illness Is a Coronavirus." *BMJ* 326 (7392): 727. http://dx.doi.org/10.1136/bmj.326.7392.727. Medline:12676826

Parry, Jane. 2003b. "China Joins Global Effort over Pneumonia Virus." *BMJ* 326 (7393): 781. http://dx.doi.org/10.1136/bmj.326.7393.781. Medline:12689957

Parry, Jane. 2003c. "SARS Shows No Sign of Coming under Control." *BMJ* 326 (7394): 839. http://dx.doi.org/10.1136/bmj.326.7394.839. Medline:12702606

Parry, Jane. 2003d. "SARS Virus Identified, But the Disease Is Still Spreading." *BMJ* 326 (7395): 897. http://dx.doi.org/10.1136/bmj.326.7395.897. Medline:12714455

Parry, Jane. 2003e. "SARS May Have Peaked in Canada, Hong Kong, and Vietnam." *BMJ* 326 (7396): 947. http://dx.doi.org/10.1136/bmj.326.7396.947. Medline:12727741

Parry, Jane. 2003f. "United Kingdom Has Its First Confirmed Case of SARS." *BMJ* 326 (7399): 1103. http://dx.doi.org/10.1136/bmj.326.7399.1103-a. Medline:12763959

Pearson, Hampton. 2003. "U.S. Health Body Seeks Help on SARS." *MSNBC.com.* April 24. http://www.msnbc.com/news/904702.asp (no longer available online, accessed May 14, 2003).

Pedersen, Kate. 2006. "Skittish SARSical: Sketch-like Musical Sends up the Marketing of the SARS Epidemic." *NOW Magazine.* June 8–14. http://www.nowtoronto.com /stage/story.cfm?content=153705 (accessed June 19, 2007).

"Penalize Quarantine Violators." 2003. Editorial. *Toledo Blade.* June 10. http://www .toledoblade.com/Editorials/2003/06/10/Penalize-quarantine-violators.html (accessed June 18, 2003).

Persell, Caroline Hodges, Richard Arum, and Kathryn Seufert. 2004. "Racial and Ethnic Educational Inequality in Global Perspective." In *Handbook of Social Problems: A Comparative International Perspective*, edited by George Ritzer, 261–80. Thousand Oaks, CA: SAGE Publications. http://dx.doi.org/10.4135/9781412973526.n16.

Peters, Ralph. 2005. "Myths of Globalization." *USA Today.* May 22. http://www.usatoday 30.usatoday.com/news/opinion/editorials/2005-05-22-oplede_x.htm (accessed on June 6, 2005).

Philip. 2010. "Official Beer of the Flu Epidemic." January 13. E-mail to author.

Picard, Andre. 2009. "Reader Questions on H1N1 Answered." *Globe and Mail.* November 2. http://www.theglobeandmail.com/life/health-and-fitness/health/conditions /reader-questions-on-h1n1-answered/article792196/ (accessed June 17, 2010).

Pilkington, Ed. 2009. "What's in a Name? Governments Debate 'Swine Flu' versus 'Mexican' Flu." *Guardian.* April 28. http://www.theguardian.com/world/2009/apr/28 /mexican-swine-flu-pork-name (accessed June 3, 2010).

"PM Hopes Meal Helps Debunk SARS Myth." 2003. CBC News. April 10. http://www .cbc.ca/news/canada/story/2003/04/10/sars_pm030410.html (accessed April 10, 2003).

"Poll: SARS Epidemic Likely in U.S." 2003. *MSNBC.com.* May 2. http://www.boston.com /news/daily/02/sars_poll.htm (accessed February 22, 2013).

Pomfret, John. 2003. "SARS Reported in Rural China." *MSNBC.com.* May 14. http:// www.highbeam.com/doc/1P2-256471.html (accessed February 22, 2013).

Preves, Sharon E. 2003. *Intersex and Identity: The Contested Self.* New Brunswick, NJ: Rutgers University Press.

ProTo Fire Fox. 2008. "A Detailed Introduction of H5N1 to New Comers." *Above Top Secret.* July 21. http://www.abovetopsecret.com/forum/thread373787/pg1 (accessed January 7, 2010).

Public Health Agency of Canada. 2003. "Update #57—Severe Acute Respiratory Syndrome." May 13. http://www.phac-aspc.gc.ca/sars-sras-gen/update/2003/update57 -eng.php?option=email (no longer available online, accessed April 2, 2008).

"Q&A: Sars." 2003. *BBC News.* September 9. http://newsvote.bbc.co.uk/mpapps /pagetools/print/news.bbc.co.uk/1/hi/health/2856735.stm (no longer available online, accessed September 9, 2003).

Radbill, Samuel X. 1976. "The Role of Animals in Infant Feeding." In *American Folk Medicine: A Symposium*, edited by Wayland D. Hand, 21–30. Berkeley: University of California Press.

Radford, Benjamin. 2005. "Ringing False Alarms: Skepticism and Media Scares." *Skeptical Enquirer* 29 (2): 34–9.

Raghav. 2009. "The Bear, the Lion and the Pig." October 30. http://raghavsubramanian. blogspot.com/2009/10/bear-lion-and-pig.html (accessed October 30, 2013).

Rayelan. 2003. "Is SARS the Bio-Weapon I Was Told about in the Early 90s?" *Rumor Mill News Reading Room.* April 28. http://www.rumormillnews.com/cgi-bin/archive.cgi /noframes/read/31563 (accessed January 24, 2004).

Razum, Oliver, Heiko Becher, Annette Kapaun, and Thomas Junghanss. 2003. "SARS, Lay Epidemiology, and Fear." *Lancet* 361 (9370): 1739–40. http://dx.doi.org/10.1016 /S0140-6736(03)13335-1. Medline:12767754

Recer, Paul. 2003. "Modified Cold Drug May Fight SARS." *Yahoo! News.* May 13. http:// www.apnewsarchive.com/2003/-dheadline-Modified-cold-drug-may-fight-SARS -/id-0b930f4be640e6474422ed37b6533843 (accessed April 2, 2008).

Reinarman, Craig, and Ceres Duskin. 2002. "The Culture's Drug Addict Imagery." In *Deviance: The Interactionist Perspective*, edited by Earl Rubington and Martin S. Weinberg, 32–42. Boston: Allyn and Bacon.

Renard, Jean-Bruno. 2005. "Negatory Rumors: From the Denial of Reality to Conspiracy Theory." In *Rumor Mills: The Social Impact of Rumor and Legend*, edited by Gary Alan Fine, Véronique Campion-Vincent, and Chip Heath, 223–39. New Brunswick, NJ: Aldine Transaction.

"Report Blasts HK Chiefs over SARS." 2004. *CNN.com.* July 5. http://tvnz.co.nz/content /434496/411361/article.html (accessed February 22, 2013).

"Report: Iran Set to Unveil Herbal AIDS Cure." 2007. *FOX News.com.* February 6. http:// www.foxnews.com/story/2007/02/06/report-iran-set-to-unveil-herbal-aids-cure (accessed October 3, 2007).

"Report: SARS Not Airborne Virus." 2003. *CNN.com.* October 20. http://thechina.biz /china-economy/report-sars-not-airborne-virus/ (accessed October 21, 2003).

Rives, James B. 1996. "The Blood Libel Against the Montanists." *Vigiliae Christianae: A Review of Early Christian Life and Language* 50 (2): 117–24.

Roberts, Dexter. 2003. "China's Healthcare Breakdown." *MSNBC.com.* April 21. http:// www.businessweek.com/stories/2003-04-27/breakdown (accessed April 4, 2008).

Roberts, J. A. G. 2002. *China to Chinatown: Chinese Food in the West.* London: Reaktion.

"Rodriguez, Rangers Taking SARS Precautions." 2003. *ESPN.com.* April 28. http://sports .espn.go.com/espn/print?id=1545940&type=news (accessed May 14, 2003).

Rosecrance, Richard N. 1999. *The Rise of the Virtual State: Wealth and Power in the Coming Century.* New York: Basic.

Ross, Emma. 2003. "SARS May Cause Deaths during Flu Season." *Yahoo! News.* May 20. http://insidecostarica.com/specialreports/sars_deaths_flu_season.htm (accessed April 3, 2008).

Rotella, Pam. N.d. "Dr. Hulda Clark's Cure for Cancer and AIDS." http://clark.pamrotella .com/ (accessed October 3, 2007).

"Russian Experts Downplay SARS Scare, Say Alarm 'Unjustified.'" 2003. *Yahoo! News.* May 12. http://www.russialist.org/7181-21.php (accessed April 2, 2008).

"SARS Antibodies Found in Wild Animal Traders in Southern China." 2003. *Yahoo! News.* May 25. http://www.chinapost.com.tw/news/detail.asp?id=37939 (accessed February 22, 2013).

"SARS Drives Chinese to Kill Pets." 2003. *MSNBC.com.* May 7. http://www.nbcnews.com /id/3076752/ (accessed April 2, 2008).

"SARS Driving Shoppers Online." 2003. *CNN.com.* May 22. http://www.financialexpress. com/news/a-masked-blessing-sars-drives-online-shopping-boom-in-china/83998/0 (accessed February 22, 2013).

"SARS Fears Continue to Exacerbate Air Canada Losses." 2003. *Yahoo! News.* June 11. http://www.accessmylibrary.com/coms2/summary_0286-23530530_ITM (accessed February 22, 2013).

"SARS Hits Airlines, Qantas Cuts Jobs." 2003. *MSNBC.com*. April 9. http://usatoday30
.usatoday.com/travel/news/2003/2003-04-09-sars-airlines.htm (accessed February
22, 2013).

"SARS Hits Asian, European Airlines." 2003. *MSNBC.com*. April 24. http://www.msnbc
.com/news/904635.asp (no longer available online, accessed May 14, 2003).

"SARS Hits Nokia Sales in Asia." 2003. *CNN.com*. June 16. http://www.totaltele.com
/view.aspx?ID=394557 (accessed February 22, 2013).

"SARS: Human Vaccine Trials Begin." 2004. *CNN.com*. May 26. http://forum.pakistani
defence.com/index.php?showtopic=31615 (accessed April 2, 2008).

"'SARSical' Sets Disease to Song and Dance." 2006. CBC News. May 25. http://www.cbc
.ca/arts/story/2006/05/25/sarsical.html (no longer available online, accessed June 19,
2007).

"SARS Impacting Higher Education." 2003. *CNN.com*. May 7. http://www.calstate.edu
/pa/clips2003/may/9may/9MaySARS.shtml (accessed May 14, 2003).

"SARS Kills Two More in Canada." 2003. *CNN.com*. June 22. http://www.abc.net.au
/news/2003-06-23/sars-kills-two-more-in-canada/1875056 (accessed April 3, 2008).

"SARS Outbreak a Medical Version of Bio-Terror?" 2003. *The Age*. April 3. http://www
.theage.com.au/articles/2003/04/03/1048962870262.html (accessed May 12, 2004).

"SARS Relapses Stump Doctors." 2003. *CNN.com*. May 3. http://www.cnn.com/2003
/HEALTH/05/03/sars.mutate/index.html (accessed May 14, 2003).

"SARS Report Faults Government." 2003. *MSNBC.com*. October 2. http://usatoday30.usa
today.com/news/world/2003-10-02-sars-report_x.htm (accessed February 22, 2013).

"SARS Tally Soaring in Taiwan." 2003. *CNN.com*. May 20. http://www.cnn.com/2003
/HEALTH/05/20/sars/ (accessed May 25, 2003).

"SARS Trials Lift Vaccine Hope." 2003. *CNN*.com. December 4. http://www.cnn.com
/2003/HEALTH/12/04/sars.vaccine.reut/index.html (accessed December 5, 2003).

"SARS under Control in China: WHO." 2003. *CNN.com*. June 12. http://edition.cnn.
com/2003/HEALTH/06/12/sars.wrap/index.html (no longer available online,
accessed June 16, 2003).

"SARS Virus Uncovered at Restaurant." 2004. *CNN.com*. January 16. http://asianfanatics
.net/forum/topic/1200-health-sars-virus-uncovered-at-restaurant/ (accessed January
16, 2004).

"SARS Won't Delay First Human Space Trip." 2003. *CNN.com*. May 12. http://www.
apnewsarchive.com/2003/SARS-Won-t-Delay-Chinese-Spaceship-Launch/id-f87e5b
7eb4fe704d19af35374f68250b (accessed February 22, 2013).

"SARS Worse than 9/11 on Industry." 2003. *CNN.com*. May 15. http://www.aardvark
travel.net/chat/viewtopic.php?t=947 (accessed February 22, 2013).

Saulny, Susan. 2003. "In Chinatown, an Outbreak of Fear." *New York Times*. April 4.
http://www.nytimes.com/2003/04/04/nyregion/in-chinatown-an-outbreak-of-fear
-herb-shops-and-rumors-thrive-on-virus-panic.html (accessed April 7, 2003).

Sayre, Joan. 2001. "The Use of Aberrant Medical Humor by Psychiatric Unit Staff." *Issues
in Mental Health Nursing* 22 (7): 669–89. http://dx.doi.org/10.1080/0161284011
9739. Medline:11881181

Schram, Justin. 2003. "How Popular Perceptions of Risk from SARS Are Fermenting Discrimination." *BMJ* 326 (7395): 939. http://dx.doi.org/10.1136/bmj.326.7395.939.

Schwartz, Nelson D. 2005. "Rumsfeld's Growing Stake in Tamiflu." *CNN Money*. October
31. http://money.cnn.com/2005/10/31/news/newsmakers/fortune_rumsfeld
/?cnn=yes (accessed June 29, 2010).

Schwartz, Richard D., and Jerome H. Skolnick. 1973. "Legal Stigma." In *Deviance: The
Interactionist Perspective*, 2nd edition, edited by Earl Rubington and Martin S. Weinberg, 203–7. New York: Macmillan.

Schwarz, Norbert, Lawrence J. Sanna, Ian Skurnik, and Carolyn Yoon. 2007. "Metacognitive Experiences and the Intricacies of Setting People Straight: Implications for Debiasing and Public Information Campaigns." *Advances in Experimental Social Psychology* 39: 127–61. http://dx.doi.org/10.1016/S0065-2601(06)39003-X.

"Scientists Say Develop New SARS Tracing Method." 2004. *Yahoo! News*. June 4. http://www.health.am/ab/more/scientists_say_develop_new_sars_tracing_method/ (accessed April 2, 2008).

Seizer, Susan. 2005. *Stigmas of the Tamil Stage: An Ethnography of Special Drama Artists in South India*. Durham, NC: Duke University Press.

Sekhri, Rajiv. 2003. "Canada Doctors Find SARS Link to U.S. Visitor." *Yahoo! News*. June 11. http://www.siliconinvestor.com/readmsg.aspx?msgid=19024561 (accessed February 22, 2013).

Seny. 2005. Interview by author. 3 August. Toronto. Tape recording.

Shields, Michael. 2003. "Roche Launches Test for SARS Virus." *Yahoo! News*. July 15. http://www.sibs.ac.cn/sars/kbdetail.asp?did=2071 (no longer available online, accessed April 1, 2008).

Shilts, Randy. 1987. *And the Band Played On: Politics, People, and the AIDS Epidemic*. New York: St. Martin's.

"Singapore, Foreign Experts Start Probe in SARS Case." 2003. *Yahoo! News*. September 15. http://www.planetark.com/dailynewsstory.cfm/newsid/22242/newsDate/16-Sep -2003/story.htm (accessed April 1, 2008).

"Singapore May Jail Patients for Dishonesty on SARS." 2003. *Yahoo! News*. June 10. http://news.yahoo.com/news?tmpl=story2&cid=574&u=/nm/20030610/wl_nm/sars _singapore_dc&printer=1 (no longer available online, accessed June 10, 2003).

"Singapore Prices Fall on SARS." 2003. *CNN.com*. June 23. http://edition.cnn.com/2003/ business/06/23/singapore.prices.reut/index.html (no longer available online, accessed June 23, 2003).

"Singapore's Hip-Hop SARS Hope." 2003. *CNN.com*. July 3. http://www.highbeam.com /doc/1P1-75345704.html (accessed April 1, 2008).

Sisci, Francesco. 2003. "SARS and Rumors of SARS." *Asia Times Online*. September 18. http://www.atimes.com/atimes/China/EI18Ad05.html (accessed October 30, 2003).

Sloan, Rennie. 2003. "Will SARS Wreak Havoc Here?" *MSNBC.com*. April 2. http://www .msnbc.com/news/894251.asp (no longer available online, accessed April 23, 2003).

Smith, Paul. 1984. *The Book of Nasty Legends*. London: Fontana/Collins.

Smith, Paul. 1990. "'AIDS—Don't Die of Ignorance': Exploring the Cultural Complex of a Pandemic." In *A Nest of Vipers: Perspectives on Contemporary Legend*, vol. 5, edited by Gillian Bennett and Paul Smith, 113–41. Sheffield, UK: Sheffield Academic Press.

Smith, Truman. 1981. "Herbs from Private Resources in the Community." In *Folk Medicine and Herbal Healing*, edited by George G. Meyer, Kenneth Blum, and John G. Cull, 197–212. Springfield, IL: Charles C. Thomas.

"South Africa: HIV & AIDS Statistics." 2010. *AVERT*. May 26. http://www.avert.org /south-africa-hiv-aids-statistics.htm (accessed June 30, 2010).

Spurgeon, David. 2003a. "Canada Reports More Than 300 Suspected Cases of SARS." *BMJ* 326 (7395): 897. http://dx.doi.org/10.1136/bmj.326.7395.897/a. Medline: 12714456

Spurgeon, David. 2003b. "Canada Insists That It Is a Safe Place to Visit." *BMJ* 326 (7396): 948. http://dx.doi.org/10.1136/bmj.326.7396.948/a. Medline:12727742

Spurgeon, David. 2003c. "Toronto Succumbs to SARS a Second Time." *BMJ* 326 (7400): 1162. http://dx.doi.org/10.1136/bmj.326.7400.1162-a. Medline:12775593

Stallings, Roger, and JoAnn Tilton. 1981. "Remedies of a Medicine Man—Curandero—a Listing." In *Folk Medicine and Herbal Healing*, edited by George G. Meyer, Kenneth Blum, and John G. Cull, 213–37. Springfield, IL: Charles C. Thomas.

Stanley-Blackwell, Laurie C. 1993. "The Mysterious Stranger and the Acadian Good Samaritan: Leprosy Folklore in 19th Century New Brunswick." *Acadiensis* 22 (2): 27–39.

Stein, Rob. 2003. "SARS Seen as Long-Term Threat." *MSNBC.com*. April 21. http://xblog .tripod.com/Apr2003/apr2003-1.htm (accessed April 4, 2008).

"Study: SARS Vaccine Shows Promise in Mice." 2004. *CNN.com*. March 31. http://usa today30.usatoday.com/news/health/2004-03-31-sars-vaccine_x.htm (accessed February 22, 2013).

Sullivan, Gerald. 1981. "Herbs Available to the Public." In *Folk Medicine and Herbal Healing*, edited by George G. Meyer, Kenneth Blum, and John G. Cull, 179–96. Springfield, IL: Charles C. Thomas.

"Swine Flu (H1N1) Vaccine." 2010. *New York Times*. January 5. http://www.nytimes.com /info/swine-flu-h1n1-vaccine/ (no longer available online, accessed January 5, 2010).

Szep, Jason. 2003a. "Singapore on Hygiene Blitz after SARS." *CNN.com*. July 3. http:// www.singapore-window.org/sw03/030703re.htm (accessed April 1, 2008).

Szep, Jason. 2003b. "SARS Returns or Lab Accident? Singapore Wonders." *Yahoo! News*. September 10. http://www.bearforum.com/cgi-bin/bbs51.pl?read=300946 (accessed April 1, 2008).

Szep, Jason. 2003c. "Singapore Labs Investigated in Mystery SARS Case." *Yahoo! News*. September 11. http://www.hurriyetdailynews.com/default.aspx?pageid=438&n =singapore-labs-investigated-in-mystery-sars-case-2003-09-12 (accessed April 1, 2008).

Szep, Jason. 2003d. "Singapore SARS Fears Recede; Patient Recovering." *Yahoo! News*. September 12. http://www.timesofmalta.com/articles/view/20030913/local/singapore-sars-fears-recede-patient-recovering.141313#.UnWyDCQXjAo (accessed April 1, 2008).

"Taiwanese Girl Ruled out as SARS Infection." 2003. *Yahoo! News*. July 24. http://www. accessmylibrary.com/coms2/summary_0286-23959280_ITM (accessed April 1, 2008).

"Taiwan Health Chief Resigns in SARS Crisis." 2003. *CNN.com*. May 16. http://www.cnn .com/2003/HEALTH/05/16/sars/ (accessed May 17, 2003).

"Taiwan Launches National Temperature Check Campaign as SARS Wanes." 2003. *Yahoo! News*. June 1. http://www.accessmylibrary.com/coms2/summary_0286-23419817 _ITM (accessed April 3, 2008).

"Taiwan SARS Crisis Worsens." 2003. *CNN.com*. May 22. http://www.cnn.com/2003 /WORLD/asiapcf/east/05/22/sars/ (accessed May 25, 2003).

"Taiwan Says SARS May Lurk among 3 Mln Flu Patients." 2003. *Yahoo! News*. October 30. http://news.yahoo.com/news?tmpl=story2&cid=571&u=/nm/20031030/hl_nm /sars_taiwan_dc_3&printer=1 (no longer available online, accessed October 30, 2003).

"Tamiflu-Maker Roche Warns against Generic Versions." 2005. *USA Today*. October 24. http://usatoday30.usatoday.com/news/health/2005-10-24-roche-tamiflu_x.htm (accessed June 28, 2010).

"There's an Ancient Cure to an Old Disease." http://www.northernwatchdog.com/cure .htm (no longer available online, accessed October 5, 2007).

"Third Suspected SARS Case in China." 2004. *CNN.com*. January 12. http://cbsnews .com/2100-204_162-592852.html (accessed January 12, 2004).

Thomas, Jeannie B. 1997. *Featherless Chickens, Laughing Women, and Serious Stories.* Charlottesville: University of Virginia Press.

Thompson, William W., David K. Shay, Eric Weintraub, Lynnette Brammer, Nancy Cox, Larry J. Anderson, and Keiji Fukuda. 2003. "Mortality Associated with Influenza and Respiratory Syncytial Virus in the United States." *Journal of the American Medical Association* 289 (2): 179–86. http://dx.doi.org/10.1001/jama.289.2.179. Medline:12517228

Thorson, James A. 1993. "Did You Ever See a Hearse Go By? Some Thoughts on Gallows Humor." *Journal of American Culture* 16 (2): 17–24. http://dx.doi.org/10.1111/j.1542-734X.1993.00017.x.

"Timeline for SARS." 2003. *MSNBC.com.* April 24. http://www.msnbc.com/news/904137.asp (no longer available online, accessed April 24, 2003).

"Timeline: Sars Virus." 2003. *BBC News.* September 9. http://news.bbc.co.uk/2/hi/asia-pacific/2973415.stm (accessed September 9, 2003).

"Toronto Is Back a Year after SARS." 2004. *CNN.com.* May 27. http://usatoday30.usatoday.com/travel/news/2004-05-26-toronto-sars_x.htm (accessed February 22, 2013).

"Toronto Reports 25 Possible New SARS Cases." 2003. *CNN.com.* May 23. http://edition.cnn.com/2003/HEALTH/05/23/sars/index.html (accessed May 25, 2003).

"Toronto Reveals SARS Source." 2003. *CNN.com.* May 26. http://edition.cnn.com/2003/HEALTH/05/26/sars.wrap.intl/index.html (accessed June 2, 2003).

"Toronto SARS Death Toll Reaches 40." 2003. *Yahoo! News.* July 14. http://www.ireland.com/newspaper/breaking/2003/0714/breaking83.htm (no longer available online, accessed April 1, 2008).

"Toronto Traces SARS Cases to 96-Year-Old Patient." 2003. *CNN.com.* May 27. http://www.cnn.com/2003/HEALTH/05/26/sars.wrap/index.html (accessed October 31, 2013).

"Toronto's Economy Takes SARS Hit." 2003. *MSNBC.com.* April 24. http://www.msnbc.com/news/904789.asp (no longer available online, accessed May 14, 2003).

Treichler, Paula A. 1999. *How to Have Theory in an Epidemic: Cultural Chronicles of AIDS.* Durham, NC: Duke University Press.

Trudeau, Kevin. 2007. *Natural Cures "They" Don't Want You to Know About.* Elk Grove Village: Alliance.

Turner, Patricia A. 1993. *I Heard It through the Grapevine: Rumor in African-American Culture.* Berkeley: University of California Press.

Twain, Mark. (1872) 2003. *Roughing It (Enriched Classic Series).* New York: Pocket.

"Two SARS Cases Confirmed in China." 2004. *CNN.com.* April 23. http://www.cnn.com/2004/WORLD/asiapcf/04/23/china.sars/index.html (accessed April 23, 2004).

"Two Taiwan Doctors Charged with SARS Cover-up." 2003. *Yahoo! News.* June 18. http://groups.yahoo.com/neo/groups/long_life/conversations/topics/22 (accessed April 3, 2008).

"UK Has First Confirmed SARS Case." 2003. *CNN.com.* May 15. http://www.cnn.com/2003/WORLD/europe/05/15/uk.sars/index.html (accessed May 25, 2003).

UNAIDS. 2009. "Sub-Saharan Africa." http://www.unaids.org:80/en/Regionscountries/Regions (accessed June 30, 2010).

"US Criticised China over Death Penalty for SARS Quarantine Violations." 2003. *Yahoo! News.* May 17. http://www.accessmylibrary.com/coms2/summary_0286-23299265_ITM (accessed April 2, 2008).

"US Holds Plane in Virus Scare." 2003. *BBC News.* April 1. http://news.bbc.co.uk/2/hi/health.com/2908021.stm (accessed March 23, 2006).

"U.S. Hospitals Ready for SARS Outbreak?" 2003. *CNN.com.* May 17. http://online.athens.com/stories/051603/hea_20030516015.shtml (accessed February 22, 2013).

"The Vanished Virus." 2003. *Guardian*. August 18. http://www.theguardian.com/society/2003/aug/18/publichealth.sars (accessed September 16, 2003).

van Wormer, Katherine, and Mary Boes. 1997. "Humor in the Emergency Room: A Social Work Perspective." *Health & Social Work* 22 (2): 87–92. http://dx.doi.org/10.1093/hsw/22.2.87. Medline:9131354

Vasagar, Jeevan. 2003. "Chinatown Hit by Sars Rumours." *Guardian*. April 18. http://www.theguardian.com/uk/2003/apr/18/sars.world (accessed December 5, 2004).

Vaskilampi, Tuula. 1982. "Culture and Folk Medicine." In *Folk Medicine and Health Culture: Role of Folk Medicine in Modern Health Care*, edited by Tuula Vaskilampi and Carol P. MacCormack, 2–16. Kuopio, Finland: University of Kuopio.

Vedantam, Shankar, and Rob Stein. 2003. "Death Rate for Global Outbreak Rising." *MSNBC.com*. April 25. http://vedantam.com/sars04-2003.html (accessed April 4, 2008).

Vogel, Virgil J. 1976. "American Indian Foods Used as Medicine." In *American Folk Medicine: A Symposium*, edited by Wayland D. Hand, 125–41. Berkeley: University of California Press.

Vogel, Virgil J. 1990. *American Indian Medicine*. Norman: University of Oklahoma Press.

Walsh, Bryan. 2003. "SARS: Are We Ready?" *TIME*. September 15. http://www.time.com/time/magazine/article/0,9171,501030922-485794,00.html (accessed September 23, 2003).

Washer, Peter. 2004. "Representations of SARS in the British Newspapers." *Social Science & Medicine* 59 (12): 2561–71. http://dx.doi.org/10.1016/j.socscimed.2004.03.038. Medline:15474209

Watson, James L. 2005. "SARS and the Consequences for Globalization." In *SARS in China: Prelude to Pandemic?*, edited by Arthur Kleinman and James L. Watson, 196–204. Stanford, CA: Stanford University Press.

Weaver, Kimberlee, Stephen M. Garcia, Norbert Schwarz, and Dale T. Miller. 2007. "Inferring the Popularity of an Opinion from Its Familiarity: A Repetitive Voice Can Sound Like a Chorus." *Journal of Personality and Social Psychology* 92 (5): 821–33. http://dx.doi.org/10.1037/0022-3514.92.5.821. Medline:17484607

Whatley, Mariamne H., and Elissa R. Henken. 2000. *Did You Hear about the Girl Who . . .?: Contemporary Legends, Folklore, and Human Sexuality*. New York: New York University Press.

White, Amy S., Renee D. Godard, Carolyn Belling, Victoria Kasza, and Rebecca L. Beach. 2010. "Beverages Obtained from Soda Fountain Machines in the U.S. Contain Microorganisms, Including Coliform Bacteria." *International Journal of Food Microbiology* 137 (1): 61–66. http://dx.doi.org/10.1016/j.ijfoodmicro.2009.10.031. Medline:19926155

White, Luise. 2005. "Social Construction and Social Consequences: Rumors and Evidence." In *Rumor Mills: The Social Impact of Rumor and Legend*, edited by Gary Alan Fine, Véronique Campion-Vincent, and Chip Heath, 241–54. New Brunswick, NJ: Aldine Transaction.

"WHO Gives Toronto SARS All-Clear." 2003. *MSNBC.com*. July 2. http://usatoday30.usatoday.com/news/health/2003-07-02-sars-canada_x.htm (accessed February 22, 2013).

"WHO: Global SARS Outbreak Over." 2003. *CNN.com*. July 5. http://edition.cnn.com/2003/WORLD/asiapcf/east/07/05/sars/index.html (accessed July 7, 2003).

"WHO Lifts Taiwan SARS Advisory." 2003. CBC News. June 17. http://www.cbc.ca/news/world/story/2003/06/17/sars030617.html (accessed June 18, 2003).

"WHO: SARS No Longer Spreading in Canada." 2003. *CNN.com*. May 14. http://www.cnn.com/2003/HEALTH/05/14/sars.canada/index.html (accessed May 17, 2003).

"WHO Sheds New Light on SARS." 2003. *CNN.com*. May 4. http://www.usj.com.my
/bulletin/upload/archive/index.php/t-3464.html (accessed May 14, 2003).

"WHO to Conduct Fresh Studies on SARS Link to Other Animal Species." 2003. *Yahoo!
News*. June 12. http://www.accessmylibrary.com/coms2/summary_0286-23538603
_ITM (no longer available online, accessed April 1, 2008).

"WHO: Worst of SARS Over in Some Countries." 2003. *CNN.com*. April 28. http://www
.cnn.com/2003/HEALTH/04/28/sars/index.html (accessed May 14, 2003).

Wong, Ian. 2003. "Policies on SARS in UK Boarding Schools Are Confused." *BMJ* 326
(7395): 929. http://dx.doi.org/10.1136/bmj.326.7395.929. Medline:12714478

Wong, Jacqueline. 2003. "Singapore Says Lab Accident Caused New SARS Scare." *Yahoo!
News*. September 23. http://www.virtualmenshealth.com/news.asp?artid=428 (no
longer available online, accessed April 1, 2008).

Wong, Margaret. 2003a. "SARS Prompts to Seek Out Fresh Air." *Yahoo! News*. May 31.
http://www.highbeam.com/doc/1P1-74281102.html (accessed April 2, 2008).

Wong, Margaret. 2003b. "WHO Removes Hong Kong from SARS List." *Yahoo! News*.
June 23. http://usatoday30.usatoday.com/news/health/2003-06-23-who-sars-list_x
.htm (accessed April 3, 2008).

Wong, Margaret. 2004. "Hong Kong Apartment Recovers after SARS." *Yahoo! News*. June
4. http://lateline.muzi.net/news/ll/english/1314210.shtml?cc=24204 (no longer
available online, accessed April 2, 2008).

Woodward, Kathleen. 1999. "Statistical Panic." *Differences: A Journal of Feminist Cultural
Studies* 11 (2): 177–203. http://dx.doi.org/10.1215/10407391-11-2-177.

World Health Organization. 2004. "Summary of Probable SARS Cases with Onset of Illness from 1 November 2002 to 31 July 2003." Global Alert and Response (GAR).
April 21. http://www.who.int/csr/sars/country/table2004_04_21/en/index.html
(accessed June 25, 2010).

World Health Organization. 2009a. "Cumulative Number of Confirmed Human Cases for
Avian Influenza A/(H5N1) Reported to WHO." June 1. http://www.who.int/csr
/disease/avian_influenza/country/cases_table_2009_06_01/en/index.html (no longer
available online, accessed June 25, 2010).

World Health Organization. 2009b. "Global Tuberculosis Control—Epidemiology, Strategy, Financing." Tuberculosis (TB). http://www.who.int/tb/publications/global
_report/2009/en/index.html (accessed June 25, 2010).

World Health Organization. 2009c. "Pandemic (H1N1) 2009—Update 81." Global Alert
and Response (GAR). December 30. http://www.who.int/csr/don/2009_12_30/en
/index.html (accessed January 6, 2010).

World Health Organization. 2010. "The International Response to the Influenza Pandemic: WHO Responds to the Critics." Global Alert and Response (GAR). June 10.
http://www.who.int/csr/disease/swineflu/notes/briefing_20100610/en/index.html
(accessed July 1, 2010).

World Health Organization. 2012a. "Background and Summary of Novel Coronavirus
Infection—as of 21 December 2012." Global Alert and Response (GAR). December
21. http://www.who.int/csr/disease/coronavirus_infections/update_20121221/en
/index.html (accessed January 9, 2013).

World Health Organization. 2012b. "Novel Coronavirus Infection in the United Kingdom." Global Alert and Response (GAR). September 23. http://www.who.int/csr
/don/2012_09_23/en/index.html (accessed January 9, 2013).

World Health Organization. 2013. "Middle East Respiratory Syndrome Coronavirus
(MERS-CoV) – Update." Global Alert and Response (GAR). October 31. http://
www.who.int/csr/don/2013_10_31/en-index.html (accessed November 3, 2013).

"Worldwide HIV & AIDS Statistics." 2010. *AVERT.* June 30. http://www.avert.org /worldstats.htm (accessed June 30, 2010).

Wroughton, Lesley. 2003. "Toronto Probes Four Deaths as SARS Cases Rise." *Yahoo! News.* May 31. http://www.hurriyetdailynews.com/default.aspx?pageid=438&n=toronto -probes-four-deaths-as-sars-cases-rise-2003-06-02 (accessed April 2, 2008).

Wu, Tiffany. 2003. "Taiwan Rethinks SARS Measures So as to Calm Fears Re: Gene Difference May Explain SARS Epidemic." *Yahoo! News.* October 31. http://www.national -anthems.net/forum/article/rec.travel.asia/187930 (accessed April 2, 2008).

Yee, Daniel. 2003a. "So Far, U.S. Succeeds in Containing SARS." *Yahoo! News.* May 19. http://www.apnewsarchive.com/2003/So-Far-U-S-Succeeds-in-Containing-SARS /id-2fb3852be25368a5065c3fb812f4e3be (accessed April 2, 2008).

Yee, Daniel. 2003b. "CDC Doctor Suspected of SARS Recovering." *Yahoo! News.* May 26. http://www.highbeam.com/doc/1P1-74152710.html (accessed April 2, 2008).

Young, Doug. 2003a. "SARS Disrupts China's Wild Game Business." *Yahoo! News.* June 21. http://www.planetark.org/dailynewsstory.cfm/newsid/21265/newsDate/23-Jun -2003/story.htm (accessed April 3, 2008).

Young, Doug. 2003b. "China Says Antibody Offers a Way to Diagnose SARS." *Yahoo! News.* June 12. http://www.royalsociety.org.nz/2003/06/12/sars-china-animals/ (accessed April 1, 2008).

Young, Saundra. 2010. "CDC: H1N1 Still Circulating; Vaccine Plentiful." *CNN.com.* January 7. http://www.cnn.com/2010/HEALTH/01/07/h1n1.virus.vaccine/index .html (accessed January 8, 2010).

Zambon, Maria. 2003. "Severe Acute Respiratory Syndrome Revisited." *BMJ* 326 (7394): 831–2. http://dx.doi.org/10.1136/bmj.326.7394.831. Medline:12702595

Zambon, Maria, and Karl G. Nicholson. 2003. "Sudden Acute Respiratory Syndrome." *BMJ* 326 (7391): 669–70. http://dx.doi.org/10.1136/bmj.326.7391.669. Medline:12663376

Zhu, Charlie. 2003. "SARS Drives Online Banking Boom in Hong Kong and Singapore." *TotalTele.com.* April 29. http://www.totaltele.com/view.aspx?ID=390097 (accessed November 2, 2013).

About the Author

Jon D. Lee is a lecturer in the English Department at Suffolk University.

Index